Fodor's 91
The Bahamas

Ian Glass

Fodor's Travel Publications, Inc.
New York and London

Fodor's The Bahamas

Editor: David Low
Contributors: Suzanne Brown, Gordon Lomer, William G. Scheller, Laurie Senz
Art Director: Fabrizio La Rocca
Cartographer: David Lindroth
Illustrator: Karl Tanner
Cover Photograph: Robert Holland/The Waterhouse

Design: Vignelli Associates

About the Author

A free-lance writer based in Miami, Ian Glass has written extensively on the Bahamas and the Caribbean for numerous publications, including *Travel & Leisure* and *The New York Times*.

Special Sales

Fodor's Travel Publications are available at special discounts for bulk purchases (100 copies or more) for sales promotions or premiums. Special editions, including personalized covers, excerpts of existing guides, and corporate imprints, can be created in large quantities for special needs. For more information write to Special Marketing, Fodor's Travel Publications, 201 East 50th St., New York, NY 10022. Inquiries from the United Kingdom should be sent to Fodor's Travel Publications, 20 Vauxhall Bridge Rd., London, England SW1V 2SA.

Contents

Foreword

We wish to express our gratitude to the Bahamas News Bureau, the Nassau/Cable Beach/Paradise Island Promotion Board, the Grand Bahama Promotion Board, and the Family Islands Promotion Board for their assistance in the preparation of this guidebook.

While every care has been taken to ensure the accuracy of the information in this guide, the passage of time will always bring change, and consequently, the publisher cannot accept responsibility for errors that may occur.

All prices and opening times quoted here are based on information supplied to us at press time. Hours and admission fees may change, however, and the prudent traveler will avoid inconvenience by calling ahead.

Fodor's wants to hear about your travel experiences, both pleasant and unpleasant. When a hotel or restaurant fails to live up to its billing, let us know and we will investigate the complaint and revise our entries where the facts warrant it.

Send your letters to the editors of Fodor's Travel Publications, 201 E. 50th St., New York, NY 10022.

Highlights '91 and Fodor's Choice

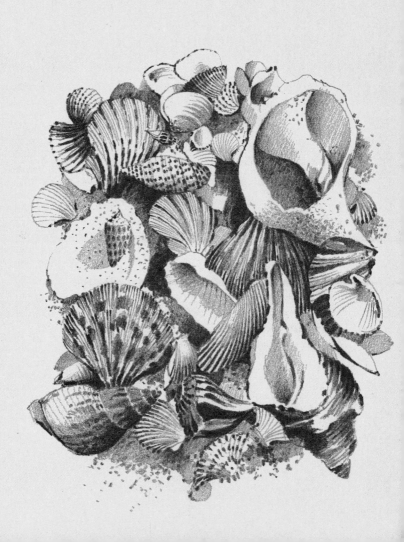

Highlights '91

En Garde Resort owners in both Paradise Island and Cable Beach continue to try to outdo one another in their quest to lure more Nassau visitors. Resorts International opened its **Paradise Island International Airport** in March 1989, with owner Merv Griffin playing host to Prime Minister Lynden O. Pindling. The 3,000-foot runway accommodates the new 50-passenger De Havilland Dash 73s, which are owned by Merv Griffin's Paradise Island Airlines' and provide 20 daily flights from Miami and Fort Lauderdale.

Griffin has brought in architect Waldo Fernandez, who has forged a reputation as interior designer to the stars (he has redone the homes of Elizabeth Taylor, Goldie Hawn, Neil Simon, Sean Connery, and Griffin himself), to give a multi-million-dollar face-lift to the Resorts International Paradise Island properties: the **Paradise Island Resort and Casino,** the **Ocean Club,** and the **Paradise Paradise Beach Resort.** Griffin's planes, the island's scenery, and even staff uniforms are also getting a new look.

Carnival Time Meanwhile, at the end of 1989, **Carnival's Crystal Palace Resort & Casino,** the hotel of many colors on Cable Beach, completed its six-tower, 1,550-room complex (making it the largest in the Bahamas and the Caribbean). The resort also introduced the ultimate in opulence with its $25,000-a-night, two-bedroom, white-and-silver penthouse **Galactic Fantasy Suite,** with its own friendly robot; changing artwork on the walls; a player piano featuring visual images along with the music; a sofa and bed that rotate 360 degrees; and a button that brings forth thunder and lighting to the touch. Carnival's Crystal Palace operates the Carnival Airlines 727 jet service, flying to Nassau twice a day from Miami and once daily from Fort Lauderdale, as well as offering regularly scheduled service from Newark, Cleveland, Baltimore, New Orleans, Nashville, and Cincinnati. That's a lot of gambling potential.

New in Freeport Several new restaurants have recently opened in Freeport to brighten the dining scene. **Le Bouquet** at the Holiday Inn serves fine French cuisine in an intimate, romantic setting reminiscent of a country home. At Port Lucaya Marketplace, visitors can try **Luciano's,** one of Freeport's most sophisticated dining spots, for Italian and French cuisine; **Fatman's Nephew,** for substantial Bahamian fare; and **Pusser's Co. Store and Pub,** for good, solid English meals.

Flying High In 1989 **Bahamasair,** the nation's main carrier, bought five new Dash 8 planes from Boeing Canada; it planned to phase out its fleet of HS-748s by the end of 1990. Work began in 1989 on the new **U.S. departure terminal** at **Nassau International Airport;** it's due to be completed and open for business during the first half of 1991. Meanwhile, at Moss Town on Great Exuma Island, the $9.3 million international airport with 7,000-foot runway has reached completion. Quite coincidentally, the Bahamas airport departure tax rose in 1989 from $5 to $7.

The Place to Go An increasing number of U.S. and international airlines find Nassau a profitable destination. **Scanair,** a Scandinavian airline, offers weekly direct service from Stockholm to Nassau and hopes to expand to take in other Bahamas destinations. The flow of German tourists has increased, now that European carrier **LTU** offers weekly service between Düsseldorf and Nassau. **Bahamasair** features nine flights a day from Miami, and **Pan Am** has increased its number of flights from Miami. **Comair** has weekly service from Jacksonville, Florida. **USAir** offers daily flights from Philadelphia. Meanwhile, **American Airlines** began daily flights from Miami to Marsh Harbour in the Abacos.

All at Sea One-day cruises to the Bahamas from Florida are more popular than ever. *Discovery I* sails daily from Fort Lauderdale to Grand Bahama, joining the long-established *SeaEscape* from Miami and Fort Lauderdale to the same island. Bimini, the closest island to the United States, also became a destination for *SeaEscape*, with daily cruises out of Miami.

Meanwhile, the $45 million expansion of **Nassau Harbour** was due to be completed by early 1991; it will accommodate 13 cruise ships at a time. **Grand Bahama Island** completed a $5 million harbor expansion. **Governor's Harbour, Eleuthera,** started a $5 million improvement program to take in small cruise ships. And Royal Caribbean Cruise Line began a $7 million renovation of **Little Stirrup Cay** (renaming it **Coco Cay**) in the Berry Islands; the *Emerald Seas* ship stops at the small island.

Hotels News At press time **Jack Tar Village** on the West End of Grand Bahama Island had closed. No date was scheduled for reopening. In 1990 the 20-room **Emerald Palms–by–the–Sea Hotel** finished construction in Congo Town, Andros. In spring 1991 a new 75-room hotel and small marina, built by the Hotel Corporation of the Bahamas, is scheduled to open in George Town on Great Exuma Island to boost accommodations during the annual Family Island Regatta, held each April. The Hotel Corporation has also signed a letter of intent with Club Méditerranée, Inc., to build a third Bahamian Club Med on San Salvador. The 375-room property will provide additional rooms for visitors attending the 1992 celebration of the 500th anniversary of Columbus's landing on the island.

On Grand Bahama, Radisson Hotels has taken over management of the **Xanadu Beach and Marina Resort.** CARN-ICON, an amalgam of Carnival Cruise Lines and Continental Hotels, has made massive improvements in the **Lucayan Beach Resort and Casino.**

Fodor's Choice

No two people will agree on what makes a perfect vacation, but it's fun and helpful to know what others think. We hope you'll have a chance to experience some of Fodor's Choices yourself while visiting the Bahamas. For detailed information about each entry, refer to the appropriate chapters (given in parentheses) within this guidebook.

Beaches

Cat Island (Chapter 5)

Great Harbour Cay, The Berry Islands (Chapter 5)

Harbour Island's pink beaches, Eleuthera (Chapter 5)

North Bimini's western coast (Chapter 5)

Saunders Beach, New Providence Island (Chapter 3)

Stocking Island, Great Exuma (Chapter 5)

Best Buys

British woolens—The Scottish Shop, Nassau (Chapter 3)

China and crystal—Bernard's, Nassau

French perfumes—The Perfume Salon, Nassau

Hand-batiked fashions—Mademoiselle, Nassau

Irish linen—The Nassau Shop, Nassau

Leather goods—Leather Masters, Nassau

Locally made gold charms—Coin of the Realm, Nassau

Watches and cameras—John Bull, Nassau

International Bazaar, Freeport (Chapter 4)

Port Lucaya, Freeport

For Kids

Glass-bottomed boat trips—Prince George Wharf, Nassau (Chapter 3)

Horseback riding—Coral Harbour, New Providence Island (Chapter 3); Harbourside Riding Stables, Paradise Island (Chapter 3); and Pinetree Stables, Freeport (Chapter 4)

Snorkeling and water sports—at most Cable Beach/Paradise Island hotels (Chapter 3)

Swimming with dolphins—UNEXSO, Lucaya (Chapter 4)

Tennis—more than 80 courts available on New Providence Island (Chapter 3)

Golf

Bahamas Princess Resort's Emerald Golf Course, Grand Bahama Island (Chapter 4)

Cotton Bay Club, Eleuthera (Chapter 5)

Great Harbour Cay, The Berry Islands (Chapter 5)

Lucaya Golf & Country Club, Grand Bahama Island (Chapter 4)

Paradise Island Club, Paradise Island (Chapter 3)

Hotels

Bahamas Princess Resort & Casino, Freeport (Chapter 4) *Expensive*

Divi Bahamas Beach Resort and Country Club, New Providence Island (Chapter 3) *Expensive*

Lucayan Beach Resort & Casino, Freeport (Chapter 4) *Expensive*

Nassau Beach Hotel, Cable Beach (Chapter 3) *Expensive*

Ocean Club, Paradise Island (Chapter 3) *Expensive*

Coral Sands Hotel, Harbour Island, Eleuthera (Chapter 5) *Moderate*

Spanish Wells Beach Resort, Eleuthera (Chapter 5) *Moderate*

Stella Maris Resort Club, Long Island (Chapter 5) *Moderate*

Local Dishes

Boiled fish, preferably grouper, highly seasoned

Conch—fritters, cracked, chowder, and salad

Guava duff, a small, peach-colored fruit used in jams and puddings

Peas 'n' rice, made with pigeon peas, tomatoes, and onions, with chicken or meat added

Soups—dried pigeon pea, turtle, breadfruit, pumpkin, and crab bisque

Nightlife

Bahamas Princess Country Club, Freeport (Chapter 4)

Le Cabaret Theatre, Paradise Island (Chapter 3)

Flamingo Club, Divi Bahamas Beach Resort, Nassau (Chapter 3)

Out Island Bar, Nassau Beach Hotel, Cable Beach (Chapter 3)

Palace Theater, Carnival's Crystal Palace, Cable Beach (Chapter 3)

Peanut Taylor's Drumbeat Club, Nassau (Chapter 3)

Restaurants

Buena Vista, Nassau (Chapter 3) *Expensive*

Café Martinique, Paradise Island (Chapter 3) *Expensive*

Frilsham's, Cable Beach (Chapter 3) *Expensive*

Graycliff, Nassau (Chapter 3) *Expensive*

Luciano's, Lucaya (Chapter 4) *Expensive*

Les Oursins, Lucaya (Chapter 4) *Expensive*

Guanahani's, Freeport (Chapter 4) *Moderate*

Romantic Hideaways

Bluff House, Green Turtle Cay, The Abacos (Chapter 5)

Cotton Bay Club, Eleuthera (Chapter 5)

Hotel Peace and Plenty, Great Exuma (Chapter 5)

Small Hope Bay Lodge, Andros (Chapter 5)

Walker's Cay, The Abacos (Chapter 5)

Windermere Island Club, Eleuthera (Chapter 5)

Sights

Ardastra Gardens' pink marching flamingos and other exotic birds, Nassau (Chapter 3)

Brightly colored spinnakers of the yachts in the Family Island Regatta at Elizabeth Harbour, George Town, Great Exuma (Chapter 5)

Coral World's sea creatures, Silver Cay (Chapter 3)

Royal Bahamas Police Band at the Changing of the Guard ceremonies, Government House, Nassau (Chapter 3)

Rand Memorial Nature Centre, Grand Bahama Island (Chapter 4)

Sunsets

Adelaide Beach, New Providence (Chapter 3)

From the veranda of the Blue Water Marina/Anchorage, North Bimini (Chapter 5)

Love Beach, West Bay Street, New Providence Island (Chapter 3)

Views

Cat Island from 206-foot-high Mt. Alvernia (Chapter 5)

Frenzied shoppers on Bay Street or the Junkanoo Parade from one of the east-wing top floors, the British Colonial Hotel (Chapter 3)

Nassau from atop Fort Fincastle's Water Tower (Chapter 3)

The ocean and Freeport from the top floors of the Atlantik Beach Hotel, Grand Bahama (Chapter 4)

The Bahamas

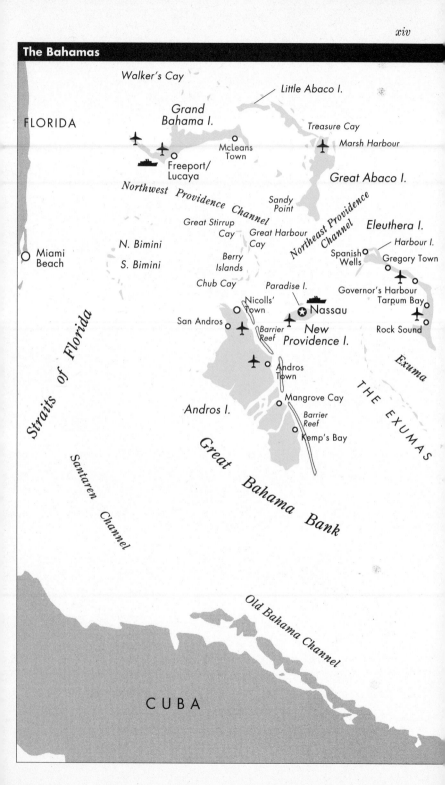

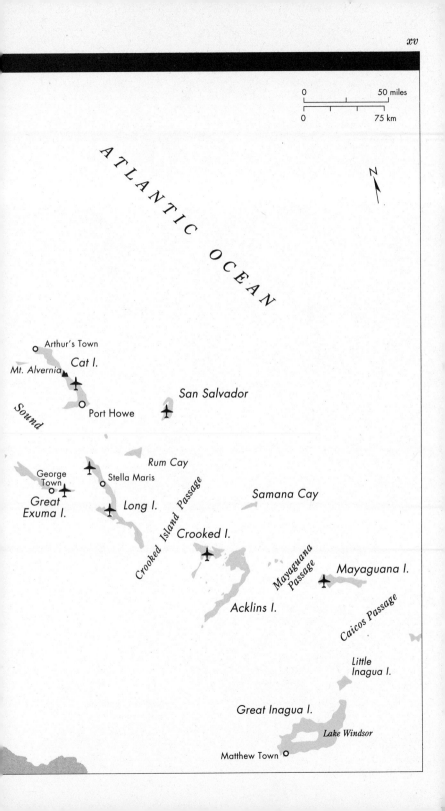

World Time Zones

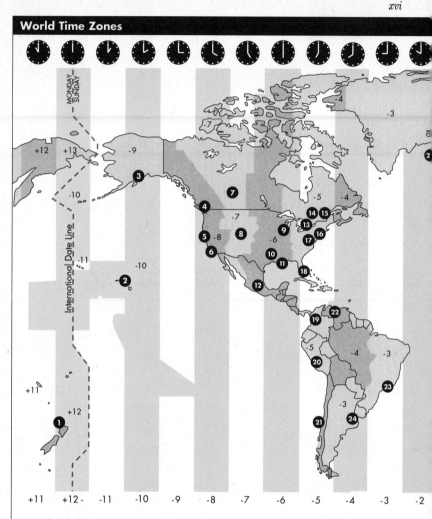

Numbers below vertical bands relate each zone to Greenwich Mean Time (0 hrs.).
Local times frequently differ from these general indications,
as indicated by light-face numbers on map.

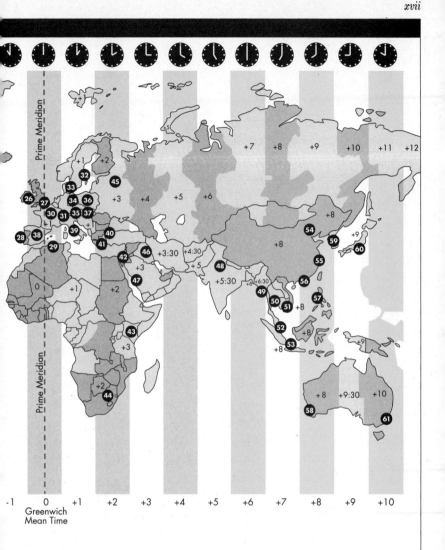

Introduction

T he Bahamas was born to become a major international resort destination, with its exquisite white-and-pink beaches, lush tropical landscape, unsullied waters, and year-round sunshine. This archipelago, which begins just 60 miles off the Floridian coast, contains more than 700 islands (only 20 of them inhabited) scattered over 100,000 square miles of the Atlantic. Vacationers first ventured here in large numbers during the Roaring '20s, and a second tourist boom occurred after World War II, with the development of several large oceanfront communities. Since then, tourism has remained the Bahamas' number-one industry; each year, its shores attract almost 3½ million visitors, among them young couples, families, rock stars, royalty, and millionaires.

Most travelers to the Bahamas make their principal stop either Nassau on New Providence Island or Freeport on Grand Bahama Island, two playgrounds where hedonism flourishes. Here they can doze in the sun, bargain at straw markets, dine at fine restaurants, and enjoy the sophisticated casino nightlife at plush resorts. In Nassau the nation's past may be rediscovered by exploring historic buildings, forts, gardens, and monuments. The life of this restless city is linked closely to two expensive resort areas, Cable Beach and Paradise Island. Freeport, which was built in the '60s, features the International Bazaar, where imported goods may be purchased at reduced prices. Adjacent to Freeport is the suburb of Lucaya, where visitors can swim with dolphins at UNEXSO, a world-renowned diving school.

Vacationers who don't like crowds may prefer a trip to one of the Family Islands, which are situated all over the archipelago. In contrast to the glittering modernity of New Providence and Grand Bahama, these islands offer a slower-paced, unspoiled way of life characterized by narrow, sandstrewn streets, pastel clapboard houses shrouded in brilliantly colored vegetation, and uncluttered beaches. Because of the small-town atmosphere of these islands, tourists will probably find local residents even friendlier than those in Nassau and Freeport.

The Family Islands offer travelers many alternatives from which to choose. The Abacos, a center for boatbuilding, have attracted sailing and yachting fans over the years because of their translucent waters and excellent marina facilities. Andros, the largest Bahamian island, offers spectacular dives off the 140-mile-long Great Barrier Reef, the third largest coral reef in the world. Deep-sea fishermen find bliss in Bimini, for in its waters roam great warriors such as marlin, swordfish, giant tuna, wahoo, sailfish, dolphin, and bonefish. (Ernest Hemingway once chose Bimini as his favorite getaway spot.) Bird-watchers marvel at the flock of over 20,000 flamingos that resides in a national park on Inagua, the southernmost of the Bahamian islands. Other visitors who simply want to relax in a quiet seaside setting may opt for the charms of Harbour Island, off the coast of Eleuthera, with a pink beach, friendly residents, and a New England–style village named Dunmore Town.

You might call Christopher Columbus the first tourist to hit the Bahamas, although he was actually trying to find a route to the East Indies with his three ships, the *Santa Maria*, the *Pinta*, and the *Niña*. Columbus is popularly believed to have made his first landfall in the New World on October 12, 1492, at San Salvador, in the southern part of the Bahamas. Researchers of the National Geographic Society, however, recently came up with the theory that he may have first set foot ashore on Samana Cay, some 60 miles southeast of San Salvador. The Bahamians have taken this new theory under consideration, if not too seriously; tradition dies hard in the islands, and they are hardly likely to tear down the New World landfall monument on San Salvador. Plans for their celebrations in 1992 to mark the 500th anniversary of the explorer's visit will take in all of the islands, with San Salvador as the focal point.

The people who met Columbus on his landing day were Arawak Indians, said to have fled from the Caribbean to the Bahamas to escape the depredations of the murderous Caribs around the turn of the 9th century. The Arawaks were a shy, gentle breed who offered Columbus and his men their hospitality. He was impressed with their kindness and more than slightly intrigued by the gold ornaments they wore. Columbus liked the place enough to spend several weeks visiting the area's other islands, such as Crooked Island, Rum Cay, and Long Island, before continuing his laborious voyage through the Caribbean.

But the voracious Spaniards who followed in Columbus's footsteps a few years later repaid the Indians' kindness by forcing them to work in the conquistadors' gold and silver mines in the New World; the Indians were virtually wiped out by 1520. Some Indian words, such as *cassava* (a vegetable) and *guava* (a fruit), remain in the Spanish language. The Spaniards' description of this part of the New World— Bajío Mar (shallow sea)—somehow ended up as *Bahama*.

In 1513, the next Spanish-speaking seafarer stumbled on the Bahamas. Juan Ponce de León had been a passenger on Columbus's second voyage, in 1493. He conquered Puerto Rico in 1508 and then began searching thirstily for the Fountain of Youth. He thought he had found it on South Bimini, but he changed his mind and moved on to visit the site of St. Augustine, on the northeast coast of Florida. However, there are still a few people on Bimini who, if you cross their palms with a little silver, will point out the spot where Ponce de León thought he had discovered the magic elixir. The majority, though, will shake their heads bemusedly if you question them about the spring.

In 1629, King Charles I claimed the Bahamas for England, though his edict was not implemented until the arrival of English pilgrims in 1647. They had fled the religious and political dissension then rocking their country to seek religious freedom; they settled on the Bahamian island they christened Eleuthera, the Greek word for *freedom*. Other English immigrants followed, and in 1656 another group of pilgrims, from Bermuda, took over a Bahamian island to the west and named it New Providence because of their links with Providence, Rhode Island. By the last part of the 17th century, some 1,100 settlers were trying to eke out a living, supplemented by the cargoes they salvaged from Spanish galleons that ran aground on the reefs. Many settlers were inclined to give nature a hand by enticing these ships onto the reefs with lights.

Inevitably, the British settlers were joined by a more nefarious subset of humanity, pirates and buccaneers like Edward Teach (better known as Blackbeard, he was said to have had 14 wives), Henry Morgan, and Calico Jack Rackham. Rackham numbered among his crew two violent, cutlass-wielding female members, Anne Bonney and Mary Read, who are said to have disconcerted their enemies by swinging aboard their vessels topless. Bonney and Read were crafty women, indeed; after being captured, they escaped hanging in Jamaica by feigning pregnancy.

For some 40 years until 1718, pirates in the Bahamas constantly raided the Spanish galleons that carried booty home from the New World. The islands had several hidden coves and harbors. During this period, the Spanish government, furious at the raids, sent ships and troops to destroy the New Providence city of Charles Town, which was later rebuilt and renamed Nassau, in 1695, in honor of King William III, formerly William of Orange-Nassau.

In 1718, King George I appointed Captain Woodes Rogers the first royal governor of the Bahamas, with orders to clean up the place. Why the king chose Rogers for this particular job is unclear; the king's thinking may well have been that it takes a pirate to know one, for Woodes Rogers had been a privateer himself. Rogers's body carried the scars of many battles, and he was well known among the pirates. But Rogers did take control of Nassau, hanging eight pirates from trees on the site of what was to become the British Colonial Hotel.

Today, a statue of the former governor stands at the hotel entrance, and the street that runs along the waterfront is named after him. Rogers also inspired the saying *Expulsis Piratis, Restitua Commercia* (Piracy Expelled, Commerce

Restored), which remained the country's motto until Prime Minister Lynden O. Pindling replaced it with the more appropriate and optimistic Forward, Upward, Onward Together, on the occasion of independence from Britain in 1973.

Although the Bahamas enjoyed a certain measure of tranquillity thanks to Rogers and the governors who followed him, the British colonies in America at the same time were seething with a desire for independence. The peace of the islanders' lives was to be shattered during the Revolutionary War by a raid in 1788 on Nassau by the American navy, which purloined the city's arms and ammunition without even firing a shot. Next, in 1782, the Spanish came to occupy the Bahamas until the following year. Under the Treaty of Versailles of 1783, Spain took possession of Florida, and the Bahamas reverted to the British.

The Bahamas were once again overrun, between 1784 and 1789, this time by merchants from New England and plantation owners from Virginia and the Carolinas who had been loyal to the British and were fleeing the wrath of the American revolutionaries. Seeking asylum under the British flag, the Southerners brought their families and slaves with them. Many set up new plantations in the islands, though they did not stay long, frustrated by the islands' arid soil. They soon opted for greener pastures in the Caribbean to the south. Their slaves were left behind and set free in 1834, retaining the names of their masters as their own. That is why you'll find many a Johnson, Saunders, and Thompson in the towns and villages throughout the Bahamas.

The Southern refugees also gave a new architectural facelift to Nassau, with churches, schools, public buildings, and gracious homes that reflected the genteel, aristocratic life they had had to abandon in the American South. Two forts, Charlotte and Fincastle, were erected as defense against any future marauders, but they were never needed, for the Bahamas, until their independence, remained undeniably British.

Because of New Providence Island's almost perfect climate, marred only by the potential for hurricanes during the fall, tourism was foreseen as far back as the 19th century when the legislature approved the building of the first hotel, the Royal Victoria, in 1861. Though it was to reign as the grande dame of the island's hotels for more than a century, its early days saw it involved in an entirely different profit-making venture. During the U.S. Civil War, the Northern forces blockaded the main Southern ports, and the leaders of the Confederacy turned to Nassau, the closest neutral port to the south. The Royal Victoria became the headquarters of the blockade-running industry, which reaped huge profits for the British colonial government from the duties it imposed on arms supplies.

A similar bonanza, also at the expense of the United States, was to come in the 1920s, after Prohibition was signed into U.S. law, in 1919. Booze brought into the Bahamas from Europe was funneled into a thirsty United States by rum-runners operating out of Nassau, Bimini, and West End, the community on Grand Bahama Island east of Palm Beach. Racing against, and often exchanging gunfire with, Coast Guard patrol boats, the rumrunners dropped off their supplies in Miami, the Florida Keys, and other Florida destinations, making their contribution to an era that is known as the Roaring '20s. Even then, tourists were beginning to trickle into the Bahamas, many in opulent yachts belonging to the likes of Whitney, Vanderbilt, and Astor. In 1929, a new airline, Pan American, started to make daily flights from Miami to Nassau. The Royal Victoria, shedding its shady past, and two new hotels, the Colonial (now called the British Colonial) and the Fort Montagu Beach, were all in full operation. What was eventually to become the islands' most profitable industry, tourism, was finally a reality.

Nassau even had instant communication with the outside world. In 1892, a few miles northwest of the Colonial, a subterranean telegraph cable had been laid linking New Providence with Jupiter, Florida. It obviously took no flash of inspiration to name the area Cable Beach. Nassau residents had access at Cable Beach to a racecourse called Hobby Horse Hall, which had been used mainly by officers of the British West India Regiment stationed on New Providence in the late-19th century. The course closed in 1975.

One of the most colorful and enigmatic characters of the era came to Nassau in the 1930s. Sir Harry Oakes was a rough-and-ready Canadian who had made his fortune in a gold strike. During the '40s, he built the Bahamas Country Club and developed the Cable Beach Golf Course, a 6,500-yard, par-72 layout that is still in operation; it stands across the street from the new Carnival's Crystal Palace Resort & Casino and the other expensive hotel complexes on Cable Beach. Oakes also built Nassau's first airport in the late '30s to lure the well-heeled and to make commuting easier for the wealthy residents. Oakes Field can still be seen on the ride from Nassau International Airport to Cable Beach.

Oakes was to die in an atmosphere of eerie and mysterious intrigue during the governorship of the Duke of Windsor. On July 8, 1943, his battered and badly charred body was found in his bed. Only his good friend, the late Sir Harold Christie, a real-estate tycoon and one of the most powerful of the Bay Street Boys (as the island's wealthy merchants were called), was in the house at the time. This was a period when all of the news that was fit to print was coming out of the war theaters in Europe and the Far East, but the Miami newspapers and wire services had a field day with the society murder. Although a gruff, unlikable character, Oakes had no known enemies, but there was speculation that mob hit men from Miami had come over and taken care of him because of his unyielding opposition to the introduction of gambling casinos to the Bahamas.

Finally, two detectives brought from Miami pinned the murder on Oakes's son-in-law, Count Alfred de Marigny, for whom the Canadian was known to have a strong dislike. De Marigny was tried and acquitted in an overcrowded Nassau court. Much of the detectives' research and testimony was later discredited. For many years afterward, however, the mysterious and still-unsolved crime cloaked New Providence like a ghostly shroud. Visitors, intrigued by the affair, learned quickly not to bring it up in conversation with Nassau residents, for they would be met with silence. A couple of books were written about the case, but the authors had to rely on their own ingenuity, for they received little cooperation on the island. In his will, Sir Harry left Nassau assets of $9.8 million.

During World War II, New Providence also played host to a noble, if unlikely, couple. In 1936, the Duke of Windsor had forsaken the British throne in favor of "the woman I love," an American divorcée named Wallis Warfield Simpson, and the couple temporarily found a carefree life in Paris and the French Riviera. When the Nazis overran France, they fled to neutral Portugal. Secret papers revealed after the war suggest that the Germans had plans to use the duke and duchess, by kidnapping if necessary, as pawns in the German war against Britain. This would have taken the form of declaring them king and queen in exile, and seating them on the throne when Hitler's assumed victory was accomplished. The plan, if it existed, would seem to have had some merit, for the duke had been popular with the common people of Britain when he was Prince of Wales, and many sympathized with, and wept over, his dilemma of choosing between royal duty and love.

Word of the plot might have reached the ears of Britain's wartime prime minister, Winston Churchill, who encouraged King George VI, the duke's younger brother and his successor, to send the couple as far away as possible out of harm's way. In 1939, the duke had briefly returned to England, offering his services to his brother in the war effort. He was given a position of perhaps less import than he had expected, for he and Wallis suddenly found themselves in the Bahamas, with the duke as governor and commander in chief. The Bahamians were nevertheless impressed; a calypso ballad, "Love Alone," was composed in honor of the couple's fairy-tale romance.

It wasn't until after the end of World War II that the first luxury resorts were built on Cable Beach—the 145-room Balmoral Beach Hotel (now Le Meridien Royal Bahamian Hotel), a private club, in 1946; and the 213-room Emerald Beach Hotel, the first with air-conditioning, in 1954. The

Crystal Palace now stands on the Emerald Beach's original site.

For more than 300 years, the country had been ruled by whites; members of the United Bahamian Party (UBP) were known as the Bay Street Boys, after Nassau's main business thoroughfare, because they controlled the islands' commerce. But the voice of the overwhelmingly black majority was being heard in the land. In 1953, a London-educated black barrister named Lynden O. Pindling joined the opposition Progressive Liberal Party (PLP); in 1956, he was elected to Parliament. Bahamian voters threw the UBP out in 1967, and Pindling led the PLP into power.

Pindling continued to stir the growing resentment most Bahamians now had for the Bay Street Boys, and his parliamentary behavior became more and more defiant. In 1965 during one parliamentary session, he picked up the speaker's mace and threw it out the window. Because this mace has to be present and in sight at all sessions, deliberations had to be suspended; meanwhile, Pindling continued his harangue to an enthusiastic throng in the street below. Two years later, Bahamian voters threw the UBP out, and Pindling led the PLP into power.

Pindling's magnetism kept him in power through independence from Britain in 1973 (though loyalty to the mother country led the Bahamians to choose to remain within the Commonwealth of Nations, recognize Queen Elizabeth II as their sovereign, and retain a governor-general appointed by the queen). For his services to his nation, the prime minister became Sir Lynden O. Pindling when the queen knighted him in her New Year's Honours List in January 1983. His deputy prime minister Clement Maynard, who is now also minister of tourism, received the same accolade in 1989.

Freeport on Grand Bahama Island was well on its way to becoming an international resort when Pindling became prime minister, while another little island, only a slingshot away from Potter's Cay, where Nassau's fishermen tie up their boats, was also jumping into prominence. This 5½-mile-long, ¾-mile-wide spit of land is now called Paradise Island, but it once labored under the ignominious name Hog Island because its population was largely porcine.

A few wealthy individuals once made Hog Island their home. One was Joseph Lynch, a partner in the Merrill Lynch brokerage firm, who lived there during the '30s. Then came Dr. Axel Wenner-Gren, a Swedish industrialist and real-estate tycoon, who bought the island and made improvements, including a man-made lake, at the suggestion of the Duke of Windsor, who wanted to create work for local Bahamians during the lean years of World War II. Wenner-Gren's guest house was later to be converted into the now-famous epicurean restaurant Café Martinique.

In 1961, supermarket-chain heir Huntington Hartford bought Hog Island from Wenner-Gren; Hartford changed its name to the more appealing Paradise Island, made improvements designed to entice Europe's jet-setters, and imported a 14th-century French cloister, which he had reassembled in the terraced gardens of his Ocean Club, formerly Wenner-Gren's home. Putting the cloister back together proved to be rather more complicated and painstaking than the process of actually getting it there, for there were no clues as to how the structure originally looked. The work was finally completed, but it took a year.

Paradise Island—now connected to Nassau by a huge arched bridge—changed hands several more times. In November 1988, popular TV talk-show host Merv Griffin acquired Resorts International, which owned 80% of the island, including three top resorts—Paradise Island Resort & Casino, the Ocean Club, and the Paradise Paradise Beach Resort—plus the Café Martinique, the golf club, and Le Cabaret Theatre. Resorts International also took over the Miami-based Chalk's International Airlines, with its fleet of amphibious planes, which flew straight to Paradise Island from Miami's Watson Island, and started its own Merv Griffin's Paradise Island Airline to bring in visitors from Miami and Ft. Lauderdale.

Meanwhile, on rival Cable Beach, billionaire Miamian Ted Arison, owner of Carnival Cruise Lines, the world's largest seagoing fleet, was putting the finishing touches to the seven-tower, 1,550-room Crystal Palace Resort & Casino, the largest resort in the area. During its two-year construction, until its completion in December 1989, Carnival was, after the government, the country's largest employer, with some 3,000 workers. The Crystal Palace management dubbed Cable Beach the Bahamian Riviera, a glitzy nickname that other hotel owners in the area happily adopted.

Today a visitor to the Bahamas will be quick to observe that local residents, for the most part, are relaxed and friendly. The last complete census showed about 27% of the population was attending school at one level or another. They are also a devoutly religious people. New Providence alone has some 20 places of worship, and on the outer islands, locals dress up for church. Women wear colorful, freshly ironed dresses with big bonnets, and men don suits, white shirts, and ties, even under the broiling sun. Inside the churches, they sing to the Lord with a resounding and spontaneous gusto.

Much of the Bahamians' music carries echoes of African rhythms, Caribbean calypso, English folk songs, and their own hearty Goombay beat. Nowhere is the Bahamians' zest for life more exuberantly expressed than in the Junkanoo celebrations held yearly on Boxing Day (the day after Christmas) and New Year's Day in Nassau and on Grand Bahama Island.

The origin of the word *junkanoo* is hazy. One apocryphal legend has it that an African chieftain named John Canoe loved to indulge in wild parties. Whatever the origin, junkanoo—which can be likened in its uninhibited and frenzied activities only to Carnival in Rio de Janeiro and Mardi Gras in New Orleans—is a time when raucous masked revelers, dressed in costumes representing everything from dragons to bats, fill the streets, playing goatskin drums, clanging cowbells, and shrieking whistles. Junkanoo, in fact, has become an organized festival, with teams of participants with names such as the Valley Boys, the Saxon Superstars, the Fox Hill Congos, and the Vikings vying for prizes for best float, best theme, and best costumes. The celebration gets more imaginative, more colorful, and noisier every year.

Similar to Junkanoo is Goombay, but it is not quite as frenetic. Goombay runs throughout the summer, with festivals on Wednesday evenings on Nassau's Bay Street. Goatskin drummers and dancers wearing shimmering costumes perform, with the added contribution of the Royal Bahamas Police Band.

Somehow, these celebrations sum up the buoyancy of the people who live in the Bahamas, with its growing prosperity, steadfast economy, and stable government. The people who forged all this are nationalistic, but nonetheless gracious in welcoming the ever-increasing numbers of outsiders who have discovered their little piece of paradise.

1 Essential Information

Before You Go

Government Tourist Offices

For information on travel to the Bahamas, visit one of the many Bahamas tourist offices scattered around the United States, or those in Canada and the United Kingdom. They will provide you with brochures on where to stay, where to dine, what to do, what to buy, and what to wear. You can contact any of these offices at the following addresses:

In the U.S. **Atlanta:** 2957 Clairmont Rd., Suite 150, Atlanta, GA 30329, tel. 404/633–1793.
Boston: 1027 Statler Office Bldg., Boston, MA 02116, tel. 617/426–3144.
Charlotte: 4801 E. Independence Blvd., Suite 100, Charlotte, NC 28212, tel. 704/532–1290.
Chicago: 875 N. Michigan Ave., Chicago, IL 60611, tel. 312/787–8203.
Dallas: 2050 Stemmons Fwy., Suite 186, World Trade Center, Dallas, TX 75258, tel. 214/742–1886.
Detroit: 26400 Lahser Rd., Suite 309, Southfield, MI 48034, tel. 313/357–2940.
Houston: 5177 Richmond Ave., Suite 755, Houston, TX, tel. 713/626–1566.
Los Angeles: 3450 Wilshire Blvd., Suite 208, Los Angeles, CA 90010, tel. 213/385–9590.
Miami: 255 Alhambra Circle, Coral Gables, FL 33134, tel. 305/442–4860. Also at this address: Grand Bahama Promotion Board, tel. 305/448–3386; Nassau Cable Beach/Paradise Island Promotion Board, tel. 305/445–3705; Bahamas Family Islands Promotion Board, tel. 305/446–4111.
New York City: 150 E. 52nd St., New York, NY 10022, tel. 212/758–2777.
Philadelphia: Lafayette Bldg., 437 Chestnut St., Room 216, Philadelphia, PA 19106, tel. 215/925–0871.
San Francisco: 44 Montgomery St., Suite 503, San Francisco, CA 94104, tel. 415/398–5502.
St. Louis: 555 N. New Balles Rd., Suite 310, St. Louis, MO 63141, tel. 314/569–7777.
Washington, DC: 1730 Rhode Island Ave. NW, Washington, DC 20036, tel. 202/659–9135.

In Canada **Montreal:** 1255 Phillips Sq., Montreal PQ H3B 3G1, tel. 514/861–6797.
Toronto: 121 Block St., East, Suite 1101, Toronto M4W 3M5, tel. 416/968–2999.

In the U.K. **London:** 10 Chesterfield St., London W1X 8AH, tel. 071/629–5238.

Tour Groups

The vast majority of travelers bound for the sun, sand, and slow pace of the Bahamas opt for independent packages. Group tours are scarce for good reason. If your goal is to relax and get away from it all, you probably won't want to crowd your itinerary with many activities other than tanning and shopping. An incredible number of packages are available from tour operators, airlines, and travel agencies. Some are land only; others include round-trip airfare. Choosing a package will depend mostly on your pocketbook. Accommodations range from modest hotels to super-glitzy casino resorts. As usual, you get what you pay for.

When considering a tour, be sure to find out (1) exactly which expenses are included, particularly tips, taxes, side trips, meals, and entertainment; (2) the ratings of all hotels on the itinerary and of the facilities they offer; (3) the additional cost of single, rather than double, accommodations if you are traveling alone; and (4) the number of travelers in your group. Note whether the tour operator reserves the right to change hotels, routes, or even prices after you've booked, and check out the operator's policy regarding cancellations, complaints, and trip-interruption insurance. Many tour operators request that packages be booked through a travel agent; there is generally no additional charge for doing so.

Listed below is a sampling of operators and packages to give you an idea of what is available. For additional resources, contact your travel agent or the Bahamas Tourist Office.

Package Deals for Independent Travelers

In the U.S.   **Globetrotters** (124 Mt. Auburn St., Cambridge, MA 02138, tel. 800/999–9696 or 617/661–4555), **Travel Impressions** (465 Smith St., Farmingdale, NY 11735, tel. 800/284–0044 or 516/845–8000), and **Pan Am Holidays** (tel. 800/THE–TOUR) all include airfare in their three- to seven-night hotel packages in Nassau/Paradise Island and Freeport/Lucaya. **TWA Getaway Vacations** (tel. 800/GETAWAY) lets you have three, four, or seven nights, including airfare and two-for-one sightseeing vouchers. **Delta Dream Vacations** (tel. 800/872–7786 or 305/522–1440) has four-day air/hotel packages. **American Express Vacations** (Box 5014, Atlanta, GA 30302, tel. 800/241–1700, or 800/282–0800 in GA) offers three- and seven-night stays at several hotels; extra nights are available. Airfare is not included. **GoGo Tours** (69 Spring St., Ramsey, NJ 07446, tel. 800/821–3731 or 201/934–3500) is a veritable supermarket of hotel packages, offering a wide number and range of accommodations for a minimum three-night stay. Airfare is not included. **Martin Empire Tours** (1865 Palmer Ave., Larchmont, NY 10538, tel. 800/232–8747 or 914/834–2805) also offers a variety of packages.

In the U.K.   Here is just a selection of companies offering packages to the Bahamas. Contact your travel agent for further details.

Club Méditerranée (106–110 Brompton Rd., London SW3 1JJ, tel. 071/581–1161) has two villages in the Bahamas: Paradise Island and Eleuthera, the latter with special facilities for children. Peak season costs for two weeks, including flights, accommodations, and meals are from £1,889 on Paradise Island and £1,898 on Eleuthera. Flights to Eleuthera are from Paris only.

Kuoni Travel (Kuoni House, Dorking, Surrey RH5 4AZ, tel. 0306/740500) offers resort holidays in four beach-side Bahamian hotels, all on New Providence Island, close to Nassau. Prices begin at around £600, including flights, for seven nights, and peak at around £820.

Speedbird Holidays (152 King St., London W6 0QU, tel. 081/741–3369) offers resort holidays in three beach-side Bahamian hotels, two on Paradise Island, one just outside Nassau itself. In addition, the company also offers one week in Nassau followed by one week in the Family Islands. Prices vary considerably, beginning at around £600 for one week.

Thomson Worldwide (Greater London House, Hampstead Rd., London NW1 7SD, tel. 071/387–1900) offers similar resort-based trips in two beach-side hotels on New Providence Island. Prices start from around £700 for one week.

When to Go

The Bahamas is affected by the refreshing trade-wind flow generated by a large area of high atmospheric pressure covering a large part of the subtropical North Atlantic, so the climate varies little during the year. The most pleasant time is between December and May, when the temperature averages 70–75 degrees Fahrenheit. It stands to reason that hotel prices during this period are at their highest—around 30% higher than during the less popular times. The rest of the year is hot, and prone to having tropical storms; the temperature hovers around 80–85 degrees.

Remember that the sun is closer to earth the farther south you go. The sun in the Bahamas burns you more quickly than the sun in Baltimore. Stock up on suntan products before you go. These range in SPF (Suntan Protection Factor) from 2, for minimal protection, to 34, for complete blocking out. Wear sunglasses, because eyes are particularly vulnerable to direct sun and reflected rays.

Climate What follows are average daily maximum and minimum temperatures for major cities in the Bahamas.

Nassau

Jan.	77F	25C	**May**	85F	29C	**Sept.**	88F	31C
	65	18		72	22		76	24
Feb.	77F	25C	**June**	88F	31C	**Oct.**	85F	29C
	65	18		74	23		74	23
Mar.	79F	26C	**July**	88F	31C	**Nov.**	81F	27C
	67	19		76	24		70	21
Apr.	81F	27C	**Aug.**	90F	32C	**Dec.**	79F	26C
	70	21		76	24		67	19

Freeport

Jan.	74F	23C	**May**	83F	28C	**Sept.**	88F	31C
	58	14		72	22		76	24
Feb.	74F	23C	**June**	85F	29C	**Oct.**	83F	28C
	61	16		74	23		70	21
Mar.	76F	24C	**July**	88F	31C	**Nov.**	79F	26C
	63	17		77	25		65	18
Apr.	79F	26C	**Aug.**	88F	31C	**Dec.**	76F	24C
	67	19		76	24		61	16

Gregory Town	**Jan.**	76F	24C	**May**	83F	28C	**Sept.**	86F	30C
		67	19		74	23		79	26
	Feb.	76F	24C	**June**	85F	29C	**Oct.**	83F	28C
		68	20		76	24		76	24
	Mar.	79F	26C	**July**	86F	31C	**Nov.**	81F	27C
		70	21		79	26		74	23
	Apr.	81F	27C	**Aug.**	88F	31C	**Dec.**	77F	25C
		72	22		79	26		72	22

WeatherTrak provides information on more than 750 cities around the world—450 of them in the United States. Dialing 900/370–8725 will connect you to a computer, with which you can communicate by touch tone—at a cost of 75¢ for the first minute and 50¢ a minute thereafter. The number plays a taped message that tells you to dial a three-digit access code for the destination you're interested in. The code is either the area code (in the United States) or the first three letters of the foreign city. For a list of all access codes, send a self-addressed, stamped envelope to: **Cities,** Box 7000, Dallas, TX 75209, or call 214/869–3035 or 800/247–3282.

Festivals and Seasonal Events

The Bahamas always seem to have celebrations or tournaments going on, both on land and in the surrounding waters, and visitors to the islands are invited to join in most of them. Listed below are some of the most important, with public holidays included.

January: Junkanoo, a Mardi Gras–style parade, but uniquely Bahamian, welcomes the New Year in both Nassau and Freeport, with more subdued celebrations in the Family Islands on **January 1,** a public holiday. Colorful, outrageous costumes are the norm, and the ear-splitting clanging of cowbells and tomtoms is the prevailing sound. Pomp and pageantry take over when the **Supreme Court** opens in Nassau, a quarterly event. The annual **Bahamas International Windsurfing Regatta,** the largest event of its kind in North America, is held at the Nassau Beach Hotel. On Grand Bahama Island, a week-long **Grand Bahama Grand Prix** features 15 car races, and runners from around the world participate in the **Grand Bahama 10K Road Race.** The annual **New Year's Day Cruising Regatta** is celebrated at Staniel Cay in the Exumas.

February: The annual **Heart Ball** in Nassau attracts the island's most prominent personalities and international socialites. The **Nassau Cup Yacht Race** brings in yachtsmen from outside the islands to compete, and powerboats traverse the waters in the **Miami/Nassau Ocean Race.** An air show with skydivers and parachutists is held on Grand Bahama.

March: The annual **Red Cross Fair** in the gardens of Nassau's Government House rounds off the winter social season. Bimini hosts the annual **Bacardi Rum Billfish Tournament** and the **Hemingway Billfish Tournament.** Up to a dozen teams take part in the **Freeport International Rugby Festival** on Grand Bahama.

April: Easter means a long weekend; **Good Friday** and the following **Easter Monday** are public holidays. The **Princess Cup Classic Women's Golf Tournament** comes to the Bahamas Princess Resort & Casino, Freeport. One of the most colorful sailing get-togethers, the **Family Islands Regatta,** can be seen at George Town, in the Exumas, and the annual **Treasure Cay Powerboat Race Week** starts at the Treasure Cay Beach Hotel & Villas on Great Abaco Island.

May: This month brings billfish tournaments at Walker's Cay and Treasure Cay, both in the Abacos, and at Cat Cay, south of Bimini. The Bahamas Ministry of Tourism sponsors an **All-Women's International Air Race** from Ft. Pierce, Florida, to the Bahamas.

June: Two public holidays are held in June, **Labour Day** on June 1 and **Whit Monday** on June 4. This is another month for deep-sea fishing tournaments: the **Bimini Blue Water Tuna Tournament,** the annual **Green Turtle Club Fishing Tournament** at Green Turtle Cay in the Abacos, and the **Blue Marlin Tournament** in Bimini. Golfers will be teeing off at the **National Open Championships** at the Paradise Island Golf Course. And the four-month-long **Goombay Summer Festival** begins, with street dancing, fairs, beach parties, concerts, arts and crafts shows, and sporting activities.

July: The Bahamas' most important public holiday falls on July 19—**Independence Day,** which was established in 1973; it marks the end of 300 years of British rule. The annual **Commonwealth Fair,** which displays industrial and commercial accomplishments, is held at the Gibson Primary School in Nassau.

August: Emancipation Day, which marks the freeing of the slaves in 1834, is a public holiday celebrated on the first Monday in August. It is followed, a week later, by **Fox Hill Day,** on which the residents of a community at the east end of New Providence Island hold their own country fair. Two annual regattas take place, at Andros and Cat Island.

September: The end of the month is the end of the **Goombay Summer Festival.** The annual **Bahamas Free Diving Championship** can be seen at the **Andros Beach Hotel,** North Andros.

October: The first Wednesday marks the fourth and final opening for the year of the **Supreme Court** in Parliament Square. **Discovery Day,** commemorating the landing of Columbus in the islands in 1492, is observed on October 12, a public holiday. The **Bahamas Princess Open Tennis Championship** and the **Michelin National Long Driving Championship** for golfers are held at the Bahamas Princess Resort & Casino, Freeport.

November: North Andros celebrates its **Thanksgiving Bonefish Championship,** and runners may compete in Freeport's **Bahamas Blenders Guinness Road Race.** The **Grand Bahama Conchman Triathlon** features a one-mile swim, a four-mile run, and a 10-mile bicycle race.

December: The final game-fish contest of the year, the **Adam Clayton Powell Memorial Wahoo Tournament,** is held in Bimini; the late U.S. congressman was a frequent visitor to the island. The **Marlboro International Tennis Open** is held at the Ocean Club on Paradise Island. **Christmas Day,** December 25, and **Boxing Day,** December 26 (named after the custom of giving boxed presents to tradesmen the day after Christmas), are both public holidays. Boxing Day coincides with the first of the Junkanoo parades, which precedes the January 1 bash.

What to Pack

Pack light: Porters and luggage trolleys can be hard to find, and baggage restrictions are tight.

Clothing The reason you're going to the Bahamas is to get away from all of that big-city suit-shirt-and-tie turmoil, so your wardrobe should reflect the informality of the experience. Aside from that bathing suit, which will be your favorite uniform, take lightweight clothing (short-sleeve shirts, T-shirts, cotton slacks, lightweight jackets for evening wear for men; light dresses, shorts, and T-shirts for women). If you're going during the "high season," between mid-December and April, toss in a sweater for the occasional cool evening. Cover up in public places for downtown shopping expeditions, and save that skimpy bathing suit for the beach at your hotel.

Only some of the more sophisticated hotels require jackets for men and dresses for women at dinner. These are listed in the Dining section of each destination chapter. But there are no such dress rules in any of the Bahamas' four casinos.

Miscellaneous An extra pair of glasses, contact lenses, or prescription sunglasses is always a good idea; it is important to pack any prescription medicines you use regularly, as well as any allergy medication you may need.

Carry-on Luggage Airlines generally allow each passenger one piece of carry-on luggage on international flights from the United States. The bag cannot exceed 45 inches (length + width + height) and must fit under the seat or in the overhead luggage compartment.

Checked Luggage Passengers are generally allowed to check two pieces of luggage, neither of which can exceed 62 inches (length + width + height) or weigh more than 70 pounds. Baggage allowances vary slightly among airlines, so be sure to check with the carrier or your travel agent before departure.

Electricity Electricity is normally 120 volts/60 cycles, providing compatibility with all U.S. appliances.

Taking Money Abroad

The Bahamian dollar has the same exchange rate as the U.S. dollar, and the two currencies are used interchangeably. Banks handle currency exchange in the Bahamas, and all branches—including airport branches—close in the late afternoon and on weekends; some hotels convert limited amounts of foreign currency but charge relatively high commission rates. It's wise, therefore, to arrive with some U.S. cash. If at all possible, try to avoid accumulating a large amount of Bahamian money; it is often difficult to exchange this money for U.S. dollars while in the Bahamas, and U.S. exchange institutions charge a fee.

Credit cards are accepted in most of the major resort centers, especially on New Providence and Grand Bahama islands (less frequently in the outlying islands), and traveler's checks are accepted by most large hotels, fine restaurants, and stores. The most recognized traveler's checks are American Express, Barclays, Thomas Cook, and those issued through major commercial banks such as Citibank and Bank of America. Some banks will issue the checks free to established customers, but most charge a 1% commission fee. Remember to take the addresses of offices where you can get refunds for lost or stolen traveler's checks.

Getting Money from Home

There are at least three ways to get money from home:

1) Have it sent through a large commercial bank that has a branch where you are staying. The only drawback is that you must have an account with the bank; if not, you'll have to go through your own bank, and the process will be slower and more costly.

2) Have it sent through **American Express.** If you are a cardholder, you can cash a personal check or a counter check at an American Express office for up to $1,000; $200 will be in cash and $800 in traveler's checks. There is a 1% commission on the traveler's checks. You can also receive money through an **American Express MoneyGram,** which enables you to obtain up to $10,000 in cash. It works this way: You call home and ask someone to go to an American Express office—or an American Express MoneyGram agent located in a retail outlet—and fill out an American Express MoneyGram. It can be paid for with cash or with any major credit card. The person making the payment is given a reference number and telephones you with that number. The American Express MoneyGram agent calls an 800 number and authorizes the transfer of funds to the American Express office or participating agency where you are staying. In most cases, the money is available immediately on a 24-hour basis. You pick it up by showing identification and giving the reference number. Fees vary with the amount of money sent. For $300 the fee is $30; for $5,000, $195. For the American Express MoneyGram location nearest your home, and to find out the locations in the Bahamas, call 800/543–4080. You do not have to be a cardholder to use this service.

3) Have money sent through **Western Union,** whose U.S. number is 800/325–6000. If you have a MasterCard or Visa, you can have money sent for any amount up to your credit limit. If not, have someone take cash or a certified cashier's check to a Western Union office. The money will be delivered to a bank where you are staying. Fees vary with the amount of money sent and the precise location of the recipient. To send $500 to Nassau, the fee is $42; to send $1,000, $47.

Currency

The U.S. dollar is on a par with the Bahamian dollar, U.K. pound sterling compares at about 58 pence, and the Canadian dollar at around $1.20. If someone offers you a $3 bill, don't think you're being conned. Bahamian money runs in half-dollar, $1, $3, $5, $10, $20, $50, and $100 bills. The $3 bill makes an unusual souvenir.

What It Will Cost

Generally, prices in the Bahamas reflect the exchange rates given above: they are about the same as in the United States, less expensive than in the United Kingdom, and more expensive than in Canada. A hotel can cost anything from $35 a night (for cottages and apartments in downtown Nassau and in the Family Islands) to $145 and up (at the ritzier resorts on Cable Beach and Paradise Island and in Freeport and Lucaya), depending on the season. Add $35 to $50 per person a day for meals. Bus fares in the two main islands, New Providence and Grand Bahama, are cheap. Four-day/three-night and eight-day/seven-night package stays offered by most hotels can cut costs considerably.

Passports and Visas

Americans For a stay of up to eight months, a passport and visa are not required of tourists with onward/return tickets, proof of citizenship, and photo ID. However, it is a good idea to take your passport for identification. A departure tax of $5 is charged at the airport. For additional information, contact the **Embassy of the Commonwealth of the Bahamas** (600 New Hampshire Ave. NW, Suite 865, Washington, DC 20037, tel. 202/944–3390) or the nearest consulate.

Canadians All Canadians need a passport to enter the Bahamas. Send your completed application (available at any post office or passport office) to the **Bureau of Passports** (External Affairs, Ottawa, Ontario K1A 0G3). Include $25, two photographs, a guarantor, and proof of Canadian citizenship. Application can be made in person at the regional passport offices in Edmonton, Halifax, Montreal, Calgary, St. John's (Newfoundland), Victoria, Toronto, Vancouver, or Winnipeg. Passports are valid for five years, after which a new application must be filed.

A visa is not required to enter the Bahamas.

Britons All British citizens require a valid passport to enter the Bahamas. British visitors' passports are not valid, however. Application forms are available from most travel agents and major post offices, or contact the **Passport Office** (Clive House, 70 Petty France, London SW1H 9HD, tel. 071/279–3434). Cost is £15 for a standard 32-page passport, £30 for a 94-page passport. All applications must be countersigned by your bank manager, or by a solicitor, a barrister, a doctor, a clergyman, or a justice of the peace, and must be accompanied by two photographs.

A visa is not required to enter the Bahamas.

Customs and Duties

On Arrival Customs allows you to bring in 200 cigarettes and a quart of liquor, in addition to personal effects and all the money you wish. But don't even think of smuggling in marijuana or any kind of narcotics. Justice is swifter in the Bahamas than in the United States. Expect conviction and severe punishment within three days, which could certainly put a damper on your vacation.

As for pets, you would be well advised to leave them at home, unless you're considering an elongated stay in the islands. An import permit is required from the **Ministry of Agriculture, Trade, and Industry** for all animals brought into the Bahamas. Applications must be made to the Ministry at Box N 3028, Nassau (tel. 809/323–1777). You'll also need a veterinary health certificate issued by a licensed vet within 24 hours of embarkation. The permit is good for 90 days from the date of issue.

On Departure   If you are bringing any foreign-made equipment from home, such as cameras, it's wise to carry the original receipt with you or register it with U.S. Customs before you leave (Form 4457). Otherwise, you may end up paying duty on your return.

Americans   You may bring home duty free up to $400 worth of foreign goods, as long as you have been out of the country for at least 48 hours and you haven't made another international trip in 30 days. Each member of the family is entitled to the same exemption, regardless of age, and exemptions may be pooled. For the next $1,000 worth of goods, a flat 10% rate is assessed; above $1,400, duties vary with the merchandise. Travelers 21 or older are entitled to bring in up to one liter of alcohol, 100 cigars (non-Cuban), and 200 cigarettes. Only one bottle of perfume trademarked in the United States may be brought in. However, there is no duty on antiques or works of art more than 100 years old. Anything exceeding these limits will be taxed at the port of entry, and may be taxed additionally in the traveler's home state. Gifts valued at under $50 may be mailed to friends or relatives at home duty free, but you may not send more than one package per day to any one addressee; packages may not include tobacco, liquor, or perfumes costing more than $5.

Canadians   You have a $300 exemption and may also bring in duty free up to 50 cigars, 200 cigarettes, 2.2 pounds of tobacco, and 40 ounces of liquor, provided these items are declared in writing to customs on arrival and accompany the traveler in carryons or checked-through baggage. These restrictions apply for absences of at least seven days and at most one year. If you are out of Canada for less than seven days but for a minimum of 48 hours, there is a $100 exemption, with the same restrictions on alcohol and tobacco products. Personal gifts should be labeled, "Unsolicited gift—value under $40." Get a copy of the Canadian Customs brochure *I Declare* for further details. Copies can be obtained at local customs offices.

Britons   There are two levels of duty-free allowance for people entering the United Kingdom: one for goods bought outside the European Economic Community (EC) *or* for goods bought in a duty-free shop in an EC country; the other for goods bought in an EC country but not in a duty-free shop.

In the **first category** you may import duty free: 1) 200 cigarettes or 100 cigarillos or 50 cigars or 250 grams of tobacco (if you live outside Europe these allowances are doubled); 2) one liter of alcoholic drink over 22% volume or two liters of alcoholic drink under 22% volume or fortified or sparkling wine; 3) two liters of still table wine; 4) 60 milliliters of perfume and 250 milliliters of toilet water; 5) other goods to the value of £32.

In the **second category** you may import duty free: 1) 300 cigarettes or 150 cigarillos or 75 cigars or 400 grams of tobacco; 2) 1.5 liters of alcoholic drink over 22% volume or three liters of alcoholic drink under 22% volume or fortified or sparkling wine; 3) five liters of still table wine; 4) 90 milliliters of perfume and 375 milliliters of toilet water; 5) other goods to the value of £250.

Note that, though it is not classified an alcoholic drink by EC countries for customs' purposes and is thus part of the "other goods" allowance, you may not import more than 50 liters of beer.

For further information, contact **HM Customs and Excise** (Dorset House, Stamford St., London SE1 9PS, tel. 071/928–0533).

Traveling with Film

If your camera is new, shoot and develop a few rolls before leaving home. Pack some lens tissue and an extra battery for your built-in light meter. Invest about $10 in a skylight filter: It will protect the lens and reduce haze.

Film doesn't like hot weather, so if you're driving in the heat, don't store film in the glove compartment or on the shelf under the rear window. Put it behind the front seat on the floor, on the side opposite the exhaust pipe.

On a plane trip, never pack unprocessed film in check-in luggage; if your bags get X-rayed, say good-bye to your pictures. Always carry undeveloped film with you through security and ask to have it inspected by hand. (It helps to keep your film in a plastic bag, ready for quick inspection.)

The old airport scanning machines, still in use in some countries, use heavy doses of radiation that can make a family portrait look like an early morning fog. The newer models used in all U.S. airports are safe for from five to 500 scans, depending on the speed of your film. The effects are cumulative; you can put the same roll of film through several scans without worry. After five scans, though, you're asking for trouble.

If your film gets fogged and you want an explanation, send it to the National Association of Photographic Manufacturers (550 Mamaroneck Ave., Harrison, NY 10528). It will try to determine what went wrong. The service is free.

Language

Bahamians speak English with a lilt influenced by their Scottish, Irish, and/or African ancestry.

Staying Healthy

Sunburn and sunstroke are chronic problems for visitors to the Bahamas. On a hot, sunny day, even people who are not normally bothered by strong sun should cover themselves with a long-sleeve shirt, a hat, and long pants or a beach wrap. These are essential for a day on a boat but are also advisable for midday at the beach. Also carry some sun-block for nose, ears, and other sensitive areas such as eyelids, ankles, etc. Be sure to drink enough liquids. Above all, limit your sun time for the first few days until you become accustomed to the heat.

A vaccination against yellow fever is required if you're arriving from an infected area. The *Summary of Health Information for International Travel*, a biweekly publication put out by the Centers for Disease Control, has updated reports on which regions of the world are infected. To obtain the latest copy, contact the Superintendent of Documents (U.S. Government Printing Office, Washington, DC 20402, tel. 202/783–3238).

The cost for a single copy, including shipping and handling, is $5.

Otherwise, no special shots are required before visiting the Bahamas. If you have a health problem that might require your purchasing prescription drugs while in the Bahamas, have your doctor write a prescription using the drug's generic name; brand names can vary widely.

International Association for Medical Assistance to Travelers (IAMAT) is a worldwide organization offering a list of approved English-speaking doctors whose training meets British and U.S. standards. Contact IAMAT for a list of physicians and clinics in the Bahamas that belong to this network. **In the United States:** 417 Center St., Lewiston, NY 14092, tel. 716/754–4883. **In Canada:** 40 Regal Road, Guelph, Ontario N1K 1B5. **In Europe:** 57 Voirets, 1212 Grand-Lancy, Geneva, Switzerland. Membership is free.

Insurance

In the U.S. Travelers may seek insurance coverage in three areas: health and accident, lost luggage, and trip cancellation. Your first step is to review your existing health and home-owner policies; some health-insurance plans cover health expenses incurred while traveling, some major-medical plans cover emergency transportation, and some home-owner policies cover the theft of luggage.

Health and Accident Several companies offer coverage designed to supplement existing health insurance for travelers:

Carefree Travel Insurance (Box 310, 120 Mineola Blvd., Mineola, NY 11501, tel. 516/294–0220 or 800/343–3553) provides coverage for emergency medical evacuation. It also offers 24-hour medical phone advice.

International SOS Assistance (Box 11568, Philadelphia, PA 19116, tel. 215/244–1500 or 800/523–8930) does not offer medical insurance but provides medical evacuation services to its clients, who often are international corporations.

Travel Assistance International (1133 15th St. NW, Suite 400, Washington, DC 20005, tel. 202/347–2025 or 800/821–2828) provides emergency evacuation services and 24-hour medical referrals.

Travel Guard International, underwritten by Transamerica Occidental Life Companies (1100 Centerpoint Dr., Stevens Point, WI 54481, tel. 715/345–0505 or 800/782–5151), offers reimbursement for medical expenses with no deductibles or daily limits and emergency evacuation services.

Wallach and Company, Inc. (243 Church St. NW, Suite 100D, Vienna, VA 22180, tel. 703/281–9500 or 800/237–6615), offers comprehensive medical coverage, including emergency evacuation, for trips of 10 to 90 days.

WorldCare Travel Assistance Association (605 Market St., Suite 1300, San Francisco, CA 94105, tel. 415/541–4991 or 800/666–4993) provides unlimited emergency evacuation, 24-hour medical referral, and an emergency message center.

Lost Luggage On international flights, airlines are responsible for lost or damaged property at rates of up to $9.07 per pound (or $20 per kilo) for checked baggage, and up to $400 per passenger for unchecked baggage. If you're carrying valuables, either take

them with you on the plane or purchase additional insurance for
lost luggage. Some airlines will issue extra luggage insurance
when you check in, but many do not. Insurance for lost, damaged, or stolen luggage is available through travel agents or
directly through various insurance companies. Luggage-loss
coverage is usually part of a comprehensive travel-insurance
package that includes personal accident, trip cancellation, and
sometimes default and bankruptcy. Two companies that issue
luggage insurance are **Tele-Trip** (Box 31685, 3201 Farnam St.,
Omaha, NE 68131, tel. 800/228–9792), a subsidiary of Mutual of
Omaha, and the **Travelers Insurance Co.** (Ticket and Travel
Dept., 1 Tower Sq., Hartford, CT 06183, tel. 203/277–0111 or
800/243–3174). Tele-Trip operates sales booths at airports, and
it also issues insurance through travel agents. Tele-Trip will in-
sure checked luggage for up to 180 days and for $500–$3,000
valuation. For one–three days, the rate for a $500 valuation is
$8.25; for 180 days, $100. The Travelers Insurance Co. will in-
sure checked or hand luggage for $500–$2,000 valuation per
person, also for a maximum of 180 days. The rate for one–five
days for $500 valuation is $10; for 180 days, $85. Other compa-
nies with comprehensive policies include **Access America, Inc.**,
a subsidiary of Blue Cross–Blue Shield (Box 807, New York,
NY 10163, tel. 212/490–5345 or 800/284–8300); **Near Services**
(1900 N. MacArthur Blvd., Suite 210, Oklahoma City, OK
73127, tel. 800/654–6700, or 405/949–2500 in Oklahoma City);
Travel Guard International and **Carefree Travel Insurance** (*see*
Health and Accident Insurance, above).

Before you go, itemize the contents of each bag in case you need
to file an insurance claim. Be certain to put your home or business address on each piece of luggage, including carry-on bags.
If your luggage is lost or stolen and later recovered, the airline
will deliver the luggage to your home free of charge.

Trip Cancellation   Flight insurance is often included in the price of a ticket when
paid for with American Express, Visa, or other major credit
cards. It is usually included in combination travel-insurance
packages available from most tour operators, travel agents,
and insurance agents.

In the U.K.   We recommend strongly that you take out adequate insurance
to guard against health problems, motoring mishaps, theft,
flight cancellation, and loss of luggage. Most major tour operators offer holiday insurance, and details are given in brochures.
But for free general advice on all aspects of holiday insurance
contact the **Association of British Insurers** (Aldermary House,
Queen St., London EC4N 1TT, tel. 071/248–4477). A proven
leader in the holiday insurance field is **Europ Assistance** (252
High St., Croydon, Surrey CR0 1NF, tel. 081/680–1234).

Car Rentals

Before leaving home, find out if your hotel and air package includes a car—many packages do, and the deals offered by tour
wholesalers are often better than the prices you'll find when
you arrive in the Bahamas. Some airlines provide car tie-ins
with a lower than normal rate. On fly/drive deals, ask whether
the car-rental company will honor a reservation rate if it must
upgrade you to a larger vehicle upon arrival.

Reserving your vehicle before you arrive is always a good idea if you plan to rent from a national chain, especially if you will be in the Bahamas during the busy travel times.

Before calling or arriving in person at the rental desk, do a bit of homework to save yourself some money. Check with your personal or business insurance agent to see if your coverage already includes rental cars. Signing up for the collision damage waiver (CDW) offered by the rental agency quickly inflates that "what a deal" rate before you ever leave the parking lot. Some credit card companies also offer rental-car coverage.

When booking over the phone, be certain to ask whether you're responsible for additional mileage and for returning the car with a full tank, even if you don't use all the gas. In addition, be sure to get a confirmation number for your car reservation, and check to see if the rental company offers unlimited mileage and a flat rate per day, which are definitely advantages. Last but not least, check beforehand on which credit cards are honored by the company.

Car rentals are available at the airports, cruise ports, and hotels on the main islands of New Providence (Nassau) and Grand Bahama (Freeport/Lucaya). Most rental firms in the Bahamas are locally owned and operated (exclusively, in the Family Islands), but if you would like to make arrangements with a U.S. agency before leaving home, call **Avis** (800/331–1212), **National** (800/227–7368), **Hertz** (800/527–0700), or **Budget** (800/527–0700). The rental rates for an automobile are between $47 and $85 a day, and from $279 a week, depending on the type of car.

Student and Youth Travel

The **International Student Identity Card (ISIC)** entitles full-time students to rail passes, special fares on local transportation, student charter flights, and discounts at museums, theaters, sports events, and many other attractions. If purchased in the United States, the $10 cost of the ISIC card also includes $2,000 in emergency medical coverage, $100 a day for up to 60 days of hospital coverage, as well as a collect phone number to call in case of emergency. Apply to the **Council on International Educational Exchange** (CIEE, 205 E. 42nd St., New York, NY 10017, tel. 212/661–1414). In Canada, the ISIC is available for CN $10 from the **Association of Student Councils** (187 College St., Toronto, Ontario M5T 1P7).

Travelers under age 26 can apply for a **Youth International Educational Exchange Card (YIEE)** issued by the **Federation of International Youth Travel Organizations** (81 Islands Brugge, DK-2300 Copenhagen S, Denmark). It provides similar services and benefits as the ISIC card. The YIEE card is available in the United States from CIEE (address above) and in Canada from the **Canadian Hostelling Association** (333 River Rd., Vanier, Ottawa, Ontario K1L 8H9, tel. 613/476–3844).

An **International Youth Hostel Federation (IYHF)** membership card is the key to inexpensive dormitory-style accommodations at thousands of youth hostels around the world. Hostels aren't only for young travelers on a budget, though; many have family accommodations. Hostels provide separate sleeping quarters for men and women at rates of $7–$15 a night, per person, and are situated in a variety of facilities, including converted farmhouses, villas, restored castles, and even lighthouses, as well as in specially constructed modern buildings. There are more than 5,000 hostel locations in 75 countries around the world. IYHF memberships, which are valid for one year from the time of purchase, are available in the United States through **American Youth Hostels** (AYH, Box 37613, Washington, DC 20013, tel. 202/783–6161). The cost for a first-year membership is $25 for adults 18–54. Renewal thereafter is $15. For youths (17 and under) the rate is $10 and for seniors (55 and older) the rate is $15. Family membership is available for $35. Every national hostel association arranges special reductions for members visiting their country, such as discounted rail fare or free bus travel, so be sure to ask for a list of discounts when you buy your membership. **Council Travel,** a CIEE subsidiary, is the foremost U.S. student travel agency, specializing in low-cost charters and serving as the exclusive U.S. agent for many student airfare bargains and student tours. CIEE's 80-page "Student Travel" catalogue and "Council Charter" brochures are available free from any Council Travel office in the United States (enclose $1 postage if ordering by mail). In addition to the CIEE headquarters (205 E. 42nd St.) and branch office (35 W. 8th St.) in New York City, there are Council Travel offices in Berkeley, La Jolla, Long Beach, Los Angeles, San Diego, San Francisco, and Sherman Oaks, CA; New Haven, CT; Washington, DC; Atlanta, GA; Chicago and Evanston, IL; New Orleans, LA; Amherst, Boston, and Cambridge, MA; Minneapolis, MN; Portland, OR; Providence, RI; Austin and Dallas, TX; Seattle, WA; and Milwaukee, WI.

The **Educational Travel Center** (438 N. Frances St., Madison, WI 53703, tel. 608/256–5551) is another student-travel specialist worth contacting for information on student tours, bargain fares, and bookings.

Students who would like to work abroad should contact CIEE's **Work Abroad Department** (205 E. 42nd St., New York, NY 10017, tel. 212/661–1414, ext. 1130). The council arranges various types of paid and voluntary work experiences overseas for periods of up to six months. CIEE also sponsors study programs in Europe, Latin America, Asia, and Australia, and it publishes many books of interest to the student traveler. These include *Work, Study, Travel Abroad: The Whole World Handbook* ($9.95, plus $1 book-rate postage or $2.50 first-class postage); and *Volunteer! The Comprehensive Guide to Voluntary Service in the U.S. and Abroad* ($6.95, plus $1 book-rate postage or $2.50 first-class postage).

The Information Center at the **Institute of International Education** (IIE; 809 UN Plaza, New York, NY 10017, tel. 212/984–5413) has reference books, foreign-university catalogues, study-abroad brochures, and other materials, which may be consulted by students and nonstudents alike, free of charge. The center is open Mon.–Fri. 10–4; closed on holidays.

Traveling with Children

Publication *Family Travel Times* is a newsletter published 10 times a year by Travel With Your Children (TWYCH, 80 8th Ave., New York, NY 10011, tel. 212/206–0688). A one-year subscription costs $35 and includes access to back issues and twice-weekly opportunities to call in for specific advice.

Getting There   On international flights, children under 2 not occupying a seat pay 10% of adult fare. Various discounts apply to children age 2–12, so check with your airline when booking. Reserve a seat behind the bulkhead of the plane, as there's usually more leg room and enough space to fit a bassinet, which the airlines will supply. At the same time, ask about special children's meals or snacks; most airlines offer them. See TWYCH's "Airline Guide," published in the February 1990 issue of *Family Travel Times* (and again in February 1992), for more information about the children's services offered by 46 airlines.

Ask the airline in advance if you can bring aboard your child's car seat. For the booklet *Child/Infant Safety Seats Acceptable for Use in Aircraft,* write to the Federal Aviation Commission (APA-200, 800 Independence Ave. SW, Washington, DC 20591, tel. 202/267–3479).

Home Exchange   Exchanging homes is a surprisingly low-cost way to enjoy a vacation abroad, especially a long one. The largest home-exchange service, **International Home Exchange Service** (Box 3975, San Francisco, CA 94119, tel. 415/435–3497), publishes three directories a year. Membership, which costs $35, entitles you to one listing and all three directories. Photos of your property cost an additional $8.50; listing a second home costs $10. A good choice for domestic home exchange, **Vacation Exchange Club, Inc.** (12006 111th Ave., Unit 12, Youngstown, AZ 85363, tel. 602/972–2186), publishes one directory in February and a supplement in April. Membership is $24.70 per year, for which you receive one listing. Photos cost an additional $9; listing a second home costs $6. **Loan-a-Home** (2 Park La., Mount Vernon, NY 10552) is popular with the academic community on sabbatical and with businesspeople on temporary assignment. There's no annual membership fee or charge for listing your home; however, one directory and a supplement costs $30. Loan-a-Home publishes two directories (in December and June) and two supplements (in March and September) each year. The set of four books costs $40 per year.

Hints for Disabled Travelers

A couple of dozen hotels throughout the Bahamas have special facilities for the physically disabled, in the way of elevators, ramps, and easy access to rooms and public areas. Your travel agent should have information on them, though prospective travelers may prefer to make their own individual inquiries. Here are some suggestions based on a survey conducted by the Bahamas Paraplegic Association:

Nassau   Cable Beach Manor (Box N 8333, tel. 809/327–7785), Nassau Beach Hotel (Box N 7756, tel. 809/327–7711), New Olympia (Box 984, West Bay St., tel. 809/322–4971), Parliament (Box N 9689, tel. 809/322–2836), The Orchard Garden (Box 1514, tel. 809/323–1297), and The British Colonial Beach Resort (Box N 7148, tel. 809/322–3301).

Paradise Island   Bay View Village (Box SS 6308, tel. 809/326–2555), Pirates Cove Holiday Inn (Box SS 6214, tel. 809/326–2101), Loew's Harbour Cove (Box SS 6249, tel. 809/326–2561), Paradise Beach Resort (Box N 4777, tel. 809/363–2541), and Paradise Island Resort & Casino (Box N 4777, tel. 809/363–3000).

Grand Bahama	Atlantik Beach (Box F 531, tel. 809/373–1444), Bahamas Princess Resort & Casino (Box F 2623, tel. 809/352–9661), Windward Palms (Box F 2549, tel. 809/352–8821).
Family Islands	Ambassador Inn (Box 484, Marsh Harbour, Abaco, tel. 809/367–2022) and Guana Beach Resort (Box 474, Guana Key, Marsh Harbour, Abaco, tel. 809/359–6194).
Cat Island	Bridge Inn (c/o New Bight Post Office, tel. 809/354–5013).
Eleuthera	Ethel's Cottages (Box 27, Tarpum Bay, tel. 809/334–4030, ext. 233) and Windermere Island Club (Box 25, tel. 809/332–2538).
Inagua	Ford's Inagua Inn (c/o Matthew Town, tel. 809/555–1222; ask overseas operator for 2277 in Inagua).
Long Island	Stella Maris Inn (Box 105, tel. 809/336–2106).
Spanish Wells	Spanish Wells Beach Resort (Box 31, tel. 809/333–4371).

The following organizations in the United States provide advice and services:

The **Information Center for Individuals with Disabilities** (Fort Point Pl., 1st floor, 27–43 Wormwood St., Boston, MA 02217, tel. 617/727–5540) offers useful problem-solving assistance, including lists of travel agents who specialize in tours for the disabled.

Mobility International USA (Box 3551, Eugene, OR 97403, tel. 503/343–1284) is an internationally affiliated organization with 500 members. For a $20 annual fee, it coordinates exchange programs for disabled people around the world and offers information on accommodations and organized study programs.

Moss Rehabilitation Hospital Travel Information Service (12th St. and Tabor Rd., Philadelphia, PA 19141, tel. 215/329–5715), for a small fee, provides information on tourist sights, transportation, and accommodations in destinations around the world.

Travel Industry and Disabled Exchange (TIDE, 5435 Donna Ave., Tarzana, CA 91356, tel. 818/368–5648), for a $15 annual fee, provides a quarterly newsletter and a directory of travel agencies and tours to Europe, Canada, Great Britain, New Zealand, and Australia, all specializing in travel for the disabled.

Hints for Older Travelers

The **American Association of Retired Persons** (AARP, 1909 K St. NW, Washington, DC 20049, tel. 202/662–4850) has two programs for independent travelers: (1) the Purchase Privilege Program, which offers discounts on hotels, airfare, car rentals, RV rentals, and sightseeing; and (2) the AARP Motoring Plan, which furnishes emergency aid (road service) and trip-routing information for an annual fee of $33.95 per person or couple. (Both programs include the member and member's spouse, or the member and another person who shares the household.) The AARP also arranges group tours, including apartment living in Europe and Australia, **American Express Vacations** (Box 5014, Atlanta, GA 30302, tel. 800/241–1700). AARP members must be 50 or older; annual dues are $5 per person or per couple.

When using an AARP or other discount identification card, ask for reduced hotel rates at the time you make your reservation, not when you check out. At restaurants, show your card to the maître d' before you're seated, because discounts may be limited to certain set menus, days, or hours. When renting a car, remember that economy cars priced at promotional rates may cost less than cars available with your discount ID card.

Elderhostel (80 Boylston St., Suite 400, Boston, MA 02116, tel. 617/426–7788) is an innovative 16-year-old educational program for people 60 and older. Participants live in dorms on some 1,200 campuses around the world. Mornings are devoted to lectures and seminars; afternoons to sightseeing and field trips. Fees for two- to three-week trips, including room, board, tuition, and round-trip transportation, are $1,700–$3,200.

Mature Outlook (6001 N. Clark St., Chicago, IL 60660, tel. 800/336–6330), a subsidiary of Sears, Roebuck & Co., is a travel club for people over 50, with hotel and motel discounts and a bimonthly newsletter. Annual membership is $9.95; there are 800,000 members currently. Instant membership is available at participating Holiday Inns.

National Council of Senior Citizens (925 15th St. NW, Washington, DC 20005, tel. 202/347–8800) is a nonprofit advocacy group with about 5,000 local clubs across the country. Annual membership is $12 per person or per couple. Members receive a monthly newspaper with travel information and an ID card for reduced-rate hotels and car rentals.

Saga International Holidays (120 Boylston St., Boston, MA 02116, tel. 800/343–0273) specializes in group travel for people over 60. A selection of variously priced tours allows you to choose the package that meets your needs.

Arriving and Departing

From North America by Plane

There are three types of flights: nonstop—no changes, no stops; direct—no changes, but one or more stops; and connecting—two or more planes, one or more stops. If you can tolerate the plane-hopping, connecting flights are often the least expensive way to go.

Airports and Airlines While the main airports of entry are **Nassau** (tel. 809/322–3344), on New Providence Island, and **Freeport** (tel. 809/352–6020), on Grand Bahama Island, there are some direct flights from Florida to **Marsh Harbour** and **Treasure Cay** in the Abacos. **Bahamasair** (tel. 800/222–4262), the national carrier, also flies to Treasure Cay and Marsh Harbour, as well as to **Acklins, Crooked Island, Andros, Cat Island, Eleuthera** (with airports at **North Eleuthera, Governor's Harbour,** and **Rock Sound**), **Great Exuma, Inagua, Long Island,** and **San Salvador. Chalk's International Airlines/Paradise Island** (tel. 800/432–8807) flies to **Bimini.**

Flying into Nassau International Airport from the United States are **Delta** (tel. 800/221–1212), **USAir** (tel. 800/428–4322), **Eastern Airlines** (tel. 800/327–8376), **Midway Airlines** (tel. 800/621–5700), **TWA** (tel. 800/221–2000), **Pan Am** (tel. 800/221–1111), **Bahamasair** (tel. 800/222–4262), **Aero Coach** (tel. 800/

327–0010), **Paradise Island/Chalk's International Airlines** (tel. 800/432–8807), **Carnival Airlines** (tel. 800/222–7466), and **Comair** (tel. 800/354–9822). Canadian airlines with flights to Nassau are **Air Canada** (tel. 800/422–6232), **Nationair First Air** (tel. 514/476–3387), **Conquest** (tel. 800/722–0860), and **Odyssey** (tel. 416/676–6220)—which also flies to Eleuthera. Freeport, Grand Bahama, is serviced by TWA, Bahamasair, Delta, Pan Am, Comair, Aero Coach, and **Airlift International** (tel. 305/ 871–1750) from the United States, and by Air Canada from Canada. Flights to the Bahamas originate from Atlanta, Baltimore, Boston, Chicago, Cincinnati, Cleveland, Columbus, Dallas/Fort Worth, Dayton, Denver, Des Moines, Detroit, Houston, Indianapolis, Kansas City, Los Angeles, Louisville, Memphis, Miami, Milwaukee, Minneapolis/St. Paul, New Orleans, New York City, Omaha, Philadelphia, Savannah, Seattle, and Washington, D.C.

Flying Time Approximate flying times to Nassau International Airport: from Miami, 35 minutes; from New York City, 2½ hours; from Toronto, 3½ hours; from San Francisco, 5¾ hours; and from Houston, 2½ hours.

Enjoying the Flight Because the air on a plane is dry, it helps to drink a lot of nonalcoholic beverages while flying; drinking alcohol contributes to jet lag, as does eating heavy meals on board. Feet swell at high altitudes, so it's a good idea to remove your shoes at the beginning of your flight. Sleepers usually prefer window seats to curl up against; those who like to move about the cabin should ask for aisle seats. Bulkhead seats (located in the front row of each cabin) have more legroom, but seat trays are attached rather awkwardly to the arms of the seat rather than to the back of the seat ahead. Generally, bulkhead seats are reserved for the disabled, the elderly, or parents traveling with babies.

Discount Flights The major airlines offer a range of tickets that can increase the price of any given seat by more than 300%, depending on the day of purchase. As a rule, the further in advance you buy the ticket, the less expensive it is and the greater the penalty (up to 100%) for canceling. Check with airlines for details.

The best buy is not necessarily an APEX (advance purchase) ticket on one of the major airlines, because these tickets carry certain restrictions: They must be bought in advance (usually 21 days); they restrict your travel, usually with a minimum stay of seven days and a maximum of 90; and they also penalize you for changes—voluntary or not—in your travel plans. But if you can work around these drawbacks (and most travelers can), they are among the best-value fares available.

Travelers willing to put up with some restrictions and inconveniences, in exchange for a substantially reduced air fare, may be interested in flying as an air courier. A person who agrees to be a courier must accompany shipments between designated points. There are two sources of information on courier deals:

A telephone directory lists courier companies by the cities to which they fly. Send $5 and a self-addressed, stamped, business-size envelope to Pacific Data Sales Publishing, 2554 Lincoln Blvd., Suite 275-F, Marina del Rey, CA 92091. *A Simple Guide to Courier Travel* is also helpful. Send $12.45 (includes postage and handling) to the Carriage Group, Box 2394, Lake Oswego, OR 97035. For more information, call 800/344–9375.

Another option is to join a travel club that offers special discounts to its members. Several such organizations are **Discount Travel International** (114 Forrest Ave., Narberth, PA 19072, tel. 215/668–2182), **Moment's Notice** (40 E. 49th St., New York, NY 10017, tel. 212/486–0503), **Stand-Buys, Ltd.** (311 W. Superior, Suite 414, Chicago, IL 60610, tel. 800/255–0200), and **Worldwide Discount Travel Club** (1674 Meridien Ave., Miami Beach, FL 33139, tel. 305/534–2082). These cut-rate tickets should be compared with APEX tickets on the major airlines.

Smoking
As of late February 1990, smoking is banned on all routes within the 48 contiguous states; within the states of Hawaii and Alaska; to and from the U.S. Virgin Islands and Puerto Rico; and on flights of under six hours to and from Hawaii and Alaska. The rule applies to both domestic and foreign carriers.

On a flight where smoking is permitted, you can request a nonsmoking seat during check-in or when you book your ticket. If the airline tells you there are no seats available in the nonsmoking section, insist on one: Department of Transportation regulations require carriers to find seats for all nonsmokers, provided they meet check-in time restrictions. These regulations apply to all international flights on domestic carriers; however, the Department of Transportation does not have jurisdiction over foreign carriers traveling out of or into the United States.

From North America by Ship

Cruise ships from the Florida ports call regularly at Nassau and Freeport on one-, two-, three-, and four-day cruises. Prices vary from a minimum $89 for a one-day trip to $325 for three days and $355 for four days. Some ships on longer Caribbean trips of seven and 14 days make Nassau their last port of call before returning home.

Admiral Cruises Inc. (1220 Biscayne Blvd., Miami, FL 33101, tel. 800/327–0271) runs three-day trips to Nassau, leaving every Friday, and four-day trips to Nassau and Freeport, leaving every Monday. The *Emerald Seas*, with space for 980 passengers, sets sail on both trips from Port Everglades.

Carnival Cruise Lines (5225 N.W. 87th Ave., Miami, FL 33166, tel. 800/327–7373) offers three-day trips to Nassau leaving every Thursday, and four-day trips to Nassau and Freeport leaving every Sunday. The *Carnivale*, which holds 950 passengers, leaves from Port Canaveral. The *Mardi Gras*, which fits 1,108 passengers, departs from Port Everglades. The 2,720-passenger *Fantasy* leaves from the Port of Miami.

Crown Cruise Line (153 E. Port Rd., Riviera Beach, FL 33419, tel. 800/841–7447) runs two-day jaunts to Nassau aboard the *Crown del Mar*, which holds 486 passengers and cruises every Friday from Palm Beach.

Chandris Fantasy Cruises (4770 Biscayne Blvd., Miami, FL 33137, tel. 800/423–2100) offers two-day trips to Nassau aboard the *Britanis*, which fits 1,110 passengers and leaves every Friday from Miami.

Discovery Cruises (8751 W. Broward Blvd., Suite 300, Plantation, FL 33324, tel. 800/749–7447) has one-day trips to Freeport aboard the *Discovery*, which fits 1,250 passengers and leaves every Sunday, Monday, and Wednesday from Port Everglades.

Dolphin Cruise Line (1997 North America Way, Miami, FL 33132, tel. 800/222–1003) offers three-day cruises to Nassau and Blue Lagoon Island aboard the *Dolphin IV*, leaving every Friday from the Port of Miami, with room for 588 passengers.

Norwegian Cruise Line (2 Alhambra Plaza, Coral Gables, FL 33134, tel. 800/327–7030) has three-day cruises to Nassau, departing every Friday, and four-day trips to Nassau and Freeport, leaving every Monday. The liner for both trips is the *Sunward II*, which holds 676 passengers and operates out of Miami.

Sea Escape Ltd. (1080 Port Blvd., Miami, FL 33132, tel. 800/327–7400) has day cruises to Freeport aboard the *Saga*, which fits 1,050 passengers, and the *Sun*, for 1,105 passengers. The *Saga* cruises every day but Friday from Miami, and the *Sun* leaves from Ft. Lauderdale all days but Tuesdays and Saturdays.

From the United Kingdom by Plane

British Airways is the only airline with direct flights to the Bahamas from Britain, with three flights a week to Nassau from Gatwick. The cheapest peak-season fare is £543 round trip. Economy fares are £405 one way (£810 round trip); business class, £713 one way (£1,426 round trip); first class, £1,323 one way (£2,646 round trip). Some tour companies offer savings on these direct flights, but most fly visitors to Miami, from where there are regular connecting flights to Nassau and Freeport in the Bahamas by Bahamasair and most major U.S. airlines. If you're traveling independently, flying via Miami, despite the delays this entails, also represents the cheapest option. Fares to Miami start from as little as £90 one way, and, with so many airlines flying to Miami from Britain, the choice of flights is wide. Flying time to Nassau and Freeport is only 35 minutes. Fares start from $114.

For reservations and information: **Bahamasair,** tel. 071/437–8766 or 3542; **British Airways,** tel. 071/897–4000; **Delta,** tel. 071/828–5905; **PanAm,** tel. 071/409–0688; **TWA,** tel. 071/439–0707; **Virgin Atlantic,** tel. 0293/38222.

Staying in the Bahamas

Getting Around

By Car A visitor's driver's license is valid in the Bahamas for up to three months. Like the British, Bahamians drive on the left side of the road, which can be confusing, because most of the cars are American with the steering wheel on the left.

By Taxi As in the United States, there are taxis waiting at every airport and outside all of the main hotels. Rates are fixed by law, and all the vehicles have meters. At press time, the stipulated rates were $1.20 for two passengers for ¼ mile, 20¢ for each additional ¼ mile. Cabs can also be hired by the hour for $12, and $6 for every additional half-hour. Upon arriving, you're likely to find that Bahamian taxi drivers are more loquacious than their U.S. counterparts, so by the time you've reached your hotel, points of interest will have already been explained.

By Plane If you want to get from point A to point B in the islands, you have to rely on Bahamasair, the national airline, though its schedule to some of the islands is limited. If you have the burning desire and the money to escape, charter a plane; you'll find these operators at Nassau International Airport:

MD Air Service Ltd. (Box N 25, tel. 809/327–7335), **Nixon's Charter Service** (Box SS 5980, tel. 809/327–7184), **Condorair International** (Box N 7772, tel. 809/327–6940), **Trans Island Airways Ltd.** (Box N 291, tel. 809/327–8329), and **Pinders Charter Service** (Box N 10456, tel. 809/327–7320).

The **Helda Charter Service** (Box F 3335, Freeport, Grand Bahama, tel. 809/352–8832) operates out of Freeport.

By Mailboat/Ferry If you're of an adventurous frame of mind, you can revert to the mode of transportation that the islanders used before the advent of air travel: ferries and the traditional mailboat, which leave regularly in Nassau from **Potter's Cay,** under the Paradise Island bridge, or from the **Prince George Wharf,** near where the cruise liners dock. You may find yourself sharing company with goats and chickens, and then making your way on deck through piles of lumber bound for Cat Island, but that's all part of the adventure. Round-trip fares vary from $16 to $35. Don't plan to arrive or depart punctually; the flexible schedules can be thrown off by bad weather. Remember, too, that they operate on Bahamian time, which is an unpredictable measure of tempo. You cannot book ahead. In Nassau, check with the Dock Master's office (tel. 809/393–1064) at Potter's Cay.

People-to-People Program

If you would like to get a more intimate glimpse of Bahamian life, you can take advantage of the Ministry of Tourism's People-to-People Program. Volunteers will take you into their homes, introduce you to their friends, tell you about their culture, and show you their city. The program, which is free, has been enormously successful in bringing tourists and Bahamians with similar interests together. You may even be invited to a tea party at Government House. In Nassau, contact the **Tourist Information Centre** (tel. 809/328–7810) in Rawson Square or call the **People-to-People Unit** (tel. 809/326–5371); in Freeport, check with the **Tourist Information Center** at the **International Bazaar** (tel. 809/352–7848) or call 809/352–8044.

Telephones

Telephone service on all the islands is controlled by the **Bahamas Telecommunications Corporation,** a government agency. To call the United States from the Bahamas, dial 1, followed by the 10-digit number. Rates for calls to the United States are $2.40–$4.65 for three minutes during the day and $1.80–$3.45 at night, and 80¢–$1.55 for each additional minute, depending on which state you're calling.

Rates for calls to Canada, depending on the province, are $6–$9.60 for three minutes during the day, $4.95–$8.40 at night.

U.K. residents calling home will pay a flat $12 fee for the first three minutes and $5 for each additional three minutes.

To make a local call from your hotel room, dial 9, then the number.

Mail

Airmail postcards to the United States, the United Kingdom, and Canada require a 40¢ stamp. If you're going to elaborate, an airmail letter costs 45¢ per half-ounce, 50¢ for Europe. The stamps must be Bahamian.

Tipping

The usual tip for service, whether it be from a taxi driver or a waiter, is 15%. Some hotels automatically add that amount to your bill, plus an average of $2 a day for maid service.

Opening and Closing Times

Banks are open Monday–Thursday 9:30–3, Friday 9–5. They are closed Saturday–Sunday. Principal banks are **Bank of the Bahamas, Bank of Nova Scotia, Barclays Bank, Canadian Imperial Bank of Commerce, Chase Manhattan Bank, Citibank N.A.,** and **Royal Bank of Canada.**

Shops in the Bahamas are open Monday–Saturday 9–5. Bahamian stores choose to remain closed on Sunday. Best shopping times are in the morning, when the streets are less crowded. And remember, if you're staying in a hotel in Nassau, you'll be competing with the hordes of passengers who pour off the cruise ships at Prince George Wharf every day.

Religion

Bahamians are a religious people, and you'll find churches representing most faiths on New Providence and the other islands: Anglican, Assembly of God, Baptist, Church of Christ, Christian Science, Greek Orthodox, Lutheran, Free Evangelical, Methodist, Presbyterian, Islamic, Jehovah's Witness, Baha'i, and Roman Catholic. For times of services, consult the "What-to-Do" guide available at your hotel desk.

Security

Crime against tourists is relatively infrequent, and, unlike some of the less economically stable Caribbean countries, you'll find little begging. But take the precautions you would in any foreign country: Be aware of your wallet or handbag at all times, and keep your jewelry in the hotel safe. In Nassau, think twice about wandering around Grant's Town at night.

Newspapers

You'll get all the Bahamas news, and a smattering of what's going on internationally, in the *Tribune* and the *Nassau Guardian* on New Providence, and in the *Freeport News* on Grand Bahama. But if you want up-to-date news on what's happening around the world, you can also get *The Miami Herald, The Wall Street Journal,* and *The New York Times* daily at newsstands.

If you would like to get more of a feel for the Bahamas, there are several books available at Nassau bookstores. *San Salvador, The Forgotten Island,* by Dr. Pedro Grau Triana ($10), deals with Columbus's landfall on that island; *Great Inagua,* by Margery Erickson ($30), is the story of a woman whisked away from her New England home to a Bahamian island; and the authoritative *Bahamas Handbook* ($15.95) gives comprehensive information about all aspects of the Bahamas.

Casinos

Hitting the blackjack and baccarat tables, shooting craps, watching the roulette wheel spin, and pulling the one-armed bandits—these are among the pleasurable diversions of a vacation in the Bahamas. Four glitzy casinos cater to gamblers. Two of them are located on New Providence Island: **Carnival's Crystal Palace Resort & Casino** on Cable Beach, and the **Paradise Island Resort & Casino** on Paradise Island, which is linked to downtown Nassau by a causeway. On Grand Bahama, there's the **Princess Casino** in Freeport and the **Lucayan Beach Resort & Casino** in Lucaya. All four have the additional attractions of above-average restaurants, lounges, and colorfully costumed revues. You must be 21 to gamble; Bahamians and permanent residents are not permitted to indulge.

Shopping

You won't find the duty-free bargains of St. Thomas in the Bahamas, but there's enough of a savings over U.S. prices (around 30% in many cases) to make shopping enjoyable on New Providence and Grand Bahama. And you'll certainly find exotic merchandise not available back home. Go to Bay Street, Nassau's main thoroughfare, and the side streets leading off it for a wide range of imported perfumes, watches, cameras, crystal, china, and tropical wear. The main shopping areas on Grand Bahama are contained in two tight communities: the exotic **International Bazaar** in Freeport, with shops representing a variety of the world's cultures, and the new **Port Lucaya Marketplace,** which has strolling musicians and a bandstand where a local group plays for dancing.

Sports and Outdoor Activities

Boating Gentle trade winds are a boon to yachtsmen, whether they've brought their own craft or rented boats to island-hop. Most of the Family Islands are equipped with marinas and docks.

Both powerboats and sailboats participate in regattas, held throughout the year, out of most of the islands. Some of the most prominent are the **Nassau Cup Yacht Race** in February; the **Long Island Regatta** in May; the **Bahamas Princess Regatta Week** and **Regatta Time** at Marsh Harbour, Great Abaco, both in June; **Green Turtle Regatta Week** at Green Turtle Cay, in the Abacos, in July; and the annual regattas at Andros and Cat Island, both in August. For details on individual tournaments, *see* Chapter 5, The Family Islands.

Fishing Fishing in the Bahamas starts in the waters of Bimini, off the Florida coast, and ends at the southernmost island, Inagua, on the northern edge of the Caribbean. This country is an angler's dream: light tackle, heavy tackle, fly-fishing, deep-sea fishing, reef fishing, flats fishing, for everything from blue marlin to bonefish. Tournaments are scheduled throughout the Family Islands during the year; Bimini alone has a dozen.

Golf The Bahamas are registered as an official PGA destination, and golfers will find some enticing courses, most of them with refreshing sea views. There are three courses on New Providence Island (four, if you include the Lyford Cay Golf Club, but that's available only to members and their guests); four in Grand Bahama; one in Treasure Cay, Great Abaco; and one at the Cotton Bay Club, Eleuthera. Paradise Island and Freeport host tournaments annually.

Scuba Diving/ Walls, drop-offs, reefs, coral gardens, and wrecks can be ex-
Snorkeling plored throughout the Bahamas, and the clear, blue-green waters attract divers from all over the world. One of the most famous scuba schools and NAUI centers in the world is **UNEXSO (Underwater Explorers Society)**, located in Lucaya, Grand Bahama.

Tennis New Providence has more than 80 courts, Grand Bahama has 37, and a few of the Family Islands such as Eleuthera and the Abacos are also in on the racket. Each year, Paradise Island sponsors the **Marlborough Bahamas International Tennis Open,** and the **Freeport Tennis Open** is held on Grand Bahama.

Beaches

Sun, sea, and sand draw most of the tourists visiting the Bahamas. In Nassau, the main hotels on Cable Beach and Paradise Island have their own stretches of beach, while inland hotels are always near public beaches, such as Love Beach and Saunders Beach on the north shore, and Adelaide Beach on the south. On Grand Bahama, only the Lucaya hotels have their own strips of sand; guests staying in Freeport have access to public spots such as Xanadu Beach, Taino Beach, and the long strip at Williams Town, all favorites with the locals. The Family Islands are similarly endowed with beautiful beaches. One of the most intriguing is the pink beach at Harbour Island, off Eleuthera.

Dining

The sea and the land have been kind to the Bahamians. Fish, such as grouper, and shellfish, such as conch (pronounce it *conk*), abound in their waters. The Bahamians boil their fish in water, lime juice, butter, and onions, and season them with red-hot peppers—an infallible cure, they say, for hangovers. The conch, which they eat in various forms, is also valued for its pink shell, which they fashion into pendants, bracelets, earrings, brooches, and other ornaments.

From the land come sugarplum, hog plum, sapodilla, pineapple, sea grape, mango, coco plum, soursop, avocado, tangerine, tamarind, and papaya. Favorite soups include pineapple, tomato, cream of coconut, white conch chowder, sweet potato, breadfruit, souse-up (if you can stand pig's feet and tails, sheep's tongue, and chicken feet), turtle, and pumpkin.

Restaurants in the Bahamas offer a lot of variety. One night you may be munching on local cusine such as conch fritters and fried grouper at an out-of-the-way spot, and the next night you may be savoring a Grand Marnier soufflé at one of the finer restaurants in Nassau or Lucaya. Bahamians go heavy on fish and seafood dishes for the simple reason that meats are imported and, consequently, expensive. You're likely to find much simpler fare on the Family Islands.

Lodging

The range of accommodations in the Bahamas is extensive, with more than 180 hotels, condominiums, cottages, and guest houses on some 20 islands. The fastest way to make hotel reservations in the islands is to call the Miami-based **Bahamas Reservation Service (BRS)**, which is able to calculate up-to-the-minute availability of rooms through a computerized network. If the hotel of your choice is full, the service can recommend another that fits your needs as close as possible to your original preference. The BRS agents can also answer questions about transportation and other facets of the islands. *Tel. 800/327–0787; in Miami, tel. 305/443–3821. Open weekdays 9–6.*

Hotels on the beaches—on Cable Beach and Paradise Island on New Providence Island, and in Lucaya on Grand Bahama Island—are among the most expensive. They also have the widest range of sports facilities, including tennis courts and sailboats. Their high room rates during the winter season (slightly less on Grand Bahama than on New Providence) are cut by as much as 30% during the slower May–December period, when managements try to outdo one another with attractive three-day or one-week packages. Prices at hotels away from the beach tend to be considerably lower, and are often a better deal, because accessible beaches are never far away.

When you check out, an 8% government and resort tax is added to your bill. Some of the larger hotels also add an additional 1%–2% room tax.

Condominiums, many of them made available at certain times of the year by owners living elsewhere, have become popular among vacationers seeking a home-away-from-home ambience and a way to cut down on the cost of dining out. Travel agents and the Bahamas Tourist Office in your area can tell you about condominium rentals.

Guest cottages and private homes for rent are also worth considering. These are abundant in the Family Islands. For names of firms that deal exclusively in this form of vacation, *see* Chapter 5, The Family Islands.

Credit Cards

The following credit card abbreviations have been used: AE, American Express; CB, Carte Blanche; DC, Diners Club; MC, MasterCard; V, Visa. It's a good idea to call ahead to check current credit card policies.

2 Portraits of the Bahamas

In Search of Columbus

by William G. Scheller

A resident of Newbury, Massachusetts, William G. Scheller *contributes travel pieces regularly to* National Geographic, Condé Nast Traveler, *and* The Washington Post Magazine.

I first heard the singing toward the middle of the night, as the mail boat M.V. *Maxine* plowed southward between Eleuthera and the Exumas. The sound drifted faintly to where I lay doubled up on a bench in the main cabin with my head on a cardboard crate of pears and a copy of the *Bahama Journal* shielding my eyes from a yellow bug light.

It was a two-part chant, almost African in its rhythm. I looked down the dim corridor to the bridge, where the crewman at the wheel was singing softly in harmony with his companion on the midnight-to-4 watch. The second man was shuffling back and forth, keeping time. It was a scene out of Conrad, and a reminder that this is still what transportation is like in much of the world: pitching through the waters of a dark archipelago, sleeping with your head on a box of fruit, while guys sing and dance on the bridge.

The *Maxine* was 14 hours out of Potter's Cay, Nassau, the Bahamas, on the 22-hour run to the island of San Salvador. I had long since abandoned my claustrophobic upper bunk in the boat's only passenger compartment and had stayed out on deck until dark, sprawling over a tarp that covered bags of cement, taking shallow breaths to ration the stench of diesel fuel. Finally, half soaked from the waves constantly breaching the port rail, I had retreated to the last remotely habitable place on board, the big common room with its table and benches and its clutter of cargo for the islands. Four dozen eggs, the cartons taped together. An oscillating fan. Gallon jars of mayonnaise, their future owners' names Magic-Markered on the labels. Two galvanized tubs. Homemade sound equipment for the band that plays in the bar on San Salvador. My pillow of pears, consigned to Francita Gardiner of Rum Cay. Bags, boxes, crates—and secured somehow on the opposite bench, with ears alert and bright, eager eyes, a life-size ceramic German shepherd, soon to be a boon companion to someone in a place where a real German shepherd probably would die of heat prostration. Every time I woke to shift positions during that endless night, I would glance across the cabin, and there would be the good dog, looking as if he were waiting for a biscuit.

It is altogether possible to fly from Nassau to San Salvador in an hour and a half, but I had cast my lot with the mayonnaise and the galvanized tubs because I wanted to reach the island by water. San Salvador is arguably the most famous landfall in history: In 1992 the New World and the Old will celebrate (or lament, depending on one's politics) the 500th anniversary of the arrival of the *Niña*, *Pinta*, and *Santa*

María at this coral-girt outcrop. Anticipation of the tourism the quincentennial will inspire is no doubt the reason
why the creaking and malodorous *Maxine* is being replaced
this fall by a new 110-foot mail boat with air-conditioned
cabins. Fruit-box pillows are finally going out of style in the
Bahamas.

My plan was to retrace, by whatever transportation was
available, the route Christopher Columbus followed through
Bahamian waters after his landing at San Salvador on October 12, 1492. On the face of it, this seems a simple enough
task: The log of the first voyage, lost in the original but substantially transcribed by the near-contemporary chronicler
Bartolome de Las Casas, describes the fleet's circuitous
route through the archipelago and the series of island landfalls it made. The problem is, the island names given are
those that Columbus coined with each new discovery. From
San Salvador he sailed to what he called "Santa María de la
Concepción," then to "Fernandina," then to "Isabela," then
to the southwest and out of the Bahamian archipelago on his
way to Cuba. With the exception of San Salvador, which
was called Watling Island until 1926, none of these islands
bears its Columbus name today. And the distances, directions and descriptions of terrain given in the surviving
version of the log are just ambiguous enough, at crucial
junctures, to have inspired nine major theories as to exactly which sequence of island landfalls was followed. Some of
the theories are more than a bit tenuous, depending heavily
on a blithe disregard of their own weak points and an ampli-
fication of everyone else's departures from the log or from
common sense. You begin to wonder, after a while, if someone couldn't take the Las Casas translation and use it to
prove that Columbus landed on Chincoteague and sailed
into the Tidal Basin by way of Annapolis.

But two plausible theories stand out. One, championed by
the late historian and Columbus biographer Admiral Samu-
el Eliot Morison, is based on a first landing at today's San
Salvador; the other says the first landing was at Samana
Cay, a smaller, uninhabited island on the eastern fringes of
the chain. Samana Cay's most recent proponent has been
Joseph Judge of the National Geographic Society; in 1986
he published an exhaustive defense of his position, based in
part on a computer's estimation of where Columbus should
have ended up after the Atlantic crossing. The jury is still
out on both major theories, as it is on the less commonly
held ones. It probably always will be. For the purposes of
my trip, though, I had to choose one version and stick with
it. On the basis of my layman's reading of the log, I decided
to go with Morison.

In this version, San Salvador *is* San Salvador, Santa María
de la Concepción is today's Rum Cay, Fernandina is Long
Island, and Isabela is Crooked Island. This was the se-

quence I planned to follow as the *Maxine* approached San Salvador's Fernandez Bay at 9 o'clock in the morning.

> *This island is fairly large and very flat. It is green, with many trees and several bodies of water. There is a very large lagoon in the middle of the island and there are no mountains. It is a pleasure to gaze upon this place because it is all so green, and the weather is delightful.*

—Columbus's log,
October 13, 1492*

We docked at Cockburn Town, the only settlement of any size on San Salvador. Cockburn Town, population several hundred souls, was the type and model of the Bahamian Out Island communities I would see along the Columbus track over the next few days: three or four streets of cinder-block-and-stucco houses, some brightly painted; a grocery store and a bar—the Harlem Square Club, site of a big dominoes tournament that week; a post office/radiophone station; and a couple of churches. On the facade of the Catholic church, Holy Savior, there was a peeling relief portrait of Christopher Columbus.

In the late morning heat I walked the half mile of blacktop —scrub brush on one side and ocean views on the other— that separates Cockburn Town from the Riding Rock Inn.

The latter is a handful of cottages, a short block of plain but cheerful motel units, and a restaurant/bar, all right on the water; up at the bar most of the talk you hear has to do with skin diving. Divers are the principal clientele here. When I arrived, the place was securely in the hands of a California club called the Flipperdippers. At the poolside cookout just after I pulled in, the first snippet of conversation I caught was a tyro Flipperdipper asking an old hand if a basket starfish would eat until it exploded. The answer was no, and without waiting around to find out why the questioner suspected such a thing I got up for more rice and crabs. That's when the *maitresse de barbecue* hove into my path and told me about the dance that night: "If you don't dance, you don't get breakfast."

With the assistance of a Flipperdipper or two, I earned my breakfast. The band was a Cockburn Town outfit of indeterminate numerical strength. Guitarists and conga drummers came and went, and everyone kept commenting that things were really supposed to start jumping when the Kiwanis meeting at the Harlem Square Club let out. Shortly after 10, the band did get a transfusion of new talent, all wearing white cabana shirts patterned with yellow-and-black Kiwanis emblems. They played a couple of good sets, but they did an even better job of exemplifying the phenom-

Excerpted from The Log of Christopher Columbus *by Robert H. Fuson, courtesy of International Marine Publishing,* © 1987.

enon scholars call the "Columbian Exchange," that cross-pollination of peoples, cultures, flora and fauna, foodstuffs, and microorganisms that followed in the wake of the admiral's fleet and has been transmogrifying the Eastern and Western hemispheres ever since. Here were six descendants of African slaves, wearing the insignia of an American fraternal organization, playing music, written by a Jamaican who thought Haile Selassie was God, for a merry throng of skin-diving orthodontists from California on an island discovered by an Italian working for Spain but settled along with the rest of the archipelago by British and American planters who imported the slaves to begin with.

About all that was missing were the Lucayans, the native Bahamians extirpated by the Spaniards—who worked them to death in the mines of Hispaniola—within a generation after Columbus's arrival. It was the Lucayans' island I set off to see the following morning, by motor scooter and on foot. The people here call this island Guanahani *in their language, and their speech is very fluent, although I do not understand any of it. They are friendly and well-dispositioned people who bear no arms except for small spears, and they have no iron. I showed one my sword, and through ignorance he grabbed it by the blade and cut himself.*

—October 12

The San Salvador of the Lucayans is but a memory, as they are. When Columbus arrived, there were tall trees on the island, but the planters of the late 18th and early 19th centuries deforested the place so that now virtually the only vegetation is the dense, stickery brush called "haulback." The island's interior, though, still conveys the same sense of impenetrability and desolation that it must have to the first Europeans who came here, and no doubt to the Lucayans themselves. Fishermen as well as cultivators must have stayed close to shore, except to travel from one end of San Salvador to the other by dugout canoe across a system of brackish lakes that covers nearly half of the interior. From a crude concrete-and-wood observation platform on a rise near the airport, you can take in the sprawl of these lakes and the lonely, thicketed hills (the terrain isn't all as flat as Columbus described it) that break them into crazy patterns. No one lives there; it's hard to imagine that anyone ever goes there.

I drove the scooter the length of the island's circuit road, past crescent beaches with white sand so fine it coats your feet like flour, past ruined plantation buildings, past "Ed's First and Last Bar," a homey little joint out in the sticks that would be beerless until the cases made it up from the mail boat dock, past four monuments to Columbus's landing at four different places (a fifth marker is underwater, where somebody decided his anchor hit bottom), and past the Dixon Hill Lighthouse ("Imperial Lighthouse Service"), billed as one of 10 left in the world that run on kerosene. Past, and then back again—I bullied the scooter up Dixon Hill, because you don't get to climb to the top of a lighthouse every day.

I went looking for the light keeper, but instead I found my ride to Rum Cay, according to Morison the second of Columbus's landfalls on his first voyage. It was a family of blue-water sailors—an American named Kent, his German wife, Britta, and their two-month-old baby, Luke, who had cruised to San Salvador from St. Thomas in their 32-foot sailboat. Having hitchhiked up from Cockburn Town, the baby in a shaded basket, they too were waiting for the light keeper to show up; after she did, and took us to the top, the sailing couple offered to let me hitch with them the next day on the 30-mile run to Rum Cay. I soon learned I would be in good hands: Later that day, Kent asked a local if he knew anything about Rum Cay.

"What do you want to know?" the man responded.

"What's the anchorage like in a southeast wind?"

I'd have asked where to eat, or if the Kiwanis had a band.

I made sail and saw so many islands that I could not decide where to go first . . . Finally, I looked for the largest island and decided to go there.

—October 14

Christopher Columbus left San Salvador on October 14, 1492, and later that day arrived at the island he named Santa María de la Concepción. My adopted family and I weighed anchor at Cockburn Town and sailed out of Fernandez Bay early in the morning of a bright June day, flying fish scudding around our bows and cottony trade clouds riding briskly above. Luke, already a veteran mariner, slept in his basket below. We sighted Rum Cay when we were 10 miles out from San Salvador—Columbus had a much higher mast to climb—but the distant shoreline was to loom for a long time before we could draw very close to it. The east shore and much of the south shore of Rum Cay are girded with lethal reefs, and both the charts and the *Yachtsman's Guide to the Bahamas* go to great pains to point out so precise a route to the anchorage that it might as well have been the directions to a parking space in Georgetown. Six other boats had negotiated the coral gauntlet that day, including one whose captain gave us half of a blackfin tuna he'd just caught. How Columbus safely pulled it off (his anchorage was at a point west of ours) is beyond imagining.

Rum Cay, which once made a living selling sea salt to Nova Scotia's cod packers, has shriveled in population until barely 60 people today inhabit its sole settlement of Port Nelson. An American, David Melville, opened a small skin-diving resort called the Rum Cay Club a mile from town a few years back; when I arrived, the place was closed for renovations. There were no Flipperdippers here—just Melville, a couple of handymen and the locals down the road. Rum Cay was, for the moment, almost out of things to do and people to do them.

Almost, but not quite. There's always Kay's Bar, where proprietor Dolores Wilson turns out lovely baked chicken and coconut bread to wash down with the Out Islands' requisite gallons of beer and rum in an atmosphere dominated by a satellite TV, an antique space-age jukebox, turtle shells with colored light bulbs in them and a giant poster of Bob Marley wearing a beatific grin and knitted hat that looks like a Rasta halo. People who sailed the Bahamas years ago have told me that Dolores was once something of a hell-raiser, but she seems to have settled into sweet grandmotherliness by now. For ethyl-powered amusement, I had to rely on an expatriate Oklahoman named Billy. Billy, whose personal style ran to the pirate-biker look, was Melville's mechanical factotum at the Rum Cay Club. His avocation, as I discovered when I took a Jeep ride with him to the other side of the island, is nonstop talking. In the space of an hour, Billy went chapter and verse on everything from his archery prowess in Oklahoma, to how he could build an ammonia-powered icehouse like the one in *The Mosquito Coast*, to his deepest feelings about the universe: "You know, I like everything and I hate everything."

"That's called having a lover's quarrel with the world," I told him, remembering Frost.

"Oh, they have a name for it now?"

I decided not to linger very long at Santa María de la Concepción, for I saw that there was no gold there and the wind freshened to a SE crosswind. I departed the island for the ship after a two hours' stay.

—October 16

It was Billy who drove me to catch a plane to Long Island— Columbus's Fernandina, his third landfall—on the following afternoon. Back on San Salvador, I'd been told that the ticket to getting off Rum Cay without waiting for the next mail boat was to "ask for Bobby with the plane." But there was no plane on the island's crushed-coral landing strip. Bobby had flown somewhere, so rather than spend another night I asked Melville to radio the Stella Maris Inn on Long Island for a plane. They sent a Cessna four-seater, which landed just as Billy was pouring me a rum-and-powdered-lemonade at his house—he insisted on this hospitable stopover, since it was a whole mile between Kay's Bar and the airstrip. Besides, his own much-loved blue plastic cup was empty.

Long Island: a day's sail from Rum Cay for the *Niña*, *Pinta*, and *Santa María* on October 17, 1492; 15 minutes in the Cessna. As we approached the landing strip, I looked down to see territory that looked almost like a manicured suburb compared with the trackless scrub forests of Rum Cay and San Salvador. Here were roads, trees, villas, broad beaches, swimming pools . . . in short, a modest but complete resort, and run by Germans to boot. This last fact is worthy of remark because of the concept known as "Bahamian time," best defined as a devil-may-care approach to the minute hand. Somehow, the Germans and Bahamians had arrived at a compromise: The shuttle to the beach leaves more or less on time, but you don't have to eat breakfast at 7:23 AM.

I wanted to follow Columbus up and down this island. Near its northern tip is a shallow cove outside of which he anchored while several of his men went ashore for water. If local legend can be trusted, they filled their casks at a deep natural well in the coral rock, which a Stella Maris driver showed me. He had drawn water there as a small boy, just 450 years after the Spanish expedition left.

A couple of miles from the well was the cove, a harbor with "two entrances," according to the 1492 log, which the admiral sounded in his ships' boats. At least it seemed to me to be the place, and "Where was Columbus?" is a game that anyone with a copy of the log can play. I explored the cove and, while snorkeling, was reminded of the entry for October 17: "Here the fishes are so unlike ours that it is amazing."

To reach Columbus's final Long Island anchorage, at a place called Little Harbor in a village with the pretty name of Roses, was not such an easy job. I rented a VW bug and drove south for nearly 80 miles to the tip of this 2-mile-wide island. The road passed through one little town after another, each with its neat cinder-block school and tiny Protestant church. At Roses I found a storekeeper who knew the road to Little Harbor. It ended at a dump a mile into the bush. I walked nearly another mile—had I been heading due east I would have been in the water. I wasn't going to find Little Harbor, not in this pounding sun on a trail narrowing to the width of an iguana, any more than Columbus was going to find Japan.

Columbus got farther than I did, though. He wandered southeast from Long Island to Crooked Island, then southwest to the southernmost of the Ragged Islands, where the tiny outpost called Duncan Town now stands. This was his last Bahamas anchorage before he sailed off to Cuba, Hispaniola, and immortality.

The odd thing is, Columbus had an easier time pressing ahead than I would have had. Although it's true that he was not only lost in the Caribbean but stuck in the 15th century, at least his fleet was self-contained, and one island was as good as another. For me, the Cessnas were too expensive, the mail boats too infrequent, the lodgings from Long Island south, on Crooked Island and at Duncan Town, nonexistent. These places are as far away as they ever were. They are, in fact, parts of the New World that haven't really been discovered yet.

Over and Under the Bahamian Waters

by Gordon Lomer

A Canadian freelance writer based in Fort Lauderdale, Gordon Lomer is a certified diving instructor who spent 10 years in the Bahamas covering diving, fishing, and yachting events for the Bahamas News Bureau.

Today seafarers who navigate around the Bahamian islands can retrace the historical routes of Christopher Columbus, Juan Ponce de León, Blackbeard the Pirate, and rumrunners from the United States during the Prohibition years. The Bahamas is only 55 miles from Florida across the Gulf Stream. Many first-time visitors to the Bahamas are deeply impressed by the striking color and clarity of its waters. Veteran yachtsmen gauge the depth of the water by its color. The deep blues of the Gulf Stream fade into lighter blues and brilliant turquoises as boaters come closer to the Bahamian shores.

The Bahamian islands fringe the edges of two major, and several smaller, sand banks. The Little Bahama Bank is bordered on the south by Grand Bahama Island, and on the east and north by the Abaco chain. The Great Bahama Bank is a vast area of shallow water split by a deep trench called the Tongue of the Ocean. Along the western side of the Tongue lies Andros, the largest of the Bahamian islands, and a spectacular barrier reef, the third longest in the world.

Across the Great Bahama Bank to the northwest is Bimini, usually the first landfall for boaters coming from Florida. At the top of the Great Bahama Bank is Great Isaac Island. Farther to the east is Great Stirrup Cay, the northern end of the Berry Islands chain. Most cruise ships use the beacons of Great Isaac and Great Stirrup to guide them to Nassau on the island of New Providence. Smaller boats generally cross the bank from Cat Cay or Gun Cay south of Bimini to Chub Cay, at the foot of the Berry Islands, before crossing the Tongue of the Ocean to Nassau.

Northeast of Nassau is Eleuthera, with Spanish Wells and Harbour Island off its north coast. East of Nassau, the long Exuma chain stretches along the western edge of Exuma Sound, another large and deep body of water within the Great Bahama Bank. Cat Island separates the sound from the Atlantic Ocean to the east. Long Island marks Exuma Sound's lower end and stretches southeast to the Crooked Island Passage. Crooked Island and Acklins Island form their own little bank, as does Mayaguana to the east. To the south, Great and Little Inagua represent the last Bahamian port of call for boats heading down to the Caribbean.

Three small islands—Rum Cay, Conception Island, and San Salvador—lie out in the Atlantic east of the northern tip of Long Island. Possibly the most obscure island in the country is Cay Lobos, a speck just 20 miles off the northern coast of Cuba. The Cay Sal Bank, which includes the Damas Cays and Anguilla Cays, lies in the middle of the Florida Straits and is also considered part of the Bahamas archipelago.

Boating

The Abacos The Abacos, a chain of islands in the northeastern Bahamas, offer superb cruising grounds. Marinas and services for yachtsmen range from rugged rustic to high-tech facilities, with more of the latter than the former. Walker's Cay at the top of the Abacos is about 55 miles northeast of West End at the tip of Grand Bahama Island, and it's also a 55-mile crossing from Palm Beach. Many cruising yachtsmen coming from the north opt for the 110-mile route from the Fort Pierce–Vero Beach area to Walker's Cay.

Walker's Cay and its neighbor, Grand Cay, former President Richard Nixon's hideaway, represent the contrasts in facilities available for yachtsmen. Walker's features a high-class 75-slip full-service marina, a 2,500-foot paved airstrip, and extravagant hotel comforts. Grand Cay, on the other hand, is a ramshackle settlement of about 200 people and four times that many dogs of mixed breed, called Bahamian potcakes. These potcakes wander and sleep on the cracked, meandering sidewalks of the community by day, and howl by night. Yachtsmen will find both the people and the dogs friendly and the anchorage off the community dock adequate. Double anchors are advised to handle the harbor's tidal current.

If they head south from Walker's Cay and Grand Cay, boaters will pass (and maybe want to stop and explore by dinghy) a clutch of tiny cays and islets, such as Double Breasted Cays, Roder Rocks, Barracuda Rocks, Miss Romer Cay, Little Sale Cay, and Great Sale Cay. Great Sale Harbour provides excellent shelter. Snorkeling in the shallows along the mangroves of these cays can be a rewarding experience—you may encounter graceful manta rays and eagle rays, basking sand sharks, and perhaps a school of small barracuda on the prowl. In the same area, you'll find other small islands, including Carter Cay, Moraine Cay, Umbrella Cay, Guineaman Cay, Pensacola and Allan's cays (which are now virtually one island since a hurricane filled in the gap between them) and the Hawksbill Cays. Most offer varying degrees of lee anchorage. Fox Town, due south of Hawksbill Cay on the western tip of Little Abaco, is the first refueling stop for powerboats traveling east from West End.

A narrow causeway joins Little Abaco to Great Abaco, where the largest community at the north end is Cooper's Town. Visitors here can stock up on supplies of groceries, hardware, marine parts, liquor, and beer. The settlement also has a coin laundry, a telephone station, a few small restaurants, bakeries, and a resident doctor. Green Turtle Cay has excellent yachting facilities at White Sound to the north and Black Sound to the south. The Green Turtle Club dominates the northern end of White Sound, while Bluff House, halfway up the sound, has docks on the inside and a dinghy dock below the club on the bank side.

Green Turtle Cay's New Plymouth will remind you of Cape Cod, with its pastel cottages flanking the narrow lanes. The New England–style ambience comes honestly, for many of the 400 or so residents are direct descendants of original 18th-century Loyalist settlers. The town also offers some little bars and restaurants, well-stocked stores, and a wide range of services, including a post office and a medical clinic.

South of New Plymouth on the Great Abaco's mainland stands the Treasure Cay Beach Hotel, a sophisticated yet relaxed international resort with a 150-slip, full-service marina and one of the finest and longest beaches in the area. A recent development, Great Guana Cay, which is part of the Treasure Cay complex, has emerged as a water-sports mecca called Treasure Island. Great Guana is a short ferry trip from the mainland and the highlight of a twice-weekly cruise-ship tour from Port Canaveral. Another New England–style charmer lies a little to the south—Man-of-War Cay, a boat-building settlement of Loyalist descendancy. This island, with the 60-slip Man-O-War Marina, is devoid of cars, women in skimpy bikinis, beer, and liquor. Despite these relative hardships, it is well worth a visit for its friendly inhabitants and the wide variety of canvas goods made and sold there.

The most photogenic lighthouse in the Bahamas sits atop Elbow Cay. This spectacular red-and-white candy-striped beacon signals the harbor opening to Hope Town, with more New England–style atmosphere. Hope Town features a little of everything, including restaurants, inns, a 20-slip marina, markets, shops, bakeries, and even a museum.

Back on the mainland, you'll find the largest settlement in the Abacos, Marsh Harbour on Great Abaco Island, which has plenty of facilities for yachtsmen. These include the modern (and growing) 140-slip Boat Harbour Marina, a full-service operation located on the east side of the island. The other side of the town has additional marinas, including the 65-slip Conch Inn Marina, Marsh Harbour Marina and its 30 slips, and a couple of smaller facilities.

The Bimini Islands The Bimini Islands are the initial taste of the Bahamas for most visiting boaters. The ghost of Ernest Hemingway still haunts the island of North Bimini, where the writer stayed and played in the late '20s and '30s. Ossie Brown's Compleat Angler Hotel serves as a veritable museum to the Hemingway mystique, though the current loud music at the hotel bar might not be to Papa's taste.

The Biminis, which also include South Bimini, Gun Cay, and Cat Cay to the south, offer several good yachting facilities. The Bimini Big Game Fishing Club, a first-class, full-service marina with 100 slips, serves as headquarters for many of the spring and summer billfish tournaments. Bimini's Blue Water Marina offers 32 modern slips and usually hosts the annual Hemingway billfish tournament. Brown's Hotel and Marina, with 22 slips and a full line of services, is another popular hangout for yachtsmen, fishermen, and divers. Weech's Dock, immediately north of Brown's, has 15 slips and a few waterfront rooms available. The Native Fishing Tournament remains one of the more vibrant events on the Bimini calendar; it's a nonstop party. If you come here during this August blowout, be prepared to lose some sleep.

Yachtsmen will enjoy the excellent fishing opportunities along the eastern edge of the Gulf Stream. The bonefishing on the flats in this area is unsurpassed. However, you should talk to local residents about where to fish. Some of the shoal and reef areas can be tricky, especially for someone unfamiliar with the Bahamas. Many years ago while interviewing an old Bahamian skipper and guide who had spent his life on the water, I suggested, "I guess you know where every reef in the Bahamas is." He thought for a long moment and replied, "Not really. But I sure know where they ain't."

The Berry Islands   The clarity of Bahamian waters is particularly evident when you cross the Great Bahama Bank from the Bimini area along the Berry Islands on the way to Nassau. The depth of the waters here is seldom more than 20 feet. Grass patches and an occasional coral head or flattish coral patch dot the light sand bottom. Starfish abound, and you can often catch a glimpse of a gliding stingray or eagle ray. You may spot the odd turtle, and if you care to jump over the side of the boat with a mask, you may also pick up a conch or two in the grass.

In the upper Berry Islands, Great Harbour Cay, which was closed for a few years, has returned to the yachting fold with an 80-slip, full-service marina that can handle boats up to 135 feet. Accessible now through an 80-foot-wide channel from the bank side, Great Harbour Cay has one of the most pristine beaches in the Bahamas running along its east side. Chub Cay, about 75 miles from Bimini and 35 miles northwest of Nassau, is a semiprivate club with public facilities that include a full-service marina and a 50-room hotel.

New Providence Island   From Chub Cay to Nassau, the sailing route goes across the mile-deep Tongue of the Ocean. The Paradise Island Light welcomes yachtsmen to Nassau Harbour, which is open at both ends. The harbor can handle the world's largest cruise liners; sometimes as many as eight will be tied up at one time. The looming Paradise Island Bridge bisects the harbor connecting the resort island to Nassau. It has a high-water clearance of 70 feet, so sailboats with taller masts heading for the marinas east of the bridge must enter the harbor from the east end. East Bay Yacht Basin and part of the Hurricane Hole Marina are the only boating facilities west of the bridge. Beyond the bridge on the Nassau side of the harbor lie several full-service marinas, including Nassau Yacht Haven, Bayshore Marina, Brown's Boat Yard, and the Nassau Harbour Club.

Across the harbor, Hurricane Hole, with 45 slips, guards the Paradise Island end of the bridge. The Nassau Yacht Club and Royal Nassau Sailing Club are situated at the eastern opening of the harbor. At the western end of New Providence, Lyford Cay, a posh development for the rich and famous, features an excellent marina.

Grand Bahama Island Grand Bahama Island offers a wide variety of boating opportunities from West End all the way around to Deep Water Cay. Jack Tar Village at West End is an all-inclusive resort with a well-protected 100-slip marina. (The resort, however, closed for renovations in spring 1990 with no definite date set for reopening; the marina remained open.) Xanadu Beach Marina has 400 feet of dockage and 77 slips, and it provides dockside valet service. The Running Mon Marina, a half-mile to the east, has 66 slips and serves as the base for a deep-sea fishing fleet that serves most of the hotels in the Freeport and Lucaya area. Inside Bell Channel at Lucaya, the 150-slip, full-service Lucayan Marina features complimentary ferry service across the harbor to the nearby Lucayan Beach Resort & Casino. Tucked in behind the bustling Port Lucaya Marketplace, the 15-slip Port Lucaya Marina boasts a broad range of water sports, including waterskiing, diving, snorkeling, Jet Skiing and paddleboating.

About 6 miles east of the Bell Channel is the opening to the Grand Lucayan Waterway, a man-made channel that goes through the island to Dover Sound on the north side. Designed mainly for powerboats, the waterway is limited by fixed bridges with 27-foot clearances. It cuts considerable time off cruising to the northern Abacos for boats coming from Fort Lauderdale or Miami. At the east end of Grand Bahama, the Deep Water Cay Club offers a few slips, 18 rooms, a small dive operation, and bonefishing opportunities.

The Exumas The Exuma island chain, stretching south and east along the western rim of Exuma Sound, may be the finest cruising area in the Bahamas. In the Upper Exumas, at the anchorage between Allan's and Leaf cays, a nature wonderland lies only about 32 miles out of Nassau. The nightly cacophony of bird calls here could shatter crystal. On a morning visit to Leaf Cay, you can discover iguanas, oversized lizards that measure up to 3 feet long. These curious critters come to the beach when travelers arrive, but you're advised not to feed them. They have sharp teeth and might mistake a hand for food. Iguanas, protected by Bahamian law, must not be killed, captured, or exported.

The Exuma Cays National Land and Sea Park, from Wax Cay to Conch Cay, is a protected area worth visiting, although no fishing is allowed. On Little Wax Cay dwells the Bahamas' only indigenous mammal, the hutia. This nocturnal animal, about the size of a rabbit, is protected by law. The west side of Hawksbill Cay offers lonely beaches, while Warderick Wells to the south is reputed to be haunted by the ghosts of hymn-singing choral groups, though there has never been any record of habitation on the island.

George Town, on Great Exuma in the lower end of the island chain, is generally the final destination of yachtsmen cruising the Exumas. The Tropic of Cancer runs through the middle of this small community, which offers excellent anchorages and businesses that carry supplies necessary for yachtsmen. Stocking Island, just a mile offshore of George Town, features a coastline of exquisite beaches and thick coconut groves.

Crossing the Gulf Stream Many sailors and yachtsmen enjoy the trip from Florida across the Gulf Stream to the Bahamas, either on their own boat or a chartered one. Most of south Florida's major marinas offer private charter boats (usually yachts, 35–60 feet) to the Bahamas; these boats generally carry four to six people and may be hired at a cost of $100–$150 per person per day. Knowing your boat and its capabilities is necessary. The average northward drift of the Gulf Stream is 2½ knots, so, if for instance you're heading from Miami or Fort Lauderdale to Bimini, you would set your course a little south of where you want to land. If you figure your crossing will take three hours, you would set your course for a point about 7½ nautical miles south of Bimini. If you estimate it will take four hours, head for a spot 10 nautical miles south. The Gulf Stream commands and deserves respect. The combination of the northerly flow with a wind out of the northern quadrant can whip up the waters to an extremely uncomfortable pitch. So pick a calm day for your first crossing.

Sailors and yachtsmen with slow-moving, trawler-type craft are advised to start their crossing of the Gulf Stream at midnight or in late evening; this will bring them into Bahamian waters at daybreak, when navigating through the shallower waters is easier. Most yachtsmen try to avoid arriving at dusk because darkness falls swiftly in the Bahamas. A night crossing should also be approached with care and a keen eye for slow-moving tankers and tugs with long invisible cables that tow barges, sometimes as far as a mile behind.

Yachtsmen reluctant to make that first crossing alone can consider the Bahama Boating Flings. This series of group crossings from south Florida to Bimini or Freeport is sponsored and organized by the Bahamas Ministry of Tourism, the Bahamas Sports and Aviation Center, and the Marine Industries Association of South Florida. One "Fling" usually runs from the Palm Beach area to Freeport. These gatherings of up to 30 boats of at least 22 feet rendezvous at a Fort Lauderdale marina and cross as a group with an experienced leader. Outings last three or four days, although many skippers stay on after the initial crossing, cruise a little on their own, and catch a later group crossing for the return to Florida. For more information or applications, contact **Bahamas Boating Fling** (255 Alhambra Circle, Suite 415, Coral Gables, FL 33134, tel. 305/442-2867 or 800/327-7678).

If you are not coming to the Bahamas in your own boat or one that you have chartered, a few other cruising options are available in the Bahamas. Most resorts have crewed charter boats available for deep-sea fishing or bonefishing. Some have small rental boats for day cruising. At press time however, only three bareboat charter companies exist in the islands. **Abaco Bahamas Charters** (tel. 800/626-5690), in Hope Town on Elbow Cay, has a fleet of 16 sailboats from 30 to 44 feet. In Marsh Harbour on Great Abaco, **Bahamas Yachting Services** (tel. 305/484-5246 or 800/327-2276) has a large fleet of 32- to 52-foot sailboats, including 38-foot Gulfstars, plus powerboats and trawlers for bareboat or crewed charters. **Eleuthera Charters** (tel. 809/332-0181), in Hatchet Bay on Eleuthera, has several privately owned 36- to 45-foot sailboats and trawlers for bareboating or with partial crew.

In early 1990, Bahamian Prime Minister Lynden Pindling announced a reduction in import duties for boats and boat parts from a prohibitive 32% to 7½% on boats 30 to 100 feet and to 5% on boats over 100 feet. The move should spawn more charter operations, particularly in Nassau and in George Town, Exuma.

Ports of Entry When entering Bahamian waters, yachtsmen must clear through customs and immigration at the first designated port of call. A yellow quarantine flag should be flown by yachts to indicate plans to check in. The captain must fill out Maritime Declaration of Health and Inward Reports, listing all crew members and passengers, who must have proof of citizenship. Birth certificates, passports and voter registration cards constitute proof, while driver's licenses do not. A cruising permit (or transire) will be issued for the boat, good for up to six months. It must be shown when requested by government officials; requests can be frequent, given the intensity of drug smuggling. Only the boat's captain can go ashore until the boat and passengers have cleared customs and immigration.

Following is a list of Bahamian ports of entry:

The Abacos: Grand Cay, Green Turtle Cay, Marsh Harbour, Sandy Point, Treasure Cay, and Walker's Cay.

Andros: Andros Town, Congo Town, Fresh Creek, Nicholl's Town, and San Andros.

The Bimini Islands: Alice Town, Big Game Fishing Club, Cat Cay Yacht Club, and Government Dock, South Bimini.

The Berry Islands: Chub Cay and Great Harbour Cay.

Eleuthera: Governor's Harbour, Hatchet Bay, Harbour Island, and Rock Sound.

Exumas: George Town.

Grand Bahama Island: Freeport, Lucaya, Xanadu Marina, and West End.

Inagua: Matthew Town.

Long Island: Stella Maris.

New Providence Island: All marinas.

Ragged Island: Duncan Town.

San Salvador: Cockburn Town.

Diving

Cruising and diving, of course, go hand in hand, and few places in the world offer a wider variety of diving opportunities than the Bahamas—wrecks and reefs, blue holes and drop-offs, sea gardens and shallow shoals can all be found here. Finding the finest dive spots is often best left to local guides. The time spent in searching unknown waters for a particular dive site can be frustrating. Some sites, of course, are obvious; you won't need a local guide to show you a sunken ship that stands 25 feet out of the water, and drop-offs aren't that hard to spot. Local experts, however, will know the best places to dive, the drop-offs, the safest places to drop an anchor, and even the best time of day for the dive.

The local dive shops and operations, though they are geared for regular scheduled dives or personalized custom diving, are willing and generous in offering correct and precise directions to many dive sites. In some cases, they will even give you the coordinates of a location. Unless you and your navigational equipment are extremely sharp, however, you could miss a site by 100 yards or so, which would still give you a lot of seabed to search.

Most dive resorts in the Bahamas are members of the Bahamas Diving Association and will require a certification card (C-card) for tank and regulator rentals. A card is not required for refills, but the tanks must show hydrostatic test marks not more than five years old. Most resort operations offer a brief course that enables a novice to dive under supervision. Some resorts offer a five-day highly concentrated certification course.

The Abacos One of the most knowledgeable diving instructors and guides in the entire Bahamas can be found in the Abacos. Dave Gale, who has been boating and diving around the Abacos for nearly 40 years, doesn't have a scheduled dive operation; he specializes in custom diving. Contact Gale at **Island Marine** (Hope Town, Elbow Cay, tel. 809/366–2822). If you're planning to dive in the Marsh Harbour area of Grand Abaco, you can seek the help of veteran Skeet LaChance, who has also been diving around the Bahamas for about 40 years; he operates his 30-foot dive boat, Michael Lee, out of Boat Harbour Marina. Contact: Skeet LaChance, **Dive Abaco** (Box 555, Marsh Harbour, Great Abaco, tel. 809/367–2787 or 367–2014).

Andros Andros, the largest island in the Bahamas, probably has the largest number of dive sites in the country. With the third longest barrier reef in the world (behind those of Australia and Belize), the island offers about 100 miles of drop-off diving into the Tongue of the Ocean. Almost all diving in Andros is connected in one way or another with the barrier reef. Uncounted numbers of blue holes are forming in the area; in some places, these constitute vast submarine/subterranean networks.

Blue holes are named for their inky blue aura when viewed from above and the light-blue filtered sunlight that is still visible from 180 or 200 feet down. Although several of these phenomena have been explored and charted, many probably haven't been discovered yet. Some of the known ones include huge cathedrallike interior chambers with stalactites and stalagmites, offshoot tunnels, and seemingly endless corridors. Others have distinct thermoclines (temperature changes) between layers of water. Some of them are subject to tidal flow.

The most venerable and possibly the best dive resort on Andros is Small Hope Bay Lodge at Fresh Creek, a very informal place where the only thing taken seriously is diving. Contact: Dick Birch, **Small Hope Bay Lodge** (Box N-1131, Nassau, tel. 809/368–2014 or 305/463–9130).

At the north end of Andros, Neal Watson's Andros Undersea Adventures handles most of the diving out of the Andros Beach Hotel (Nicholl's Town, Andros, tel. 809/329–2582). Watson also has franchised operations at Bimini, Chub Cay, and Nassau. All of these can be reached at **Undersea Adventures**, tel. 800/327–8150, for both diving and accommodation packages.

The Bimini Islands Though better known for its big-game fishing and macho billfish tournaments, Bimini has a wide range of excellent dive sites; one of the most controversial is Atlantis, or The Road, as some call it. Scientists argue over what might be evidence of an ancient civilization in the shallow waters west of North Bimini. Atlantis is the name given to huge blocks that form three sides of a rectangle more than 300 feet long. The foundations measure 30 feet across; some scientists think the site could be a former roadbed. A few of the stones measure 16 feet square. Radioactive tests indicate this area was above water 5,000 years ago, according to one scientist. Others scoff. For most of the diving around Bimini, contact: Bill and Nowdla Keefe, **Bimini Undersea Adventures** (Box 21766, Fort Lauderdale, FL 33335, tel. 800/327–8150).

The Exumas Every conceivable sort of diving is available in the Exumas; it is all virtually virgin diving. Few facilities exist, so most exploration must be done from a self-contained boat, with its own compressor for filling tanks. Tank refills are available at Staniel Cay, Sampson Cay, and George Town. Diving is uniformly good all over the Exumas, but again, it is recommended that you seek the advice of local guides at any of the marinas.

Grand Bahama Grand Bahama Island offers some fascinating diving sites **Island** near the West End. An extensive reef system runs along the edge of the Little Bahama Bank from Mantinilla Shoals down through Memory Rock, Wood Cay, Rock Cay, and Indian Cay. Sea gardens, caves, and colorful reefs rim the bank all the way from the West End to the Freeport/Lucaya area and beyond. Sunn Odyssey Divers runs three daily reef trips and handles the resort diving for most of the hotels in Freeport/Lucaya. Contact: Nick and Karen Rolle, **Sunn Odyssey Divers** (Atlantik Beach Hotel, Box F 532, Freeport, tel. 809/373–1444).

In the center of Lucaya you'll find the renowned Underwater Explorers Society (UNEXSO), one of the most up-to-date diving schools in North America. UNEXSO's facilities include an 18-foot-deep training tank with observation windows, a recompression/decompression chamber, the Museum of Underwater Exploration, and, most recently constructed, a set of pens for the increasingly popular Dolphin Experience. This program offers participants a short lecture and the chance to hear dolphins communicating through a hydrophone (an underwater mike). Visitors then go down to the dolphin pens to take pictures of the dolphins and talk with the trainers. Participants can put their feet in the water and let the dolphins swim up and touch them, and visitors also have the option of swimming with the mammals. UNEXSO also offers educational courses and specialized training for experienced divers seeking upgraded or specialized certification. Contact: **UNEXSO** (Box F 2433, Freeport, tel. 800/992–DIVE or 305/359–2730).

New Providence Diving operations remain plentiful throughout the island of **Island** New Providence Island, where Nassau is situated. Most hotels have dive instructors who teach short courses, followed the next day by a reef trip. New Providence area diving

runs the gamut of underwater experiences—ocean holes
and caves, drop-offs, wrecks and reefs, sea gardens, and
even a few old underwater movie sets. Many small operations have sprung up in recent years in which experienced
divers with their own boats run custom dives for one to five
people. A lot of these are one-man efforts. In many cases,
the custom dive will include a picnic lunch with freshly
speared lobster or fish cooked on an open fire on a private
island beach. A fast boat reaches excellent diving sites in
North Eleuthera, the cays east of Nassau, and the upper
Exuma Cays within easy range of Nassau for a day trip.

Dive Sites

With more than 700 islands, the Bahamas offer literally
thousands of dive sites within its vodka-clear waters. Following are some of the more popular ones, but the list just
touches the surface, so to speak.

The Abacos

Site	Location and Depth (in feet)	Description
USS Adirondack	Man-of-War Cay 20	This 125-year-old wreck lies among a host of cannon on the outside of the reef. The coral heads off Man-of-War are large and spectacular, and have a wide variety of coral and fish life.
Pelican Cay Land and Sea Park	Marsh Harbour 10–30	Pelican Cay Land and Sea Park is a 2,000-acre preserve under the protection of the Bahamas National Trust. It contains a full range of marine life. Excellent for novice divers, snorkelers, and photographers.
Ocean Holes	Hole in the Wall 45–100+	To the southwest of Hole in the Wall are several ocean holes starting at 100 feet. They have not been fully explored yet. Closer to shore are several prolific reefs at about 45 feet.

Andros

Site	Location and Depth	Description
The Barge	Fresh Creek 55–70	An old landing craft was sunk about 30 years ago. Now encrusted with coral, it has become home for a group of groupers and a blizzard of tiny silverfish. There is a fish-cleaning station where miniature cleaning shrimp and yellow gobies clean grouper and rockfish, swimming into the mouths and out the gills of the larger fish picking up food particles. Excellent subject matter for close-up photography.

Over the Wall	Fresh Creek 80–185	This split-level dive takes novices to the 80-foot ledge, and experienced divers to a pre–Ice Age beach at 185 feet. The wall is covered with black coral and a wide variety of tube sponges.
Blue Hole	Fresh Creek 40–100	Discovered only a few years ago, this dramatic site provides an insight into the complex Andros cave system. Not much coral growth but plenty of midnight parrot fish, big southern stingrays, and some blacktip sharks.
	North Andros 40–200+ South Bight 40–200+	Similar blue holes are located all along the barrier reef, including several at Mastic Point in the north and the ones explored and filmed off South Bight.

Bimini Islands

Site	Location and Depth	Description
Sapona	South Bimini 15–20	This landmark wreck of a concrete-and-steel ship is of historical interest. A hapless victim of two hurricanes, it has served as a rock carrier, bootleg liquor warehouse, and World War II bombing target. Home for hundreds of tiny tropical fish, it makes a particularly fascinating night dive, with lights playing mysteriously through the openings from hold to hold.
Piquet Rock	Gun Cay 5–30	Wreck debris from a Spanish galleon includes ballast rocks, cannonballs, and ribs; it has produced brass spikes and other artifacts. A fish-cleaning station for grouper and jewfish and many coral and sponge stands can be found here.
Atlantis	North Bimini 10–40	Divers and scientists ponder the origin of the huge blocks forming a 300-foot long rectangle in shallow water off North Bimini.

Eleuthera

Site	Location and Depth	Description
Train Wreck	Near Harbour Island 15–25	In 15 feet of greenish water lies the carriage of an old narrow-gauge railway train that was headed for Cuba when the barge carrying it went down off North Eleuthera. Nearby are the remains of a 180-foot steamship with huge boilers you can swim through. Both sites make excellent photo subjects.
Current Cut	Current Cut 55	An incoming-tide ride through Current Cut makes one of the most exhilarating

dives imaginable. The narrow cut is
loaded with barracuda, eagle rays and
stingrays, crawfish, grunts, snapper,
and the odd rockfish and grouper. The
whole roller-coaster ride takes about
seven minutes.

Devil's Backbone	North Eleuthera 5–30	Though treacherous for boaters, this tricky reef area has an infinite number of dive sites, including deep and shallow reefs and a large number of wrecks. The reef stretches in a wide straggling arc to the west and southwest past Russell and Royal islands to Egg Island, where it is known as Egg Island Reef. The area has abundant and dazzling marine life.

The Exumas

Site	Location and Depth	Description
Exuma Cays National Land and Sea Park	North/Central Exumas 10–200+	This 7-mile-wide fish-and-bird sanctuary runs 22 miles from Wax Cay Cut to Conch Cut and is administered by the Bahamas National Trust. The many dive sites in the park include the full range of coral stands—brain, elkhorn, staghorn and oscillating corals reaching almost to the surface. A wide variety of drop-off diving sites are located in Exuma Sound.
Thunderball Grotto	Staniel Cay 10–20	Nature made this spot spectacular. The grotto occupies the interior of one of three rocks north of the Staniel Cay Yacht Club. It is pierced by eerie shafts of sunlight through holes in the roof of the partly submerged cave. At low tide, snorkelers can enter two of the eight openings without submerging. Stalactites creep down the limestone walls. There are coral and sponge growths usually found only on deep drop-offs.
Stocking Island Cave	George Town 10–80	This tunnel, about 12 feet wide and 8 feet high throughout, has been explored as far as 355 feet back into the island. From the mouth, ablaze with schools of milling fish, the cave dips and rises, the deepest to 80 feet. Fish swim upside down on the ceiling. The walls are covered with an orange spongelike substance. Lifeline and lights are needed. For experienced divers only.

Grand Bahama Island

Site	Location and Depth	Description
Theo's Wreck	Freeport/Lucaya 100	This 230-foot steel freighter is perched on its side on the edge of the Grand Bahama ledge. It was sunk as a dive site in 1982. The stern hangs out over the 2,000-foot drop-off. Divers can sit on the prop and rudder and contemplate the deep blue abyss below.
Angel's Camp	Lucaya 35–50	About 1¼ miles off Lucayan Beach, this medium reef is a scattering of small coral heads surrounding one large head. They are covered with gorgonians as well as sponge life, and are the habitat for a nation of angelfish.
Pygmy Caves	Lucaya 80	In the same area as Angel's Camp, these caves are formed by overgrown ledges and cuts in the reef, the edges and undersides of which are covered with colorful sponges.
Zoo Hole	West of Lucaya 35–185	This large hole in the ocean floor starts at 35 feet. At 75 feet, two huge caverns angle down; they have been explored to 185 feet. Both contain schools of large angelfish, cobia, crabs, and a plethora of shells.
Indian Cay Light	West End 30–80	Off Indian Cay Light are several reefs that form a vast sea garden with schools of grunts, snapper, chub, and tiny tropical fish. Royal grammas are everywhere, and the rare Atlantic long-nosed butterfly fish is common.

New Providence Island

Site	Location and Depth	Description
Lost Ocean Hole	East of Nassau 40–195	This elusive (and thus exclusive) hole is aptly named, difficult as it is to locate. The rim of the 80-foot opening in 40 feet of water is dotted with coral heads and teeming with small fish—grunts, margate, and jacks, as well as larger pompano, amberjack, and sometimes nurse sharks. Divers will find a thermocline at 80 feet, a large cave at 100 feet, and a sand ledge at 185 feet that slopes down to 195 feet.
Lyford Cay Drop-off	West of Nassau 40–200+	Starting from a 40-foot plateau, the cliff plummets almost straight into the inky blue mile-deep Tongue of the Ocean. The wall offers endless varieties of sponges, black coral, and wire coral.

Along the wall, grunts, grouper, hogfish, snapper, and rockfish abound. Off the wall are pelagic game fish, such as tuna, bonito, wahoo, and kingfish.

Rose Island Reefs	Nassau 5–35	The series of shallow reefs along the 14 miles of Rose Island are popular with locals on weekends and visitors on scheduled dives. The coral is varied, though the reefs are showing the effects of the heavy traffic. Plenty of tropical fish still make these reefs home.

3 New Providence Island

Introduction

New Providence Island, the home of more than 60% of the Bahamas' nearly 2½ million residents, is best known internationally for the bustling city of Nassau, a transportation hub on the northeast coast. Nassau also thrives as a banking center for the Bahamas, which offers the benefits of strict bank secrecy laws rivaling those in Switzerland, and no income, sales, or inheritance taxes. In recent years, a growing number of sun seekers who have a perference for plush hotels and close proximity to casinos have headed to two other areas: Cable Beach, a stunning stretch of sand west of Nassau, and Paradise Island, linked to northern Nassau by an arched bridge. Here they find long expanses of beach and clear, blue-green waters that draw yachtsmen, anglers, divers, water-skiers, parasailers, and windsurfers. Landlubbers can choose from three golf courses and abundant tennis courts.

New Providence Island has served as the setting for nearly all of the major historical events in the country. Residents have survived Spanish invasions and piratical dominance, as well as the arrival of English Loyalists and their slaves from the United States after the Revolutionary War. They became involved in blockade-running in the 18th century and rum-running during the 20th century. Eventually, British rule and law prevailed. Even after the black Bahamians' Progressive Liberal Party won control of the government of their country in 1967 and independence from the mother country six years later, the English influence has continued into the present.

Reminders of the British heritage may be seen throughout Nassau: in the pomp and ceremony that attends the opening of Supreme Court sessions and its bewigged judges; in the discipline of the policemen meticulously attired in starched white jackets, red-striped trousers, and pith helmets; and in the unchanged tradition of driving on the left side of the road. The locals speak English, softened by an easy island drawl. They also play cricket and rugby; their football is round, not elliptical. Behind the walls fronting Nassau's narrow streets are Colonial-style buildings with shutters and sculpted shrubbery as well tended as any you might find in an English garden.

Aside from the Bahamas' easy access from the United States (a 35-minute flight from Miami), perhaps this British ambience helps to attract American vacationers—86% of the more than 3 million tourists who come annually to New Providence, one of the smallest islands in the nation. A constant flow of planes arrives daily at Nassau International Airport from all over the United States and, to a lesser extent, from Canada and Europe. Meanwhile, approximately 800,000 annual visitors to New Providence are passengers on the more than 20 cruise ships that regularly drop anchor at Prince George Wharf on short trips from Florida or as the final stop on Caribbean cruises. These passengers disembark to enjoy the colorful harborside market with out-island sloops bringing catches of fish and conch, open-air fruit and vegetable stalls, street hawkers vending local foods, and women weaving their magic on hats and baskets. If the daytime charm of old Nassau isn't enough, travelers can always end their days with the glamour and glitter of Continental-style casinos and tropical entertainment.

Essential Information

Arriving and Departing by Plane

Airports and Airlines   More and more planes are flying in and out of **Nassau International Airport** (tel. 809/322–3344) daily, and more and more carriers are eager to make this their destination. **Eastern** (tel. 800/327–8376) and **Pan Am** (tel. 800/221–1111), both of which had dropped the island as a destination, resumed service from Miami toward the end of 1989—Eastern with daily flights, Pan Am with flights three times a day.

Delta (tel. 800/221–1212) is one of the busier carriers, with daily flights from, among other cities, Chicago, Milwaukee, Detroit, Cincinnati, New York City, Atlanta, Denver, Houston, Los Angeles, and San Francisco.

Bahamasair (tel. 800/222–4262), the national carrier, has daily flights from New York City, Philadelphia, and Washington, DC. Flights from Miami are scheduled six times a day; from Orlando, four times a week.

Among other main carriers, **Comair** (tel. 800/354–9822) began a weekly flight to Nassau from Jacksonville, Florida. The carrier already flies daily from Ft. Lauderdale and West Palm Beach, also in Florida. Miami and Fort Lauderdale are also served by **Chalk's International/Paradise Island Airlines** (tel. 800/432–8807), and **Carnival Airlines** (800/222–7466).

USAir (tel. 800/842–5374) flies in daily from Atlanta, Baltimore, Memphis, Philadelphia, and Charlotte, NC. **Midway Airlines** (tel. 800/621–5700) flies daily from Chicago, Des Moines, Detroit, Cincinnati, Baltimore, and Philadelphia. **TWA** (tel. 800/221–2000) has frequent flights from Chicago, Detroit, Boston, Memphis, Denver, Los Angeles, and Seattle.

Air Canada (tel. 800/422–6232) flies from Montreal and Toronto.

For a charter plane to Nassau, call **Airlift International** (tel. 305/871–1750).

Between the Airport and Hotels   No bus service is available from the airport to the New Providence hotels, except for guests on package tours. A taxi ride from the airport to Cable Beach costs about $12; to Nassau, $16; and to Paradise Island, $20 (this includes the causeway toll of $2).

For names of taxi companies, *see* Getting Around, below.

Arriving and Departing by Ship

For information concerning cruise ships sailing to Nassau, *see* From North America by Ship in Chapter 1.

Getting Around

By Car   For exploring at your leisure, you'll want to have access to a car. Rental automobiles are available at Nassau International Airport and downtown. Reckon on paying $47–$85 a day, $279–$545 a week, depending on the type of car. At press time, gasoline cost $1.63–$1.77 a gallon. And don't forget to observe the rule of the road in the Bahamas—drive on the left side of the road. A visitor's driver's license is valid on New Providence for up to three months.

Avis Rent-A-Car has branches at the Nassau International Airport (tel. 809/327–7121), on Paradise Island at the Pirates Cove Holiday Inn (tel. 809/363–2061), and on West Bay Street (tel. 809/322–2889). **National Car Rental** (tel. 809/327–7301) is also located at the airport. **Budget** has offices at the airport (tel. 809/327–7405), in downtown Nassau (tel. 809/327–7403), and on Paradise Island (tel. 809/363–3095). **Hertz** (tel. 809/327–6866) has an office in downtown Nassau. Also try **Wallace's U-Drive** (tel. 809/325–0650 or 325–8559) on Marathon Road.

By Taxi Taxis are generally the best and most economical way of getting around in New Providence. Fares are fixed by the government at $1.20 for the first ¼ mile, 20¢ for each additional ¼ mile. You can also hire a taxi for sightseeing for $20–$23 an hour.

Bahamas Transport (Box N 8517, tel. 809/323–5111 or 323–5112) has radio-dispatched taxis. **Calypso Taxi Tours** (tel. 809/327–7031) has a stand at Cable Beach; there are also stands at **Montagu** (tel. 809/393–1148) on East Bay Street, **Nassau Beach Lodge** (tel. 809/327–7865) on Cable Beach, **Paradise Taxi Co.** (tel. 809/363–5475) on Paradise Island, and **Perry's Transportation Service** (tel. 809/325–7494) at Dewgard Plaza.

By Bus Frequent jitney (bus) service is available around Nassau and its environs. These buses can be hailed at bus stops and go to hotels, Cable Beach, public beaches, and residential areas; 75¢ will get you a Cook's tour. When you're ready to return to your hotel from downtown Nassau, you'll find jitneys congregated and leaving one by one from Frederick Street between Bay Street and Woodes Rogers Walk.

Some hotels offer complimentary bus service (or water-taxi service) to downtown Nassau.

By Water Taxi Water taxis operate during daylight hours (usually 9–5:30) at 20-minute intervals between Prince George Wharf and Paradise Island. The round-trip cost is $2 per person.

By Scooter Two people can ride around the island on a motor scooter for $18 a half-day or $23 a full-day, including insurance. Helmets are mandatory and are included in the rental price. Many hotels have scooters on the premises. You can also try **Bowe's Scooter Rentals** at Prince George Wharf (tel. 809/326–8329) and at Cable Beach (tel. 809/327–6000, ext. 6374); **B&S Scooter Rentals** (tel. 809/322–2580) at Union Dock on Bay Street; or **Moss Scooter Rentals** (tel. 809/323–2210) on Mackey Street.

By Surrey Horse-drawn carriages with fringes on top (the animals wear straw hats) will take two people around Nassau at a rate of $8 for a half-hour.

Important Addresses and Numbers

Tourist Information The Ministry of Tourism has information booths at Nassau International Airport (tel. 809/327–6833), Rawson Square (tel. 809/328–7810 or 328–7811), and Prince George Wharf (tel. 809/325–9155), where the cruise ships tie up.

Embassies **U.S.:** Mosmar Bldg., Queen St., Box N 8197, tel. 809/322–4753 or 322–1181. **Canadian Consulate:** Out Island Traders Bldg., E. Bay St., tel. 809/323–2123. **British High Commission:** Bitco Bldg., East and Shirley sts., tel. 809/325–7471.

Emergencies **Police** and **Fire,** dial 919.

Nassau Hospitals: Princess Margaret Hospital (Shirley St., tel. 809/322–2861) is government-operated; **Doctors Hospital** (Shirley St., tel. 809/322–8411) is private.

Drugs Action Service (tel. 809/322–2308).

Opening and Closing Times

Banks are open on New Providence Island Monday–Thursday 9:30–3 and Friday 9–5. They are closed Saturday and Sunday. Principal banks on the island are Bank of the Bahamas, Bank of Nova Scotia, Barclays Bank, Canadian Imperial Bank of Commerce, Chase Manhattan Bank, Citibank, and Royal Bank of Canada.

Shops are open Monday–Saturday 9–5; they are closed Sunday, except the Strawmarket on Bay Street, which is open seven days a week.

Guided Tours

Types of Tours More than a dozen local tour operators are available to show you New Providence Island's natural and commercial attractions. Some of the many possibilities available include sightseeing tours of Nassau and the island; glass-bottom boat tours to sea gardens; and various cruises to offshore cays, all starting at $11. A full day of ocean sailing will cost around $40. During the evening you can choose among sunset and moonlight cruises with dinner and drinks (at a cost between $35 –$40) and nightlife tours to casino cabaret shows and nightclubs (at a cost between $20–$30). Tours may be booked at all hotel desks in Nassau, Cable Beach, and Paradise Island, or directly through one of the tour operators listed below, all of which offer air-conditioned cars, vans, or buses, knowledgeable guides, and a choice of tours.

Tour Operators Nassau tour operators offering similar tours and prices include: **B&B Tours** (Box N 8246, tel. 809/326–5036), **Bahamas Pleasure Tours** (Box SS 5454, tel. 809/326–5036), **Curtis Brothers Travel & Tour** (Box N 3573, tel. 809/323–5977), **Emerald Green Sightseeing** (Box N 8288, tel. 809/323–6641), **Happy Tours** (Box N 1077, tel. 809/323–5818), **Howard Johnson Tours** (Box N 406, tel. 809/322–8181), **Island Sun Tours** (Box N 1401, tel. 809/322–2606), **IST Tours** (Box N 4516, tel. 809/323–8200), **Majestic Tours** (Box N 1401, tel. 809/322–2913), **Playtours Ltd.** (Box N 7762, tel. 809/322–2913), **Reliable Tours** (Box N 1093, tel. 809/323–3149), **Richard Moss Tours** (Box N 4442, tel. 809/323–1989), **Sunshine Travel Tours** (Box FH 14359, tel. 809/323–4350), **Tropical Travel Tours** (Box N 448, tel. 809/322–4091).

Short Cruises **Calypso I and II** (Box N 8209, Nassau, tel. 809/363–3577) offers cruises to a private island for swimming and snorkeling. Cost: $35, including lunch.

El Galeon (Box N 4941, Nassau, tel. 809/393–8772) has day cruises from 10 to 4, with swimming and lunch at nearby Discovery Island, and dinner cruises in the bay from 7:30 to 10. Cost: $35.

Nautilus (Box N 7061, Nassau, tel. 809/325–2871) provides glass-bottom boat trips so you can peer down at sea creatures and reefs for 1¾ hours. Cost: $20 adults, $10 children under 11.

Wild Harp Cruises (Box N 1914, Nassau, tel. 809/322–1149) will take you out on a sunset cruise for three hours. Cost: $40, including buffet and good music.

Horticultural The lofty casuarina trees that bend with the wind, the palms used to make the umbrellalike chikee huts, the jumbey trees whose beans may be used in place of coffee, the yucca used in salads or fried, and the sisal used in making rope—all are part of the Bahamian landscape. If you would like to know more about the island's flowers and trees, the **Horticultural Club of the Bahamas** meets at 10 AM at the homes of members on the first Saturday of each month. They'll take you on field trips and even pick you up at your hotel. Call club president Stephanie Harding at tel. 809/326–4549.

Walking A free walking tour around historic Nassau, arranged by the Rawson Square tourist office, is offered on an irregular basis by the Ministry of Tourism. Call ahead for information and reservations at 809/328–7810.

Exploring New Providence Island

Orientation

After you've settled into your Nassau, Cable Beach, or Paradise Island hotel and relaxed, (perhaps, with one of the islands' celebrated Goombay Smash drinks), you'll probably want to explore downtown Nassau and its historic buildings and myriad shops. After that, it's worth looking around the rest of New Providence Island during your stay, an undertaking that can be accomplished in a day, with stops to take in beautiful beaches, local cuisine, and historic buildings.

Be aware before you set out that most of the action on New Providence is concentrated on the northern shore and eastern side of the 7-by-22-mile island. So don't be disillusioned when you drive for 5 miles through wilderness that consists mostly of palmetto and pines, for much of New Providence is undeveloped. This terrain is not the sort you find in Jamaica or Dominica, with their lush greenery and cloud-wreathed mountains. New Providence is quite flat. Renting a car is your best bet, though younger or more adventurous visitors may want to do the trip by scooter. You'll have no problems after you pick up a copy of the Bahamas Trailblazer map at your hotel desk. One side has a map of the island, the other a detailed map of the downtown Nassau area.

Highlights for First-time Visitors

The British Colonial Resort (Tour 1: Nassau)
Casino at Carnival's Crystal Palace (Tour 2: Western New Providence)

Casino at Paradise Island Resort (Tour 3: Paradise Island)
Changing of the Guard at Government House (Tour 1: Nassau)
Coral World (Tour 2: Western New Providence)
Ft. Charlotte (Tour 1: Nassau)
The French Cloisters atop the Ocean Club (Tour 3: Paradise Island)
Parliament Square (Tour 1: Nassau)
The Royal Victoria Hotel and Gardens (Tour 1: Nassau)
Potter's Cay (Tour 1: Nassau)
The Strawmarket on Bay Street (Tour 1: Nassau)

Tour 1: Nassau

Numbers in the margin correspond with points of interest on the Nassau map.

① Begin your walking tour of old Nassau at **Rawson Square.** You're advised to wear sneakers or very comfortable shoes; Bay Street, the main drag, and its environs are always crowded, which can make walking a somewhat slow and hot-footed process. (You can, alternatively, take your tour in one of the horse-drawn surreys lined up at the square, with their straw-hatted beasts of burden.)

② The square is the first part of Nassau that passengers encounter after they tumble off the cruise ships berthed at **Prince George Wharf.** This area has a Ministry of Tourism information center, which offers brochures and maps. After viewing the liners (whose passengers are taking round-trip cruises from Miami to the Bahamas or returning to Miami after seven-day

③ Caribbean trips), you can continue along **Woodes Rogers Walk,** which is named after the first royal governor of the Bahamas. Appointed in 1718, he was an ex-privateer who restored order by purging the island of pirates and other ne'er-do-wells.

Woodes Rogers Walk runs parallel to Bay Street, for about two blocks. Along the way, you'll see and smell much of Nassau's lively seafaring life at the harbor's edge, with its tugs, charter boats, yachts, glass-bottom sightseeing boats, and water taxis that ply back and forth across the harbor to Paradise Island every 20 minutes.

④ At the intersection of Woodes Rogers Walk and Charlotte Street is the **Nassau International Bazaar,** with merchandise from around the world. Here you'll find a Greek shop, French fashions, an art gallery, jewelry, and straw goods. At the foot of Frederick Street, still on Woodes Rogers Walk, you'll find a fleet of buses ready to take you to various points on the island.

⑤ Eventually, you'll have to turn left, and on your right you'll discover the island's oldest and most revered hostelry, the **British Colonial Hotel** (1 Bay St., tel. 809/322–3301), now run by Best Western. This imposing, six-story, pink-and-white structure was once an outpost of the British Empire, a dowager queen on a par with Singapore's Raffles or Hong Kong's Peninsula hotels. Originally built in 1899 on the site where Ft. Nassau stood from 1696 to 1837, it was razed by fire in 1921; it reopened in 1923 as the New Colonial Hotel, the kind of serene place where bonneted ladies crooked their pinkies when they lifted their teacups. Now, flags of five nations flutter at the main entrance, and there is also a fine statue of Woodes Rogers that recalls the hotel's colorful history. The British Colonial, fondly referred to

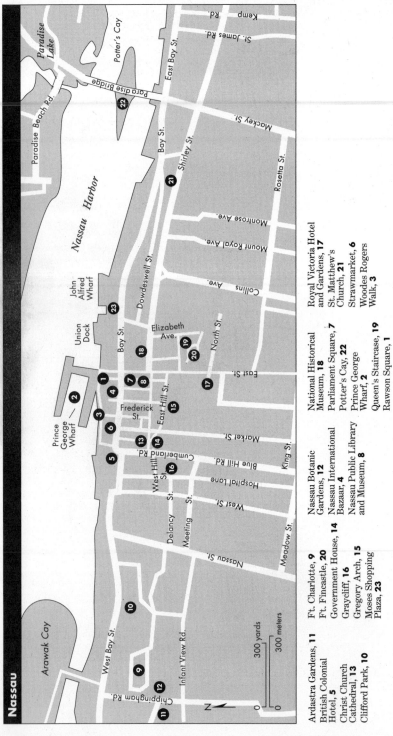

Nassau

Ardastra Gardens, **11**
British Colonial
Hotel, **5**
Christ Church
Cathedral, **13**
Clifford Park, **10**

Ft. Charlotte, **9**
Ft. Fincastle, **20**
Government House, **14**
Graycliff, **16**
Gregory Arch, **15**
Moses Shopping
Plaza, **23**

Nassau Botanic
Gardens, **12**
Nassau International
Bazaar, **4**
Nassau Public Library
and Museum, **8**

National Historical
Museum, **18**
Parliament Square, **7**
Potter's Cay, **22**
Prince George
Wharf, **2**
Queen's Staircase, **19**
Rawson Square, **1**

Royal Victoria Hotel
and Gardens, **17**
St. Matthew's
Church, **21**
Strawmarket, **6**
Woodes Rogers
Walk, **3**

by Bahamians and generations of visitors as "the B.C.," remains one of Nassau's most popular hotels.

Next, head toward the western part of the island, where Bay Street becomes West Bay Street. The **U.S. Embassy** (tel. 809/322–4753) is a block away from the British Colonial on Queen Street.

For an alternative walk, return to Rawson Square, where you'll find another Ministry of Tourism office. This area is also the site of the **Strawmarket**, sprawled through the arched open-air Market Plaza on Bay Street. From early morning until evening, seven days a week, vendors among hundreds of stalls are waiting to sell you straw hats and handbags, clothing, and coral pendants. Here you can also purchase Androsia fabric, a floral batik cloth made on the island of Andros. (Be sure to bargain; it's part of the game.) In the Market Plaza stands a statue of the first governor-general of the Bahamas, Sir Milo B. Butler.

Nassau is the seat of the national government, which has a two-house Parliament consisting of the 16-member Senate (Upper House) and the 43-member House of Assembly (Lower House), and a ministerial cabinet headed by a prime minister. Across Bay Street from Rawson Square is **Parliament Square.** Its pink, colonnaded government buildings were constructed during the early 1800s by Loyalists who came to the Bahamas from North Carolina. The buildings were patterned after the southern Colonial architecture of New Bern, the early capital of North Carolina. Parliament Square is dominated by a statue of the young Queen Victoria on her throne, erected in 1905 on the date of her birthday, May 24. The statue is flanked by a pair of old cannons, and nearby is the **House of Assembly.** Behind the House is the **Supreme Court;** its four-times-a-year opening ceremonies (held the first weeks of January, April, July, and October) recall similar wigs-and-mace pageantry at the Houses of Parliament in London. The Royal Bahamas Police Band is usually on hand. If you would like to take in all of the colorful hoopla, call 809/322–7500 for times when the ceremonies begin.

Also in this immediate area are a half-dozen magistrates' courts, open to the public, and the **Nassau Public Library and Museum,** in an octagonal building that used to be the Nassau Gaol (the Old World spelling for *jail*), circa 1797. Pop in and browse; you can have a quiet look around at the small prison cells, which are now lined with books, and can examine a collection of historic prints and old colonial documents. *Bank La., tel. 809/322–4907. Admission free. Open weekdays 10–9, Sat. 10–5.*

Start west along Bay Street, where the traffic is one-way. You will probably want to make frequent stops here at the various stores (*see* Shopping, below) or at the Strawmarket. You can also take time out at one of the small Bay Street area restaurants for a refreshing Kalik, the local beer.

You'll also come back to the British Colonial Hotel. If you continue for a few blocks on West Bay Street, you'll approach several of Nassau's popular attractions.

First, visit the most interesting fort on the island, **Ft. Charlotte,** built in the late-18th century with a waterless moat, drawbridge, ramparts, and dungeons. Lord Dunmore, the builder, named the massive structure in honor of George III's wife. At the time, some called it Dunmore's Folly because of the staggering expense of building it—£32,000, eight times more than originally planned. (Dunmore's superiors in London were less than ecstatic when they saw the bills, but he managed to survive unscathed.) Ironically, no shots were ever fired in anger from the fort. Ft. Charlotte is located at the top of a hill and commands a fine view of Nassau Harbor and Arawak Cay, a small man-made island that holds huge storage tanks of fresh water barged in from Andros Island. *Off W. Bay St. at Chippendale Rd., tel. 809/322–7500. Admission free. Local guides conduct tours Mon.–Sat. 8:30–4.*

⑩ At the foot of Ft. Charlotte lies **Clifford Park,** where colorful Independence Day ceremonies are held on July 10. The park has a large reviewing ground, grandstands, and playing fields, where you can watch the local soccer, rugby, field hockey, and cricket teams in action.

⑪ A block farther west, on Chippingham Road, are the **Ardastra Gardens,** with 5 acres of tropical greenery and flowering shrubs, an aviary of rare tropical birds, and exotic animals from different parts of the world. The gardens are renowned for the parade of pink, spindly legged, marching flamingos that performs daily at 11, 2, and 4. The flamingo, by the way, is the national bird of the Bahamas. *Near Ft. Charlotte, off Chippendale Rd., tel. 809/323–5806. Admission: $7.50 adults, $3.75 children under 10. Open daily 9–5.*

⑫ Across the street is the **Nassau Botanic Gardens,** which has 18 acres featuring 600 species of flowering trees and shrubs; two freshwater ponds with lilies, water plants, and tropical fish; and a small cactus garden that ends in a grotto. The many trails wandering through the gardens are perfect for leisurely strolls. *Near Ft. Charlotte, off Chippendale Rd., tel. 809/323–5975. Admission: $1 adults, 50¢ children. Open daily 8–4:30.*

If you retrace your steps to the British Colonial and turn right **⑬** (south) on George Street, you'll pass the Anglican **Christ Church Cathedral,** a gothic building erected in 1837 on the site of a parish church. Then at the intersection of Market and Duke streets (where the one-way traffic now goes east past delightful old bougainvillea-shrouded pastel houses), you'll find the **⑭** imposing pink-and-white **Government House,** which since 1801 has been the official residence of the governor-general of the Bahamas.

This distinguished mansion is one of the finest examples in the country of Bahamian-British and American-Colonial influenced architecture. Its graceful columns and broad, circular drive could be found in Virginia or the Carolinas, but its pink color and distinctive quoin corners, which are painted white, are typically Bahamian. Quoins are an architectual embellishment found on many old Bahamian homes and public buildings. Notice, too, the Bahama shutters—wooden louvers that often completely enclose large upper and lower verandas on many well-preserved old mansions and are designed to keep out the tropical sun.

White steps lead up to this stately mansion; halfway up is an imposing statue of Christopher Columbus, dressed ostentatiously in plumed hat and cloak and looking as if he were preparing to make his entrance at the court of Ferdinand and

Isabella to give a vivid account of his discoveries. The building's most notable occupants, the Duke and Duchess of Windsor, made this their home during the first half of the 1940s.

Here you can also catch the spiffy, flamboyant Changing of the Guard every other Saturday morning at 10 (call 809/322–7500 for specific days and times). The stars of the pomp and pageantry are the Royal Bahamas Police Band, which is decked out in white tunics, red-striped navy trousers, and white, spiked pith helmets with red sashes; the drummers sport leopard skins.

15 Just past Government House on Market Street, look up the hill for a view of **Gregory Arch,** which separates downtown from the old, "over-the-hill" neighborhood of **Grant's Town,** where most of Nassau's population lives. Grant's Town was laid out in the 1820s by Governor Lewis Grant as a settlement for freed slaves. The arch was named after John Gregory, governor from 1849 to 1854.

There was a time when visitors would enjoy late-night mingling with the locals over rum drinks in the small, dimly lit bars of Grant's Town. But times and social circumstances change; nowadays, in pondering such a foray, tourists should exhibit the same caution they would if they were visiting the more impoverished areas of a large city.

16 Across the street from Government House stands the gracious **Graycliff** (W. Hill St., tel. 809/326–6188), once a stately home and now Nassau's classiest hotel and restaurant (*see* Dining and Lodging, below). This superb example of Georgian colonial architecture dates from the mid-1700s. It is said that it was built by a Captain Gray, whose privateering vessel was named the *Graywolf;* the landmark's colorful history includes its use as an officers' mess by the British West Indian garrison; it acquired a certain notoriety during the Prohibition rumrunning days. Until the 1970s, it was the private winter home of the Earl and Countess of Dudley.

17 Continuing east on Shirley Street, you'll come to Parliament Street. A block and a half to the right stands the one time **Royal Victoria Hotel,** which was built in 1861; it soon became headquarters for blockade runners, Confederate officers, and English textile tycoons who traded guns for cotton. Along with the British Colonial, the Royal Victoria was also where many of the wealthy winter visitors to the Bahamas rested their heads. The hotel closed its doors in 1971, and the building now houses government offices.

Dominated by a giant banyan tree that once shaded bands playing for parties, the **Royal Victoria Gardens** are a bit overgrown, but they do feature hundreds of varieties of tropical plants. Visitors can roam around at will. There are plans afoot to build a national museum on the grounds in time for the 1992 Columbus quincentenary. *Admission free.*

18 Return to Shirley Street, turn right, and within a couple of blocks you'll reach Elizabeth Avenue, where you'll find, on your left, the **National Historical Museum.** This institution traces the history of the Bahamas with a modest collection of maps, prints, and artifacts. It is staffed by volunteers. *Tel. 809/322–4231. A small contribution is happily accepted. Open Tues.–Wed. 10–4.*

Turn right from the museum and climb Elizabeth Avenue to another island landmark, the **Queen's Staircase,** with 65 steps
carved out of solid limestone by slaves in the late-18th century.
The staircase was named in honor of the 65 years of Queen
Victoria's reign.

The steps lead up to **Ft. Fincastle,** a ship-shaped structure built
in 1793 by the ever-imaginative Lord Dunmore to serve as a
lookout post for marauders trying to sneak into the local harbor. The view of most of Nassau and the harbor from the 126-
foot-tall water tower and lighthouse is quite spectacular. The
tower, more than 200 feet above sea level, is the highest point
on the island. *Guided tours cost 50¢. Open Mon.–Sat. 9–4.*

At the corner of Elizabeth Avenue on Shirley Street is the
government-operated 455-bed **Princess Margaret Hospital;**
next to it is the **Chamber of Commerce.** On the other side of
Shirley Street is a white-colonnaded building, the site of *The
Tribune* (founded 1903). This has long been the Bahamas' most
influential newspaper; its fiery publisher, Sir Etienne Dupuch,
has been an unswerving critic of Sir Lynden O. Pindling's government since Pindling's Progressive Liberal Party ousted the
white merchant–dominated United Bahamian Party in 1967.

(Influential it may be, but *The Tribune* must yield in age to its
rival, the *Nassau Guardian*, which has been published since
1844. It was started by Edwin Charles Moseley, whose **Bank
House** on East Hill Street is one of the island's oldest homes,
built in the 1780s.)

Still on Shirley Street, and close to a mile farther on, you'll
come to **St. Matthew's Church,** also Anglican, and the oldest
church in the Bahamas. Built between 1800 and 1804, the
church was designed by a transplanted American Loyalist, Joseph Eve; the structure is a well-preserved example of neoclassic forms and gothic proportions that were popular during
this period.

Past the church you'll arrive at Mackey Street; on the left is the
entrance to New Providence's own special world of hedonism,
Paradise Island (*see* Tour 3, below), linked to the mainland by a
giant arched causeway. Underneath the bridge is **Potter's Cay,**
one of Nassau's most charming spots.

Here, sloops bring in fish and conch, which the fishermen clean
on the spot and sell to everyone from local housewives to hotel
chefs. Vegetables, herbs, and limes are also available at nearby
stalls, along with fruits such as pineapples, papaya, and bananas. If you don't have the cooking facilities or, more important, the know-how, to handle the preparation of the rubbery
conch (getting the diffident creature out of its shiny pink shell
requires boring a hole at the right spot to sever the muscle that
keeps it entrenched), you'll find a stall selling the crustacean in
soup, stew, and salad (raw and marinated in lime juice), or as
deep-fried fritters.

If you return to Bay Street and head west, you'll pass some of
Nassau's older haberdashery, dress, and shoe shops; the new
Moses Shopping Plaza (with department stores, boutiques,
and a pharmacy); and modest hotels, such as the 30-room **New
Harbour Moon Hotel** (tel. 809/325–1548), whose rates are
considerably more reasonable than those at the dazzling new
mega-resorts.

Soon you'll find yourself back at where you started, Rawson Square—where a uniformed police officer is usually directing traffic efficiently, almost right under the nose of the statue of Queen Victoria.

Tour 2: Western New Providence

Numbers in the margin correspond with points of interest on the New Providence Island map.

Whether you start your driving exploration of the most unpopulated part of New Providence from your hotel in Nassau, on Paradise Island, or on Cable Beach, make your first stop **Coral World,** about a mile west of the British Colonial Hotel on Bay Street. This 16-acre marine extravaganza occupies the entire island of Silver Cay, which is linked to the mainland by a bridge. To say you can't miss Coral World is an understatement, except possibly to the nearsighted. Its Observation Tower soars 100 feet above the surface of the ocean. Visitors can descend a winding staircase to a depth of 20 feet below the water's surface to observe such sea denizens as turtles, stingrays, moray eels, and starfish. The tower has two viewing decks and a gift shop.

In the adjacent Marine Park, the Marine Gardens feature the Reef Tank, home of the world's largest man-made living reef. Visitors have a 360-degree view of coral, sponges, tropical fish and other forms of sea life. Nearby you'll find the Shark Tank, where these predators native to the Caribbean can be observed from an overhead deck or from windows around the tank. All together, the Marine Gardens Aquarium has 24 aquariums that tell the story of life on the reef. You can also enjoy nature trails with tropical foliage, waterfalls, and exotic trees. Flamingos occupy another area of the park. *Silver Cay, tel. 809/328–1036. Admission: $12 adults, $8 children 3–12. Open daily Nov.–Mar. 9–6, Apr.–Oct. 9–7.*

Farther west of Coral World, past popular **Saunders Beach** and **Brown's Point,** off West Bay Street, is **Cable Beach,** which is sometimes referred to as the Bahamian Riviera. The area is dominated by its celebrated oceanfront hotels, running from the Wyndham Ambassador Beach to Casuarinas and taking in, along the way, the competing resorts of the Nassau Beach Hotel, Carnival's Crystal Palace Resort & Casino, Le Meridien Royal Bahamian, and Cable Beach Manor.

You may want to stop briefly at **Carnival's Crystal Palace Resort & Casino** (tel. 809/327–6200), the giant 1,550-room hotel complex with a multicolored facade. Start with a visit to the casino, which is a casual, friendly place, or stroll through the shopping mall that connects it with The Tower, another part of the hotel. Showcases on the upper level exhibit very good examples of Junkanoo art, the Bahamian craft that comes into play during the lavish Boxing Day and New Year's Day festivities.

Continue west along Cable Beach, past another huge strawmarket and the Sandyport shopping complex on your left, onto the dual carriageway—British for divided highway—that leads to the condominium complex of **Delaporte Point.** A little farther on, you'll come to a rambling pink house on a promontory at **Rock Point.** Here much of the James Bond movie

New Providence Island

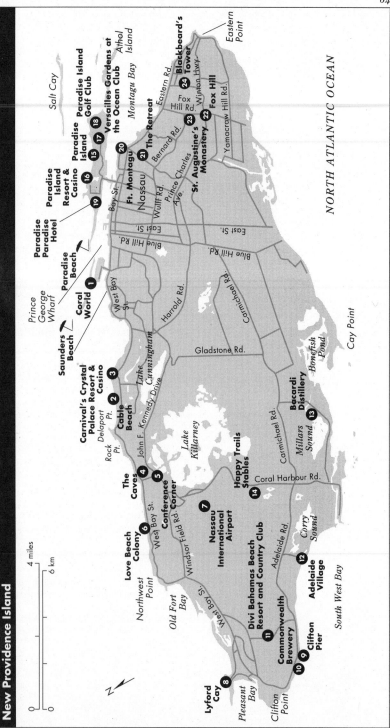

NORTH ATLANTIC OCEAN

Eastern Point

Salt Cay

Athol Island

Paradise Island Golf Club

Versailles Gardens at the Ocean Club

Montagu Bay

Blackbeard's Tower **24**

Fox Hill Rd.

Fox Hill **22**

Winton Hwy.

The Retreat **23**

Eastern Rd.

Paradise Island **18** **17**

Paradise Island **15**

20

Bernard Rd.

St. Augustine's Monastery

Yamacraw Hill Rd.

Paradise Island Resort & Casino **16**

Ft. Montagu **21**

Prince Charles Ave.

Wulff Rd.

Bay St.

Nassau

Paradise Paradise Hotel

19

East St.

East St.

Prince George Wharf

Paradise Beach

Blue Hill Rd.

Coral World **1**

West Bay St.

Blue Hill Rd.

Saunders Beach

Harrold Rd.

Carmichael Rd.

Cay Point

Carnival's Crystal Palace Resort & Casino

3

Lake Cunningham

Gladstone Rd.

Bonefish Pond

2

Cable Beach

Delaport Pt.

John F. Kennedy Drive

Lake Killarney

Bacardi Distillery

13

Rock Pt.

Millars Sound

Carmichael Rd.

The Caves **4** **5**

Conference Corner

Happy Trails Stables

Coral Harbour Rd.

14

Love Beach Colony

6

West Bay St.

Windsor Field Rd.

7

Nassau International Airport

Corry Sound

Northwest Point

Old Fort Bay

Adelaide Rd.

Adelaide Village

12

Divi Bahamas Beach Resort and Country Club

South West Bay

West Bay St.

Commonwealth Brewery

11

Clifton Pier **9**

10

Lyford Cay **8**

Pleasant Bay

Clifton Point

Clifton Pt.

4 miles

6 km

N

Thunderball was made; the shark scenes were shot at the owner's two connected pools. Those who saw the film will recall the chilling scene in which one of the villain's henchmen, who had failed in an attempt to eliminate Bond, was fed to the sharks for supper.

❹ Drive along West Bay Street, and you'll see on your left **The Caves,** large limestone caverns that have been sculpted into their present shape over the aeons by the waves. Legend has it that The Caves sheltered the early Arawak Indians. It's a plausible idea, because they had to sleep somewhere. Then, almost **❺** as soon as you leave The Caves, you'll come to **Conference Corner,** where President John F. Kennedy, Canadian Prime Minister John Diefenbaker, and British Prime Minister Harold MacMillan planted trees to commemorate their summit meeting in Nassau in 1962.

Time Out Stop on West Bay Street for a break at the white-and-green-shuttered **Traveller's Rest** (Box F 1462, tel. 809/327–7633) bar and restaurant, a popular meeting place with Nassau's permanent residents. Tropical paintings and prints line the walls, and the guest book contains the signatures of such celebrities as Sidney Poitier (who was born in the Bahamas), Diana Ross, and Sean Connery. Owner Joan Hanna mixes mean Goombay Smashes and banana daiquiris; serves up native peas and rice, fried grouper fingers, and conch fritters; and pours English Watney's draft beer, all at modest prices. Before leaving, look in the adjoining Seagrape boutique for locally made print shirts.

As you near the northwest corner of New Providence, you'll **❻** come to the **Love Beach Colony,** where one of the loveliest stretches of beach on the island is lined with expensive private homes. Across from the beach, a partially hidden pink house named Capricorn is owned by singer Julio Iglesias. Just off Love Beach are 40 acres of coral and sea fan, with forests of fern, known as the Sea Gardens. The gin-clear waters are a favorite with snorkelers. Glass-bottom boats with guides make frequent excursions to the Sea Gardens from Prince George Wharf. *Boat fare: $10 per person.*

West Bay Street then turns sharply south, past the intersec- **❼** tion of Windsor Field Road, which connects with **Nassau International Airport,** and meanders for 4–5 miles past the huge Esso refinery tanks on your left and seemingly endless rows of pine trees until you run into the most exclusive enclave on the **❽** island, **Lyford Cay.**

This 4,000-acre preserve is where Nassau's old-money pioneers started settling more than 30 years ago when a wealthy Canadian named E. P. Taylor developed it as an exclusive colony. There are a private golf course and more than 200 homes here, many of them owned by wealthy people from around the world who return only to spend winter in a kindlier clime. Unfortunately, your experience of Lyford Cay will be voyeuristic at best, for a gate at the entrance keeps out visitors who are not residents or friends.

❾ Continue on West Bay Street to **Clifton Pier,** where the cruise ships used to dock. Now the pier handles only tankers bringing in cargoes of oil and cement. Just past the pier, where the street name changes to Southwest Road, you'll see on your left

⑩ the vast **Commonwealth Brewery,** which turns out Nassau's own very good beer, Kalik. The brew has become so popular that it has lent its name to a lilting chant sung during the Junkanoo parades.

Almost immediately after this point, turn left (north) to the is-
⑪ land's most secluded hotel complex, the **Divi Bahamas Beach Resort and Country Club** (tel. 809/362–4391). The resort is far from the hustle and bustle of Cable Beach and Paradise Island, but it has all of the indoor and outdoor amenities. During excavations to build the resort's 18-hole golf course, the ruins of two buildings and extensive stone walls were uncovered, leading to speculation that the property might have been a plantation established by Loyalists after the Revolutionary War.

Return to Southwest Road, which, a five-minute drive away, changes its name again to Adelaide Road. A sign on the right
⑫ side of the road points to the small community of **Adelaide Village,** which sits almost on the ocean. Adelaide was first settled in the early 1800s by blacks who were captured from their African homes and loaded aboard slave ships bound for the New World; they were rescued on the high seas by the British Royal Navy. The first group of liberated slaves reached Nassau in 1832.

Today, only a few dozen families live in Adelaide; they raise vegetables and chickens and inhabit well-worn, pastel-painted wooden houses, sheltered in vegetation such as crotons and bougainvillea. The village has a primary school, some little grocery stores, and a tiny bar. On the beach, you may find a patient old man huddled over a table containing conch shells for sale. He is rarely disturbed, for few tourists come this way.

Returning to Adelaide Road, turn east and drive for about 5 miles (Adelaide Road becomes Carmichael Road), then veer
⑬ south again down Bacardi Road; you'll come to the **Bacardi Distillery,** where large quantities of its well-known rums and liqueurs are produced each year. *Tel. 809/326–1412. Open for free tours weekdays–12:30 and 2–4, but you must call ahead for an appointment.*

Retrace your route along Carmichael Road until you come to
⑭ Coral Harbour Road, and then turn north past **Happy Trails Stables** (tel. 809/326–1820), where you may want to stop off for a one-hour trail ride on horseback. The road continues east of the airport to the junction of Windsor Field Road, where you should turn right along John F. Kennedy Drive, cutting between the island's two lakes. On your right is Lake Killarney, and on your left, the smaller Lake Cunningham.

At the foot of Lake Cunningham, the road swerves left, past the **Lutheran Church of Nassau** (tel. 809/323–4107) and the headquarters of the Bahamas Red Cross, until it joins the easternmost point of the dual carriageway on Cable Beach.

Tour 3: Paradise Island

During your walking tour of downtown Nassau, you will have come, toward the end, to the junction of Bay Street and Mackey Street. This marks the entrance to the arched causeway ($2 car and motorbike toll, 75¢ for bicyclists and pedestrians) that takes you to the extravagant man-made world of
⑮ **Paradise Island.**

At the other side of the causeway, you'll run into Casino Drive,
which leads into the **Paradise Island Resort & Casino** (tel. 809/
326–2000), with Paradise Lake, where trained porpoises frolic,
on the left. The famed Café Martinique—yes, James Bond ate
here, too, in *Thunderball*—sits at the bottom of the driveway
(*see* Dining, below). This imposing resort was originally the
Britannia Beach Hotel, which once had a whole upper floor tak-
en over for several months during the '70s as a hideout by
eccentric millionaire Howard Hughes and his faithful entou-
rage during his final years of hibernation.

Now the complex is home to restaurants, glitzy shopping malls,
a theater with Las Vegas–type after-dark shows, and a giant,
30,000-square-foot casino. In the afternoons, the casino is fairly relaxed and considerably less crowded, so if you are not too
casually dressed (shirtless, barefoot, or otherwise scantily covered sightseers are not welcome), you can try your luck at the
slot machines, roulette wheels, and blackjack tables. The resort and the other hotels lined along the shore are linked by a
road and by biking and jogging paths.

Turn on to Paradise Island Drive and you will eventually run
into a haven of peace on the island, the **Versailles Gardens at the
Ocean Club** (tel. 809/326–2501 or 326–2509). Fountains and
statues of luminaries (such as Napoleon and Josephine, Frank-
lin Delano Roosevelt, David Livingstone, Hercules, and Meph-
istopheles) grace the seven terraces of the club, once owned by
Huntington Hartford. Fittingly, it is a favorite locale for weddings.

At the top of the terraced gardens, on the other side of the road
overlooking the channel that links the island to Nassau, stand
The Cloisters, remains of a 14th-century French stone monastery that were imported to the United States in the '20s by
newspaper baron William Randolph Hearst. Forty years later,
grocery-chain heir Hartford bought The Cloisters and had
them installed on their present commanding sight; at their center, you'll find a graceful contemporary white marble statue
called *Silence,* by U.S. sculptor Dick Reid.

Just before getting to The Cloisters, if you turn right down
onto Bayview Drive, you will find what is probably the most opulent (and most private) estate on the island. In fact, this
sprawling house, where an Arab sheikh and family rest their
heads, runs the length of the drive, with 16 four-lamp lampposts dotted along the way in front of a high protective wall.
Rarely is anyone seen in this sanctum sanctorum, though the
occasional gleaming limousine exits through the front gate,
which is guarded by a statue of Neptune. Other statues dot the
grounds, and there are eight—count them—garages at the end
of the property.

Farther along Paradise Island Drive and to the left is the
Paradise Island Golf Club (tel. 809/326–3000), one of three on
New Providence, and farther along still is the small airport
Merv Griffin opened in the spring of 1989 with great flourish—
Prime Minister Sir Lynden O. Pindling was the honored guest.

On your way back off the island, you'll come to a roundabout, or
traffic circle. Turn to the right along Paradise Beach Drive,
past pine and palmetto, then right again onto Casuarina Drive
until you come to the **Paradise Paradise Hotel** (tel. 809/326–
2541), a low-rise resort that offers a range of active water-

sports; it's situated on **Paradise Beach,** one of the most beautiful stretches of white sand to be found anywhere in the islands. You can enjoy the beach, which is dotted with chikees (thatched huts), for a $3 fee; that includes towels and changing rooms.

Tour 4: Eastern New Providence

If you return to Bay Street from Paradise Island, go left (east) past the **Nassau Yacht Haven,** and at a curve in the road where it ❷⓿ becomes Eastern Road you'll see, on your left, **Ft. Montagu,** oldest of the island's three forts, which was built in 1741 of local limestone.

The fort was built to repel possible Spanish invaders, but the only action it saw was when it was occupied for two weeks by rebel American troops—including a lieutenant named John Paul Jones—seeking arms and ammunition during the Revolutionary War. The fortification is well maintained, though there is no admission price or set hours. There also are no guided tours, but you're welcome to wander around. A broad public beach stretches for more than a mile beyond the fort; it overlooks **Montagu Bay,** where many international yacht regattas and Bahamian workboat races are held annually. Nearby stand the remains of the long-abandoned, once-recherché Fort Montagu Beach Hotel.

Back on Eastern Road, almost immediately you'll find Village Road, which veers to the southwest. Here are 11 acres of tropi- ❷❶ cal gardens known as **The Retreat,** home of a world of some 200 species of exotic palm trees. It is also the headquarters of the Bahamas National Trust. *Tel. 809/393–1317. Tours of The Retreat, Tues.–Thurs., cost $2.*

Back on Eastern Road, you turn right, and right (south) again ❷❷ on Fox Hill Road, and you'll find the little community of **Fox Hill,** which has its own festival on the second Tuesday of every August. Fox Hill Day is celebrated with goombay music, home cooking, arts-and-crafts booths, and gospel singing. It comes one week after the rest of the island has celebrated Emancipation Day; legend says that it took a week for the original news of freedom to reach the community.

❷❸ Here, too, on Fox Hill Road, is the Romanesque **St. Augustine's Monastery,** home of the Bahamas' Benedictine monks. It was built in 1946 by a monk named Father Jerome, who is also famed for his carving of the Stations of the Cross up Mt. Alvernia on Cat Island, the highest (206 feet) point in the Bahamas. He is buried in a hermitage he built at the top of Alvernia. The St. Augustine buildings overlook beautiful gardens, and the monks will be pleased to give you a tour of their home, including their own bakery, where you may buy their homemade guava jelly.

Near the foot of Fox Hill Road, just before it ends at the south shore, stands an out-of-the-way building in which few visitors would care to spend much time: **Her Majesty's Fox Hill Prison.** Turn east here onto Yamacraw Hill Road as it curves around the easternmost point of New Providence, and continue driving ❷❹ until you see **Blackbeard's Tower** on a hill to your left.

The more pragmatic people of Nassau dismiss this edifice as the remains of an old stone water tower; the more romantic insist it was used by the piratical Edward Teach, aka Blackbeard, as a lookout for Spanish ships ripe for plundering. Whatever its background, it is worth the short climb to the top to view the surrounding area. *Admission free. No set hours.*

Continue west on Eastern Road until it runs into Bay Street and downtown—by which time you can say you've seen just about all of the island of New Providence.

Shopping

Most of the shopping on New Providence is centered on Nassau. Unlike some of the Caribbean destinations such as St. Thomas and St. Maarten, Nassau is not a duty-free paradise; and although some shops will be happy to mail bulky or fragile items home for you, no one delivers your purchases to your hotel, plane, or cruise ship. Still, Nassau offers bargains on imported items like crystal, watches, cameras, sweaters, and perfumes; they can cost you up to 30%–40% less than back home. Opening hours for most shops are Monday–Saturday 9–5, but some close at noon on Thursday. Only drugstores, and the Strawmarket, are open on Sundays.

Most of Nassau's shops are located on Bay Street between Rawson Square and the British Colonial Hotel and on the side streets leading off Bay Street. You can bargain at the stalls in the Strawmarket Plaza, midway along Bay Street, but prices in the shops are fixed. And do observe the local dress customs when you go shopping; shorts are acceptable, but bathing suits are not.

Note: All shops listed below are located on Bay Street, unless otherwise noted.

Specialty Stores

China and Crystal
Check out the Wedgwood, Royal Copenhagen, Royal Doulton, Baccarat, and Lalique items at **Bernard's** (tel. 809/322–2841). The **Island Shop** (tel. 809/322–4183) has Dema crystal. For unusual English and European antique china, explore **Marlborough Antiques** (tel. 809/328–0502), not far from the British Colonial. (In fact, Marlborough offers a treasure trove of Victorian and Edwardian furniture and bric-a-brac.) The **Scottish Shop** (tel. 809/322–4720), on Charlotte Street just off Bay Street, carries a good selection of St. Andrews and Highland bone china and Scottish stoneware.

Fashion
Clothing and accessories are no great bargains in Nassau, but if you hunt through the racks you're sure to latch onto something you won't find at your home boutique. The long-established **Mademoiselle** (tel. 809/322–5130), which has 19 shops throughout the Bahamas, is one of the smartest of the boutiques; take a look at their hand-batiked Androsia fashions. **Barry's** (tel. 809/322–3118), at the corner of Bay and George streets, carries English woolen suits, Irish linen handbags, crochet blouses, and Philippine-made Guayabera shirts for men. Try the **Nassau Shop** (tel. 809/322–8405), the largest and oldest family-run department store in town, for Pringle and Braemar cashmeres.

For Gucci clothing and accessories, as well as a wide range of leather luggage, wallets, and handbags, stop off at **Leather Masters** (tel. 809/322–7597), on Parliament Street. **National**

Hand Prints (tel. 809/393–1974), on Mackey Street, is well stocked with Bahamian fabrics, shirts, and dresses. **Galaxy** (tel. 809/322–5537), at Patton and Rosetta streets, has a reputation for the most extravagant shoes and accessories in Nassau.

Jewelry **Greenfire** (tel. 809/326–6564) has the market cornered on exquisite Colombian emeralds in 14k and 18k settings. The **Nassau Shop** (tel. 809/322–8405) is known to have the most comprehensive jewelry selection in town. You'll find costume jewelry by Monet, Nina Ricci, and Yves St. Laurent at **John Bull** (tel. 809/322–3328), which has been in business on Bay Street for 60 years, immediately east of Rawson Square. **Little Switzerland** (tel. 809/322–8324) has a large selection of European sapphires and diamonds, as well as Spanish pieces of eight in settings. **Coin of the Realm** (tel. 809/322–4862) on Charlotte Street has Bahamian coins in settings.

Perfumes A wide selection of eaux de toilette, cologne, and fragrances can be found at **City Pharmacy** (tel. 809/322–2061); **John Bull** (tel. 809/322–3328), which carries Chanel, Yves St. Laurent, and Estée Lauder; **Little Switzerland** (tel. 809/322–8324), which stocks Giorgio Beverly Hills, Eternity, and Passion; the **Nassau Shop** (tel. 809/322–8405); and the **Perfume Shop** (tel. 809/322–2375), on Frederick Street. A new perfume store on Bay Street, **Cameo** (tel. 809/322–1449), is selling La Prairie skin-treatment and sun products from Switzerland.

Watches You'll find the best selections at **John Bull** (tel. 809/322–3328), the **Nassau Shop** (tel. 809/322–8405), **Little Switzerland** (tel. 809/322–8324), and **Old Nassau** (tel. 809/322–2057).

Miscellaneous Art collectors will find original Bahamian paintings and prints at **Spectrum** (tel. 809/325–7492), at Charbay Plaza on Charlotte Street. Camera buffs can try **John Bull** (tel. 809/322–3328) and the **Island Shop** (tel. 809/322–4183). If you're searching for English toys, check out **City Pharmacy** (tel. 809/322–2061). Try the **Nassau Shop** (tel. 809/322–8405) or **Linen & Lace** (tel. 809/322–4266) for fine linens. For pottery and figurines, stop off at **Little Switzerland** (tel. 809/322–8324) and the **Island Shop** (tel. 809/322–4183). Silver vases, plates, and other items are carried at **Coin of the Realm** (tel. 809/322–4862), **Little Switzerland** (tel. 809/322–8324), and **Marlborough Antiques** (tel. 809/328–0502) with specialties from the Victorian period.

Markets and Arcades

The **Strawmarket** on Bay Street is one of the world's largest, and a main action spot of old Nassau. Hundreds of women hawk their wares, including brilliantly decorated woven hats and bags, baskets and totes, mats and slippers, wall hangings, and dolls. You'll also find necklaces and bracelets strung with pea shells, sharks' teeth, and bright beans, berries, or pods; handsewn clothing; original oils, prints, and wooden carvings by local artists; and shells and corals in myriad shapes from the Bahamian sea. Here bargaining with vendors is part of the fun—all prices are negotiable.

Don't forget those little arcades off Bay Street. **Colony Place** features arts and crafts. The **Nassau Arcade** has the Bahamas Anglo-American bookstore (tel. 809/325–0338). The **Prince George Plaza** has 14 shops with varied offerings and a rooftop restaurant. A few blocks east of Rawson Square, the **Moses Plaza Arcade** includes a greeting cards store, a fancy lingerie boutique, and a gift shop.

Incidentally, if you're checked into one of the Cable Beach or Paradise Island hotels, you'll find that many of the top Bay Street shops, such as Little Switzerland, Leather Masters, and Mademoiselle, have branches in the hotel malls.

Sports

Participant Sports

Bowling There's an alley with 20 lanes called **The Village Lanes** (Box N 8030, Village Rd., tel. 809/323–2277). A game costs $1.65 from 9–5; $1.90 after 5 PM. You can rent shoes for 50¢, and there's a snack bar and lounge.

Fitness Clubs Because you're away from home, that's no excuse to get away from your normal exercise routine, especially because the majority of your time in Nassau will be spent stretched out on the beach or eating more than you should. For exercise only, try **Kicks Aerobics** (tel. 809/328–7666) on Royal Avenue. If you're into heavier things, call in at **Windermere** (tel. 809/393–0033) on East Bay Street, with aerobics, weights, and Jacuzzi; or **Total Fitness Centre** (tel. 809/323–8105) in Centreville, with whirlpool, weights, and rowing machines.

Le Meridien Royal Bahamian Hotel (tel. 809/327–6400 or 800/543–5400), on Cable Beach, has one of the best health spas in the Bahamas, open to guests and nonguests. The spa features an aerobics room, Universal machines, an outdoor freshwater pool, a steam room and a sauna, a whirlpool, Swedish massages, facials, and mud baths.

Golf Pioneer Sir Harry Oakes built the first golf course in the Bahamas in the '30s, so there's a certain nostalgia attached to his former **Cable Beach Hotel Golf Club**; 7,040 yards, par 72. *Box N 4919, tel. 809/327–6000, 800/822–4200 in the U.S. Cost: $18 for 18 holes, $10 for nine; Mandatory electric cart: $25 and $13; clubs: $10. Open winter 7:30–3:30, summer 7:30–4:30.*

Divi Bahamas Beach Resort and Country Club, on the secluded southern part of New Providence, is the newest course to surrender its divots to visiting players; 6,707 yards, par 72. *Box N 8191, tel. 809/362–4391, 800/367–3484 in the U.S. Cost: guests $12 for 18 holes, nonguests $20; guests $6 for nine holes, nonguests $10. Mandatory electric carts till noon: $20 and $10; pull carts after noon: $5 and $2.50. Clubs: $12. Open winter 7:30–5, summer 7:30–7:30.*

Paradise Island Golf Club was designed by Dick Wilson; it is a challenging 6,976 yards, par 72. *Box N 4777, tel. 809/326–3000, 800/321–3000 in the U.S. Cost: winter $25 for 18 holes, $15 for nine holes; summer $20 and $10, respectively. Electric carts: $25 for 18 holes, $15 for nine holes. Pull carts after 1 PM: $5. Clubs: $10. Open winter 7:30–6, summer 7:30–8.*

Horseback Riding You can sign up for guided rides along the golf course and beaches at the **Harbourside Riding Stables** on Paradise Island. English and Western saddles are available. *Box N 1771, tel.*

*809/326–3733. Cost: $20 per hour. Open daily 9–5, though sum-
mer hours may vary. Reservations recommended.*

Happy Trails, on Coral Harbour, has an experienced guide accompany all rides through the surrounding wooded areas. Two
to 10 persons participate in each ride. English and Western
saddles are available. During July and August, there's an afternoon trek with picnic lunch on the beach. *Box N 7992, tel.
809/326–1820. Cost: $50 with a minimum of six persons by ap-
pointment.*

Squash The **Nassau Squash and Racquet Club** (Box N 9764, tel. 809/
323–1838), with three courts, charges $7 per hour. The **Village
Club** (Box SS 6015, tel. 809/323–1580) charges $6 per hour for
play on its three courts, with a $1.50 charge for racket rental,
$2.50 for balls.

Tennis (Fees quoted at hotel courts are for nonguests.)

The **British Colonial Hotel** (Box N 7148, tel. 809/322–3301) has
three hard courts with night play, and it charges $2 per hour.

Le Meridien Royal Bahamian Hotel (Box N 7528, tel. 809/327–
6400) has two Flexipave courts and charges $5 per hour.

Nassau Beach Hotel (Box N 7756, tel. 809/327–7711) charges $3
per hour for play on its six Flexipave courts.

Nassau Squash and Racquet Club (Box N 9764, tel. 809/323–
1854) has three Har-Tru courts. Cost: $6 per hour.

Paradise Island Resort & Casino (Box N 4777, tel. 809/326–
2000) offers the largest tennis complex on the island; you can
play on any of its 12 asphalt courts for $2 per hour.

Pirates Cove Holiday Inn (Box SS 6214, tel. 809/326–2101) on
Paradise Island offers four asphalt courts. Cost: $3 per hour.

Sheraton Grand Hotel (Box SS 6307, tel. 809/326–2011) on Paradise Island has four asphalt courts and charges $3 per hour,
with a $3 racket-rental fee.

Wyndham Ambassador Beach Hotel (Box N 3026, tel. 809/327–
8617), with eight asphalt courts, is open at night. Cost: $2.50
per hour.

Water Sports Nassau Harbour can handle the world's largest cruise liners.
Boating and The Paradise Island Bridge, which bisects the harbor, has a
Fishing high water clearance of 70 feet, so that sailboats with taller
masts heading for marinas east of the bridge must enter the
harbor from the east end. **East Bay Yacht Basin** and part of the
Hurricane Hole Marina are boating facilities located west of
the bridge. Beyond the bridge on the Nassau side of the harbor
lie **Nassau Yacht Haven, Bayshore Marina, Brown's Boat Yard,**
and the **Nassau Harbour Club,** all of them full-service marinas.
Hurricane Hole with 45 slips is situated at the Paradise Island
end of the bridge. The Nassau Yacht Club and Royal Nassau
Sailing Club can be found at the harbor's eastern opening. The
posh development, Lyford Cay, at the western end of New
Providence, offers an excellent marina.

The waters are generally smooth and alive with all sorts of reef
and species of game fish, which is why the Bahamas has more
than 20 fishing tournaments, open to visitors, every year. A favorite spot just west of Nassau is the **Tongue of the Ocean,** so
called because it looks like that essential organ when viewed

from the air; it stretches for 100 miles. For boat rental, parties of two to six will pay $350 or so for a half-day, $450 for a full day. Don't forget to take your suntan lotion when you go fishing. The breezes won't prevent you from getting sunburned.

The following companies offer fishing-boat rentals: **Bayshore Marina** (Box SS 5453, tel. 809/322–8323), **East Bay Marina** (Box SS 5549, tel. 809/322–3754), **Nassau Yacht Haven** (Box SS 5693, tel. 809/322–8173), and **Hurricane Hole Marina** (Paradise Island, Box N 1216, tel. 809/326–3601).

Parasailing **Cable Beach Hotel** (Box N 4914, tel. 809/327–7070) gives you 10 minutes on the water for $40.

Nassau Beach Hotel (Box N 7756, tel. 809/327–7711) charges $30 per ride.

Paradise Island Resort & Casino (c/o Resorts International, 915 N.E. 125th St., North Miami, FL 33161, tel. 305/891–2500 or 809/326–3000) offers six minutes of whizzing through the water for $25.

Sheraton Grand Hotel (Box SS 6307, tel. 809/326–2011), on Paradise Island, charges $20 for eight minutes.

Skin Diving and New Providence Island provides several sites that are popular
Scuba Diving with the underwater set: **Gambier Deep Reef** off Gambier Village, which goes to a depth of 80 feet; the **South Side reefs** (snorkeling only, because of the shallowness of the water); the **Rose Island Reefs** close to the Nassau harbor; the **wreck of the steel-hulled ship Mahoney,** just outside the harbor; **Lost Ocean Hole,** an 80-foot opening east of Nassau; **Lyford Cay Drop-off,** a cliff that plummets into the Tongue of the ocean; and **Sea Gardens,** off the north shore. The following experts will arrange trips:

Bahama Divers Ltd. (Box SS 5004, tel. 809/326–5644) at the Pilot House Hotel has a full line of scuba equipment for rent. Destinations are drop-off wrecks, coral reefs and gardens, and an ocean blue hole. They are three-hour trips, three times a day.

Peter Hughes' Dive (Box N 8191, tel. 809/326–4391), at the Divi Bahamas Beach Resort and Country Club on the island's south shore, rents scuba and snorkel equipment, and arranges dive trips.

Smugglers Rest Resort BDA (Box N 8050, tel. 809/326–1143) also has all the equipment you need. You can visit a coral reef wall, a night cave, and a wreck. A PADI course is available.

Sun Divers Ltd., BDA (Box N 10728, tel. 809/322–3301), at the British Colonial Hotel, has air fills and snorkeling gear; it takes guests to a shallow reef, a deep reef, and a drop-off. Trips last from 1 PM to 5 PM.

Waterskiing A ride on the water at **Carnival's Crystal Palace Resort & Casino** (Box N 8306, tel. 809/327–7070) costs $10 for 3 miles. **Nassau Beach Hotel** (Box N 7756, tel. 809/327–7711) charges $20 for 3 miles. **Paradise Island Resort & Casino** (Box N 4777, tel. 809/326–3000) charges $20. A ride at the **Wyndham Ambassador Beach Hotel** (Box N 3026, tel. 809/327–8231) costs $12.

Spectator Sports

In the Bahamas, the British handed down, among other imperishable traditions, sports such as **soccer, rugby** (somewhat comparable to American football, except that rugger types hate to be burdened with all of that armor—hence, many a shoulder is broken), and **cricket** (that languid game whose players occupy positions on the field such as silly mid-on, third slip, long leg, and square leg; it is absolutely essential that someone versed in the rules of the game and long on patience accompany you). Many of these games are played at **Clifford Park,** in the shadow of Fort Charlotte. To find out what's going on, and when, call 809/322-7500.

Beaches

New Providence is blessed with stretches of white sand, studded with sea-grape plants; some of the beaches are small and plants; crescent-shape, while others stretch for miles. The **Western Esplanade** sweeps westward from the British Colonial Hotel on Bay Street, across the street from shops and restaurants; it has rest rooms, a snack bar, and changing facilities. A little farther west, just past the bridge that leads to Coral World, is **Saunders Beach,** a popular weekend rendezvous spot. Still on the north shore, about 7 miles from downtown, just before the turnoff on Blake Road that leads to the airport, is the little, crescent-shape **Caves Beach.** Farther along the north shore is **Love Beach,** which faces the rich underwater world of Sea Gardens; the area is technically the domain of Love Beach residents, but they haven't been known to shoo away anyone.

On Paradise Island, **Paradise Beach** has an exquisite stretch of sand, with facilities, but you'll pay $3 for the privilege of getting your tan there. On the south shore, drive down to **Adelaide Beach,** at the end of Adelaide Village, for sand stretching down to Coral Harbour. Also on the south shore, the people who live in the east end of the island tend to flock to **South Beach,** at the foot of Blue Hill Road.

Dining

You can still get the traditional Bahamian fare of peas 'n' rice, conch fritters, and grouper fingers at the two dozen restaurants serving local cuisine that are scattered around Nassau and its environs. Those ubiquitous fast-food places—Kentucky Fried Chicken, Burger King, and McDonald's—have also made inroads into the island's eating habits. But over the past few years, alongside the escalation of Bahamian tourism and the subsequent growth of Cable Beach and Paradise Island hotels and their in-house restaurants, the preparation of meals at some of the better dining spots has become as sophisticated as you'll find in any leading U.S. city. European chefs brought in by the top restaurants on the island have trained young Bahamians in the skills of fine cooking; artfully prepared dishes with delicate sauces incorporate local seafood and herbs. Gourmet French, Oriental, Mexican, Creole, Northern Italian, and Polynesian fare have all become available on menus. Fish is usually the most economical dining choice, for meats often have to be imported from the States.

The island chefs, banded together in the Bahamian Culinary
Association, have also developed a new Bahamian cuisine that
consists of local products not generally known or used before,
such as coconuts, tamarinds, wild spinach, and a pepper-sour
sauce made of limes and red-hot bird peppers. They've even
come up with something new to do with conch, the popular national shellfish. The red parts from fresh conch are sliced very
thin, dipped in a special sauce, and—voilà—conch sushi! This
new dish is promoted as being nutritious and nonfattening, unlike conch fritters, which are fried in flour and oil. Most of the
local chefs' new recipes are dictated by the tastes of their
health-conscious customers.

While we're on the subject of food and health, we pass on this
tidbit given to us by a prominent Nassau chef, but suggest that
no conclusions should be hastily drawn: When Bahamian fishermen catch a grouper whose skin is brown and white, they keep
it; if it is black, they believe it has come from Florida waters,
and they throw it back.

Highly recommended restaurants in each price category are indicated by a ★.

Category	Cost*
Expensive	over $45
Moderate	$25–$45
Inexpensive	under $25

per person, excluding drinks and including 15% gratuity

Nassau/Cable Beach

Expensive **Buena Vista.** This establishment, which has been open for a
quarter of a century, occupies what was originally a rambling
house, built in the early 1880s; some of the elegant, slower-
paced atmosphere of that period has been kept alive here.
Tasteful china, crystal, and silver grace the tables. The menu
mostly features Continental cuisine; the chef applies his magic
to grouper in a variety of ways; you can order the fish au gratin
or baked in wine sauce. Visitors can dine in one of the intimate
dining rooms or on the estate's garden patio. *Delancy St. up the
hill from Bay St., tel. 809/322–2811. Reservations required.
Jacket required. AE, DC, MC, V. Dinner only.*
Da Vinci Ristorante. The Renaissance-style salons, the prints
of Leonardo's paintings on the walls, the formal chandeliers,
and the large Italian stained-glass windows provide a romantic
setting for dining on French-Italian cuisine featuring veal,
fresh seafood, and pasta. For those who favor the outdoors, a
garden in the front of the restaurant and a patio are open when
the weather is fair. Conveniently located a few blocks west of
the British Colonial Hotel, Da Vinci has long been a local favorite for fine dining. *W. Bay St., tel. 809/322–2748. Reservations
advised. Jacket required. AE, DC, MC, V. Dinner only.*

★ **Frilsham House.** Built in the late '40s by Lord Iliffe, an English
newspaper baron, Frilsham House, which adjoins the Nassau
Beach Hotel, was one of the last works of noted Bahamian architect William Castle, whose design made use of Bahamian
stone floors and walls of cypress and fir. The superb menu features Bahamian cuisine with a French influence. Some rec-

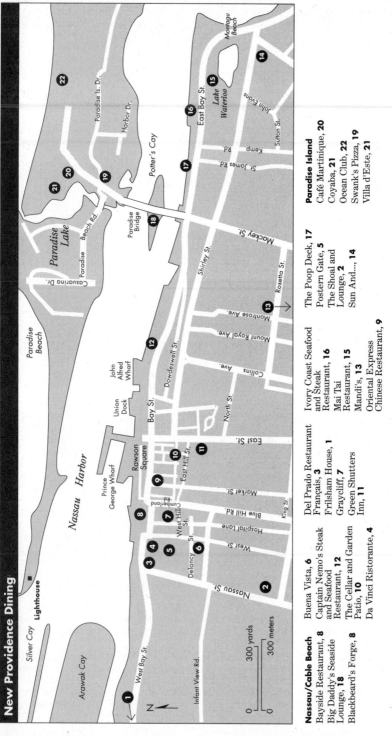

New Providence Dining

76

Nassau/Cable Beach
Bayside Restaurant, **8**
Big Daddy's Seaside
Lounge, **18**
Blackbeard's Forge, **8**

Buena Vista, **6**
Captain Nemo's Steak
and Seafood
Restaurant, **12**
The Cellar and Garden
Patio, **10**
Da Vinci Ristorante, **4**

Del Prado Restaurant
Français, **3**
Frilsham House, **1**
Graycliff, **7**
Green Shutters
Inn, **11**

Ivory Coast Seafood
and Steak
Restaurant, **16**
Mai Tai
Restaurant, **15**
Mandi's, **13**
Oriental Express
Chinese Restaurant, **9**

The Poop Deck, **17**
Postern Gate, **5**
The Shoal and
Lounge, **2**
Sun And..., **14**

Paradise Island
Café Martinique, **20**
Coyaba, **21**
Ocean Club, **22**
Swank's Pizza, **19**
Villa d'Este, **21**

ommended dishes are a puff pastry filled with asparagus tips in a chive butter sauce, and local grouper oven-baked in a butter pastry. The two dining rooms that face the ocean seat 100; try to get a table in the veranda overlooking the beach. *Nassau Beach Hotel, tel. 809/327–7639. Reservations required. Jacket required. AE, CB, DC, MC, V. Dinner only.*

★ **Graycliff.** Once the private home of a pirate, this magnificent restaurant has seven dining areas, among them the original dining room with a chandelier and an impressive mahogany table; the original library overlooking the garden; the aquarium (or Green Porch), with a tank that contains coral and windows that open on to the garden; and a serene outdoor dining section. French doors, antique furniture, and ruffled linen all add to the aristocratic ambience. The European cuisine benefits from the poignant accents of Bahamian seasoning, in the expert hands of the owner Enrico Garzaroli, who studied cooking in Europe, and his Bahamian chef, Phillip Bethel. Consider the cold appetizer called Chiffonade Tiède: smoked goose, wild boar pâté, pickled papaya, thinly sliced truffles, and Bahamian chili peppers in coriander sauce. The other dishes on the menu are just as unusual. Garzaroli values his wine collection at about $3 million; he keeps it in a cool cellar deep underneath the building. *W. Hill St., tel. 809/322–2796. Reservations advised. Jacket required at dinner. AE, DC, MC, V.*

Sun And . . . Walk through an archway and over a drawbridge, and you'll find yourself in a former old Bahamian home that has been converted into an elegant restaurant featuring French cuisine. You can dine by candlelight indoors or alfresco under the palms. Try the Norwegian salmon with scallops sautéed in olive oil and a special lemon sauce. Rack of lamb for two is a favorite with meat eaters. You can start with a cocktail at the bar overlooking the pool. *Lakeview Dr., off Shirley St., tel. 809/393–1205. Reservations required. Jacket required. AE, DC, MC, V. Dinner only.*

Moderate **Big Daddy's Seaside Lounge.** This charmer of a restaurant, popular with the locals, may be found at Potter's Cay Dock, where the Bahamian fishermen bring in their catches. The outside dining area looks out to the sea, while the room inside has a fisherman's net suspended from the ceiling and ropes along the wall. The down-to-earth Bahamian atmosphere complements a menu that features fresh seafood, such as stew fish, grouper fingers, conch patties, and lobster. For dessert, sample the cheesecake or the Key-lime pie; both are baked fresh daily. *E. Bay St., tel. 809/393–4702. No reservations required. Dress: casual. MC, V.*

Blackbeard's Forge. Beef, chicken, and seafood are the specialties here, all cooked on a grill right at your table. Savor the lobster tail with lemon and garlic butter, or, for those with an eclectic palate, the filet Mignon and lobster tail. The decor is suitably piratical: Old prints and maps hang on the wall, and the huge bay window's shape resembles the stern of a sailing vessel. The rich red velvet decor adds to the cozy feeling. *British Colonial Beach Resort, 1 Bay St., tel. 809/322–3301, ext. 278. Reservations required. Dress: casual. AE, DC, MC, V.*

Captain Nemo's Steak and Seafood Restaurant. After peering at Nassau's underwater life from a small submarine that is docked near this restaurant, you can get off and dive into a seafood platter called Treasure of the Deep—conch, shrimp, fritters, grouper, and lobster tail. The restaurant is suspended over the Nassau harbor, which means you're often aware of a swishing wake under your table as boats pass underneath. *Deveaux St., John Alfred Wharf, off Bay St., tel. 809/323–8426. Reservations advised. Dress: casual. AE, DC, MC, V.*

The Cellar and Garden Patio. A live steel band plays as you dine by a waterfall on the outdoor shady patio. The inside of this restaurant just off Bay Street has traditional Bahamian decor, with varnished wood tables and a bar. Seafood is the specialty, with a menu that features conch chowder, grouper, lobster tail, grilled snapper, and cracked conch. You can choose among five seafood appetizers. This spot is a favorite with the local crowd, who pop in at lunchtime for a bite of quiche or a roast beef sandwich. *11 Charlotte St., tel. 809/322–8877. Reservations advised. Dress: casual. AE, DC, MC, V.*

★ **Del Prado Restaurant Français.** As the name suggests, the main-course list here is predominantly Gallic; the chef's pièce de résistance is his entrecote Diane flambéed in cognac, though his grilled swordfish with cream of red bell pepper is more than acceptable. The chef is persnickety enough to grow his own herbs. You'll appreciate the attentive service and the extensive wine list. The dining room has stained-glass windows, and fresh flowers and glass candle holders decorate the tables. *W. Bay St., tel. 809/325–0324. Reservations advised. Jacket required. AE, DC, MC, V.*

Green Shutters Inn. Don't be surprised to find pinstripe-suited English barristers here perched on bar stools as they pore over the fine print in the London *Daily Telegraph* and quaff pints of Watney's beer. Actor Richard Harris, who has a home on Paradise Island, may also be present, trying for a winning double at darts. Little of the English ambience has changed since a gent named Ben Warrick opened this late-18th-century–style home for business in the late '50s. Hunting scenes, as well as stuffed heads of foxes and owls, hang on the wall. The menu includes traditional English fare, such as steak and kidney pie, bangers (sausages) and mash, and shepherd's pie. *Parliament St., tel. 809/325–5702. No reservations. Dress: casual. AE, MC, V.*

Ivory Coast Seafood and Steak Restaurant. A thoroughly African world—Ivory Coast masks, stuffed wild animals, and waiters wearing khaki walking shorts and pith helmets—surrounds you at this exotic spot with its wraparound porch overlooking the harbor. The steaks and seafood served here are grilled or broiled. Don't expect a gourmet meal—come here for the singular atmosphere. *E. Bay St., on the top floor of the Harbour Club, tel. 809/393–5393. Reservations advised. Dress: casual. AE, MC, V.*

Mai Tai Restaurant. The lovely setting is Waterview Lodge, the mansion of the late Sir Stafford Sands, a former Bahamas tourism minister. The building borders a lake and overlooks gardens with European statuary. The dining room's East Asian decor, with bamboo poles on the walls, candles on the tables, and a stark red carpet, complements the Chinese and Polynesian dishes, such as Mai Tai curry chicken, beef chop suey, and spare ribs. *E. Bay St. near Ft. Montagu, tel. 908/393–3088. No reservations. Dress: casual. AE, MC, V.*

The Poop Deck. The harbor and marina form a picturesque backdrop for this favorite of Nassau residents. Dine on the open veranda that faces the water, or in the interior dining room, where decorative plants hang from the walls and paintings depict the maritime life of the island. The restaurant specializes in Bahamian dishes, with names such as Mother

Mary's Grouper, Rosie's Chicken, and Cracked Conch. For dessert, the Guavaduff, a spongy cake topped with guava sauce, is a popular selection. The owners say their wine list offers the best selection in Nassau, an audacious claim, considering the competition. *E. Bay St., tel. 809/393–8175. Reservations advised. Dress: casual. AE, DC, MC, V.*

Postern Gate. This pleasant restaurant is housed in an old Bahamian mansion with rambling gardens and plentiful foliage. Tables are set in the gardens and in the spacious inside dining room, where a green-and-white motif makes for a lively yet conservative atmosphere. The menu, which features Bahamian and European entrées, includes grouper, conch, lobster, and filet Mignon *au poivre vert*. On weekends, go early for the boiled-fish breakfast, served from 9:30. *W. Hill St., tel. 809/ 326–8028. No reservations. Dress: casual. AE, MC, V.*

Inexpensive **Bayside Restaurant.** A hearty buffet is the specialty here, with a choice of pasta salads, ribs, sliced roast turkey, baked ham, roast pork, mounds of salad, and rich desserts. After you pile up your plate, you'll enjoy dining by the unusually tall windows looking out at the cruise ships docked at Prince George Wharf. A menu is available, if you can't stand buffets. *British Colonial Beach Resort, 1 Bay St., tel. 809/322–7479. No reservations required. Dress: casual. AE, DC, MC, V.*

Mandi's. This totally Bahamian restaurant is the only dining spot on the island to specialize solely in conch dishes—cracked, as fritters, in salad, or in chowder—with side dishes of cole slaw and french fries. A huge conch shell is displayed on a pedestal outside the small establishment. The tasty cheesecake and pies that are served here are homemade. You can eat in, take out, or drive through. *Corner of Arundel and Mt. Royal aves., tel. 809/322–7260. No reservations. Dress: casual. AE, MC, V.*

Oriental Express Chinese Restaurant. This popular place with local residents features Cantonese and Szechwan cuisine prepared by Hong Kong–trained chefs. The Cantonese-style lobster with green onion, or Kung-Po shrimp, are both sure to please. *Corner of Bay and Frederick sts., tel. 809/326–7127. No reservations. Dress: casual. AE, MC, V.*

The Shoal and Lounge. Boiled fish, perhaps the best on the island, is the dish that draws this unpretentious little restaurant's customers, who are happy to eat it for breakfast, lunch, and dinner. *Nassau St., tel. 809/323–4400. No reservations. Dress: casual. MC, V.*

Paradise Island

Expensive **Café Martinique.** Limestone walls and huge glass windows that overlook a lagoon distinguish the fin de siècle setting of this former private home. Although the beef Wellington and Continental dishes are still done with skill, this renowned restaurant, where James Bond dined in the movie *Thunderball*, can be a hustle-bustle experience with vexing service. Off-season, though, you may have more luck. The food is considerably above average. *Paradise Island Resort & Casino, tel. 809/363– 3000. Reservations required. Jacket required. AE, DC, MC, V.*

Coyaba. This is one of the best of the dozen restaurants tucked away in the Paradise Island casino complex, with an offering of Cantonese, Szechwan, and Polynesian dishes, such as Yu Shong beef and lobster Cantonese. Visitors will probably admire the small wooden monkey figures and the huge four-legged dragon-head statues scattered about; these ornaments, along with the thatch roof, are part of the restaurant's Polynesian-Chinese decor. Coyaba is located in Bird Cage Walk. *Britannia Towers, Paradise Island Resort & Casino, tel. 809/ 363-3000. Reservations advised. Dress: casual. AE, DC, MC, V.*

Ocean Club. An elite clientele congregates here, dining on Continental and American dishes to the music of a calypso combo. The staff at this refined former mansion may not serve the best food on the island, but the Wedgwood settings, Irish linen, lighted fountains, and accompanying sculpture gallery help to make the evening worthwhile. As you enjoy the surroundings, you can sample the grilled duck's breast with raspberry peppercorn sauce, or the stuffed breast of chicken with lobster and mushrooms in a saffron sauce. *Paradise Island, tel. 809/363– 2501. Reservations required. Jacket required. AE, DC, MC, V. Dinner only.*

Villa d'Este. The dimmed chandelier and mustard-and-white decor complement the impressive painting of Italy's Lake Como on the wall in the back. Notable Italian cuisine is served graciously in a tasteful Old World setting with classical guitar playing for musical accompaniment. Veal parmigiana and fettuccine Alfredo receive top honors, and the broiled swordfish deserves an honorary mention. A tempting tray of pastries is also available. *Britannia Towers, Paradise Island Resort & Casino, tel. 809/363–3000. Reservations advised. Dress: casual. AE, DC, MC, V.*

Inexpensive **Swank's Pizza.** The locals have been ordering their pizzas here for years in an informal setting. Fifteen varieties in different sizes are offered, along with French bread and some pastas. *Paradise Island Shopping Centre, tel. 809/363–2765. No reservations. Dress: casual. AE, MC, V.*

Southwestern New Providence

★ **Papagayo.** If you're not staying at the Divi Bahamas Beach Resort, where this restaurant is located, it's a long drive to the south coast of the island. The classic Italian cuisine and seafood, however, backed up by excellent service, makes the trip worthwhile. The specialty of the house is lobster, prepared in several enticing ways. You can dine in a traditionally furnished room with floral designs on the walls and carpet, or on the cozy outdoor terrace overlooking the golf course. *Divi Bahamas Beach Resort and Country Club, S. W. Bay Rd., tel. 809/362– 4391. Reservations advised. Jacket required. AE, DC, MC, V.*

Lodging

New Providence Island is blessed with an extensive range of hotels, from the small, family owned guest houses, where you can rent a room for $30 a night, to the new mega-resorts of Cable Beach and Paradise Island, which cater to the $150-a-night high rollers.

The homey, friendly little spots, where you get to be on nodding terms with your fellow guests, will probably not be on the beach (though the walk to the beach will rarely be far). In such situations you'll have to go out to eat unless you have access to a kitchen, in which case you'll have no problem picking up groceries at one of the local supermarkets. Getting to a store is inexpensive; buses will take you anywhere in Nassau and the environs for 75¢.

The plush resorts leave little to be desired, except perhaps—in the case of the two that boast casinos—some quiet outside of the gambling areas. The battle for the tourist dollar rages unceasingly between Cable Beach and Paradise Island; their hotels are continually refurbishing and developing (with good reason, since the annual tourism figure for the Bahamas is creeping toward the 3½ million mark). All of this competition, of course, has led to a wide variety of all-inclusive packages from which the potential visitor can choose (including such enticements as free snorkeling gear, free scuba lessons, free admission to a Las Vegas–style revue, etc.).

If you're trying to choose between Cable Beach and Paradise Island for accommodations, there is, in general, a better choice of beaches on Paradise Island; it also offers a more intimate atmosphere in which to stroll around and explore attractions such as The Cloisters atop the Ocean Club. Cable Beach guests are more likely to stick to their own hotel and beach; when they leave, it's usually to explore and shop in downtown Nassau.

Highly recommended hotels in each price category are indicated by a ★ .

An 8% tax is added to your hotel bill, representing resort and government levies. Some hotels may add an additional service charge and a $2–$3 maid/pool gratuity.

Category	Cost*
Expensive	over $130
Moderate	$75–$130
Inexpensive	under $75

All prices are for a standard double room, excluding tax and service charge.

Nassau/Silver Cay

Expensive   **Coral World Villas.** Each villa has its own private pool and terrace on the private island of Silver Cay and its own cute appellation, such as Queen Angelfish, Queen Triggerfish, Rock Beauty, or Porkfish. This property has one advantage over the rest of Nassau's hotels: It is next door to the island's most prominent tourist attraction, the watery Coral World, with free admission to the Marine Park and the Underwater Observatory. The rooms have ceiling fans, and the bathrooms feature Italian marble floors. The hotel also has a private beach. If you get tired of the seclusion, you can take a ferry or bus over to the more frenetic world of Cable Beach. *Box N 7797, Nassau, tel. 809/328–1036. 22 villas. Facilities: kitchens with refrigerator and microwave ovens; free harbor cruise. AE, MC, V.*

★   **Graycliff.** Built around 1750 by a retired English pirate, this noble Georgian colonial mansion, which is enveloped in tropical foliage, has played host to the likes of the Duke and Duchess of Windsor, press baron Lord Beaverbrook, Lord Mountbatten, Aristotle Onassis, and, more recently, the types who appear on

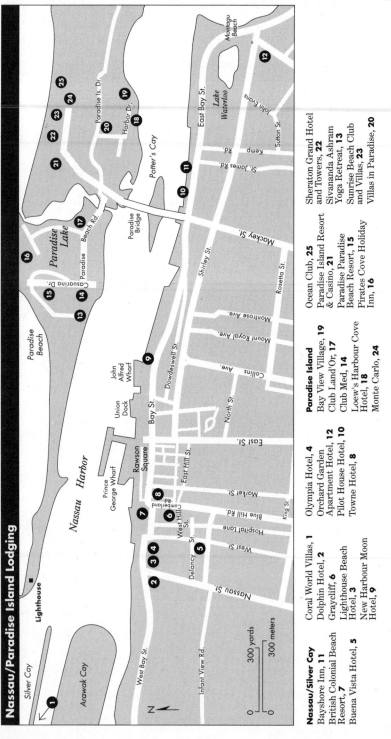

Nassau/Paradise Island Lodging

82

Nassau/Silver Cay
Bayshore Inn, 11
British Colonial Beach Resort, 7
Buena Vista Hotel, 5
Coral World Villas, 1
Dolphin Hotel, 2
Graycliff, 6
Lighthouse Beach Hotel, 3
New Harbour Moon Hotel, 9
Olympia Hotel, 4
Orchard Garden Apartment Hotel, 12
Pilot House Hotel, 10
Towne Hotel, 8

Paradise Island
Bay View Village, 19
Club Land'Or, 17
Club Med, 14
Loew's Harbour Cove Hotel, 18
Monte Carlo, 24
Ocean Club, 25
Paradise Island Resort & Casino, 21
Paradise Paradise Beach Resort, 15
Pirates Cove Holiday Inn, 16
Sheraton Grand Hotel and Towers, 22
Sivananda Ashram Yoga Retreat, 13
Sunrise Beach Club and Villas, 23
Villas in Paradise, 20

the television program "Lifestyles of the Rich and Famous." In 1974, the property was purchased from Lord Dudley by Enrico Garzaroli, a native of Lombardy and a graduate of hotel management programs in Italy and Switzerland. The following year, this private home across the street from Government House opened as a hotel, and it has retained its original elegance; it is the only member of the prestigious Relais et Château organization in the West Indies and has a classic gourmet restaurant. The lounge evokes the atmosphere of an old English club. On the walls you'll find *Cries of London* Victorian prints and a sentimental relic of Empire days, a photograph of King George VI, Queen Elizabeth's father. Each room has its own individual style; some feature antique furniture, while others have a tropical decor. The poolside honeymoon suite is nestled in its own tropical garden. *Box N 10246, W. Hill St., Nassau, tel. 809/322–2796. 11 rooms. Facilities: pool, restaurant, lounge. AE, DC, MC, V.*

Moderate **British Colonial Beach Resort.** Once the toast of the town, this imposing pink resort right on the beach in downtown Nassau is still owned by the pioneering Oakes family, but it has long since lost its urbanity. At press time, it was being run by Best Western. The same clientele has returned for the past 30 to 40 years, which says a lot for their sense of nostalgia and loyalty. Rooms are adequate (the owners recently spent $5 million in refurbishing), but the atmosphere is somewhat less than sophisticated. Still, the historic hotel, set on 8 lush acres, continues to dominate Bay Street; it is located near Nassau's main shopping area. *Box N 7181, Nassau, tel. 809/322–3301 or 800/528–1234. 325 rooms. Facilities: private beach, pool, 3 tennis courts, water sports, 3 restaurants, 4 bars. AE, DC, MC, V.*

Lighthouse Beach Hotel. Across from a beach a mile west of Nassau, this pleasant four-story pink resort has a sun lounge and a pool on its rooftop. The small, charming rooms have phones and cable TV, and some overlook the ocean. The restaurant serves American and Bahamian cuisine. The hotel is a five-minute walk from Bay Street shopping. *Box N 915, Nassau, tel. 809/322–4474. 92 rooms. Facilities: pool, restaurant, bar. AE, MC, V.*

Pilot House Hotel. This five-story hotel sits on the Nassau side of the bridge that connects with Paradise Island, right near Potter's Cay and all the conch, fresh fruit, and vegetable stalls. Frequent complimentary water-taxi service is available to downtown Nassau and Paradise Island. Spacious rooms overlook a tropical courtyard and a pool. The hotel is a favorite with sailing enthusiasts. *Box N 4941, Nassau, tel. 809/393–3431; 800/223–9815. 120 rooms. Facilities: pool with new sun deck, 2 restaurants, 2 bars. AE, DC, MC, V.*

Inexpensive **Bayshore Inn.** The location isn't exactly ideal—a short bus ride (or a longish walk) to the main Bay Street shops and a half-mile from the nearest beach—but the Bayshore remains a small and pleasant two-story motel across from the bridge that leads to Paradise Island. *Box N 9689, Nassau, tel. 809/323–2989. 12 rooms. Facilities: pool, laundry, scooters and bicycles available. No restaurant. AE, MC, V.*

Buena Vista Hotel. This small, agreeable 200-year-old former private home is set in a beautiful garden on Delancy Street, a half-mile from downtown Nassau. The two-story building is better known as an elegant place to dine than as a spot to stay (*see* Dining, above); only five high-ceilinged, rather plain guest rooms are available, and there's no pool. *Box N 564, Nassau, tel. 809/322–2811. 5 rooms. Facilities: refrigerator, restaurant, bar. AE, DC, MC, V.*

Dolphin Hotel. The airy rooms in this pink, four-story resort have refreshingly bright drapes and bedspreads, as well as private balconies that overlook palm trees, a large pool, and the Western Esplanade beach and harbor. The restaurant serves Bahamian-style dishes, and the lively Boomerang Bar adds to the nightlife. *Box N 3236, Nassau, tel. 809/322–8666. 66 rooms. Facilities: pool, restaurant, bar. AE, MC, V.*

New Harbour Moon Hotel. On Bay Street, this three-story hotel overlooks Nassau's harbor; its location is midway between the Nassau shops and the Paradise Island Bridge. There's a clean look about the place, and the small rooms are above average in appeal. *Box N 646, Nassau, tel. 809/325–1548. 30 rooms. Facilities: dining room with Chinese cuisine, bar, laundry. MC, V.*

Olympia Hotel. This compact, no-frills hotel on West Bay Street near downtown Nassau has private balconies on its outside rooms overlooking the water. In the comfy, British-style pub named Alexander's, you can fling darts, challenge someone to backgammon, play video games, and snack on pizza and sandwiches with your beer. *Box 984, Nassau, tel. 809/322–4971. 53 rooms. Facilities: restaurant, bar. AE, MC, V.*

Orchard Garden Apartment Hotel. This secluded cottage colony, east of downtown and opposite Fort Montagu, is grouped around the pool amid a 2-acre tropical garden. The owners welcome children. *Box 1514, Nassau, tel. 809/323–1297. 34 studios and cottages. Facilities: kitchens or kitchenettes, bar, 500 yards from beach. No restaurant. AE, DC, MC, V.*

Towne Hotel. White cockatoos in cages greet you as you enter this pleasant but no-frills hostelry on George Street, a block off Bay Street. It's a favorite with business travelers, and it's convenient for shoppers, though you do have to find your own beach. You'll find guests playing ping-pong, or backgammon by the Talking Stick Bar. Two free cocktail parties are offered weekly. *Box N 4808, Nassau, tel. 809/322–8451. 46 rooms, some with balconies, all with private bath, phone, TV. Facilities: swimming pool, sauna, sun deck, restaurant, bar. AE, MC, V.*

Paradise Island

Expensive   **Club Land'Or.** A three-story orange-roofed hotel set on the Paradise Island Lagoon, Club Land'Or recently expanded its apartment units by two thirds; all units have full kitchens, separate sleeping areas for up to four adults, living rooms, and patios that overlook the lagoon, the gardens, or the pool. The third-floor restaurant gives a beautiful panoramic view of the island, and there's also an attractive courtyard. The service is personal and attentive. *Box SS 6429, Nassau, tel. 809/363–2400. 72 rooms. Facilities: kitchens, pool, disco, restaurant with show, 2 bars, baby-sitting, laundry. AE, DC, MC, V.*

Club Med. This Club Med property, set on 21 acres, has all of the usual all-inclusive, don't-pay-anything-after-you've-left-home privileges of the Vacation Villages. The rustic accommodations consist of three-story bungalows of double occupancy rooms, recently refurbished with white-tile floors and bamboo furniture; third-floor rooms offer king-size beds for couples only. This vacation club is popular among families with children over 12, who are inundated with nonstop activities. Among the water sports offered are windsurfing, sailing, and snorkeling. *Box N 7137, Nassau, tel. 800/258–2633. 300 rooms. Facilities: private beach, pool, restaurant, bar, boating, fishing, golf, tennis. AE, MC, V.*

Monte Carlo. In this intimate resort, the 13 yellow-and-white villas feature rooms decorated in colorful fabrics. The place has a private-club atmosphere, away from the bustle of the nearby casino; it's well suited for families. *Box 85-5055, Nassau, tel. 809/363–2893. 13 villas. Facilities: pool, fully equipped kitchens, laundry machines, easy access to the island's resort facilities. AE, MC, V.*

★ **Ocean Club.** Once a private, two-story home, then a private club, this resort provides most of the refined ambience to be found on Paradise Island. A quiet, tasteful mood surrounds the property, from the lounge with its antique furniture, to the lovely courtyard and fountains, to the beauty of the 35-acre terraced Versailles Gardens built by a former owner, millionaire Huntington Hartford. The elegant rooms, with pastel green and yellow decor, have ceiling fans and look on to the ocean or the garden courtyard. Villas have their own enclosed patios with Jacuzzis. *Box N 4777, Nassau, tel. 809/363–2501 or 800/321–3000. 70 rooms, suites, and villas with minibars. Facilities: Beach, pool, 9 tennis courts, baby-sitting, laundry, 2 restaurants, 3 bars. AE, DC, MC, V.*

Paradise Island Resort & Casino. One of the world's largest island resort and casino complexes in the world, this glittering property run by Resorts International includes two opulent oceanside hotels, the 600-room Britannia Towers and Paradise Towers, with 500 rooms and a two-story atrium lobby. Rooms are attractively furnished, and each has 24-hour room service, a refrigerator, and balconies with ocean, pool, or lagoon views. The hotels are linked by arcades and restaurants that lead to the 30,000-square-foot Paradise Island casino. Owner Merv Griffin set up his own suite here, an opulent two-bedroom, $2,250-a-night hideaway complete with a butler happy to serve you and your dozen guests when Mr. Griffin isn't using it. The 100-room Beach Tower houses guests participating in the Club Paradise program, an all-inclusive package that provides meals (with dinner at any of 12 gourmet restaurants), airport transportation, and complimentary sports activities. The Paradise Concierge program on the top three levels of Britannia Towers offers private check-in, breakfast, and bathrobes. *Box N 4777, Nassau, tel. 809/363–3000 or 800/321–3000. 1,200 rooms. Facilities: 12 tennis courts, health club, 2 pools, 12 restaurants, 12 lounges, Las Vegas–style revue, calypso show, disco. AE, CB, DC, MC, V.*

Paradise Paradise Beach Resort. This hotel on the western tip of Paradise Island caters to a younger crowd. The simple, inviting rooms have white-washed walls, bleached wood furniture, and balconies on the second floor. Water-sport activities are all free, including sailing, snorkeling, windsurfing, and water-skiing; bicycling and aerobics are available as well. The resort features a gorgeous beach, to which outsiders are admitted for a small fee. The Paradise Pavillion restaurant serves steaks, ribs, and seafood, and it also offers a barbecue lunch; a dining plan is available at $29 per day, plus tip. Guests have access to a private road lined with casuarina trees. *Box N 4777, Nassau, tel. 809/363–2541 or 800/321–3000. 100 rooms. Facilities: restaurant and bar. AE, DC, MC, V.*

Sheraton Grand Hotel and Towers. All the large, pastel-colored rooms in this fine high-rise hotel offer a magnificent view of the beach and the various water sports going on, such as scuba diving, sailing, and tennis. The tastefully done refurbishing that was concluded recently added refrigerators to the rooms. The very expensive top floors, reached by a keyed elevator, offer full concierge service, breakfast, and evening cocktails. You can have a massage or get the salt out of your hair at a beauty parlor downstairs. The elegant Rotisserie dining room has an expansive view of the water and serves steak and the catch of the day. The hotel is located within walking distance of the casino. *Box SS 6307, Nassau, tel. 809/363–2011 or 800/325–3535. 360 rooms. Facilities: lounge, disco, pool, 2 restaurants, patio bar, lounge, gift shop, baby-sitting, laundry, scooters, bicycles. AE, CB, DC, MC, V.*

Moderate **Bay View Village.** This 4-acre condominium resort, where guests get to know one another fairly easily around the three swimming pools, features lush tropical landscaping (including several varieties of hibiscus and bougainvillea) and an intimate atmosphere. Visitors can choose among one- and two-bedroom apartments and two- and three-bedroom villas, all of them equipped with kitchens. Some villas have a good view of the harbor. On the minus side, there's no restaurant or beach, but the nearest stretch of sand is only a six-minute walk away. All the units offer private balconies and patios or garden terraces. A golf course is conveniently located a mile and a half away. *Box SS 6308, Nassau, tel. 809/363–2555. 75 units and villas. Facilities: 3 pools, tennis, bicycle rentals, bar. AE, MC, V.*

Loew's Harbour Cove Hotel. A high-rise complex overlooking a man-made beach, this 250-room resort includes 55 deluxe rooms and four suites. Located on the harbor side of the island, the resort also overlooks a marina, which means you can take the hotel's 46-passenger water taxi to town for $1 round-trip. The beach is tucked in a protective cove. *Box SS 6249, Nassau, tel. 809/326–2561. 250 double rooms with direct-dial phones. Facilities: beach, pool, tennis, free bicycles, jogging, 3 complimentary cocktail parties weekly, 3 restaurants (including the Captain's Table), 3 bars. AE, CB, DC, MC, V.*

★ **Pirates Cove Holiday Inn.** Situated on the crescent-shape private beach of Pirates Cove, but also in a woodsy setting, this 18-story resort, the tallest in the Bahamas, has undergone $12 million in renovations that give it a luxury look at moderate prices. The cheerful, newly furnished rooms with bright green and peach tropical decor offer good balcony views of the sunset. A 90-foot-long replica of the pirate ship *Bonny Anne* dominates the pool area, which also has a bar for evening cocktails. The hotel is only a mile from the casino and a five-minute drive from an 18-hole golf course. *Box SS 6214, Nassau, tel. 809/326–2100. 535 rooms. Facilities: cable TV, pool, game room, shops, live show nightly, daily activities program, baby-sitting, new exercise room, boating, deep-sea fishing, 4 tennis courts, snorkeling, scuba diving, 3 restaurants (including the Paradise Grill and the Junkanoo Café), 2 bars. AE, DC, MC, V.*

Sunrise Beach Club and Villas. This relaxing two-story resort next to the Paradise Island casino complex brings in many return guests, possibly drawn by the singular charm of the place. The property is replete with coconut palms, bougainvillea, hibiscus, and crotons; it also features two pools—one of them is multilevel and has a waterfall—and its own Cabbage Beach.

Guests find complimentary groceries in the refrigerator, and their hosts are happy to whisk them off to the nearest grocery store to stock up. *Box SS 6519, Nassau, tel. 809/363–2234. Facilities: kitchen, laundry, scooter rentals, water sports. AE, MC, V.*

Villas in Paradise. This property consists of studios and two-bedroom suites with kitchen facilities and a shared pool, as well as two- and three-bedroom villas with full kitchens and private pools in enclosed patios. At press time, the facilities would have benefitted from renovation. The 6-mile Cabbage Beach is located 50 yards away. A minimum stay of seven nights includes a free car or Jeep for three nights. *Box SS 6379, Nassau, tel. 809/ 326–2998. 20 units. Facilities: kitchens, cable TV, clock radios, pool, free snorkeling, tennis, golf, baby-sitting. AE, MC, V.*

Inexpensive **Sivananda Ashram Yoga Retreat.** The name says it all. The retreat was founded in 1967 as a yoga vacation spot; the property was donated to Swami Vishnu Devananda by Mrs. Natalie Bosswell in appreciation of the guidance given to her by the swami. Only vegetarian food is served here. Guests participate in group meditations twice daily, yoga breathing, relaxation, and exercise classes, as well in workshops that the director, named Bharata, describes as dealing with "new age disciplines." A rising bell wakes visitors at 5:30 AM. Lodgings range from semiprivate cottages on the ocean and in palm groves to dormitory rooms in the main building. Most rooms are shared. Two meals of organic vegetables, grown in the retreat's own garden, are served daily. Guests are advised to bring their own drinking water. *Box N 7550, Nassau, tel. 809/363–2902. 35 cottages. Facilities: shared washrooms, restaurant. No pool. AE, MC, V.*

Cable Beach

Expensive **Carnival's Crystal Palace Resort & Casino.** Your senses will probably need a few minutes to attune to the orange pillars, the purple-and-orange canopy at the entrance, and the matching horizontal stripes across the six towers, which make up the largest resort in the area. The resort has become known locally (and rather disdainfully) as the Rainbow Inn, but the enormous, glitzy world inside the complex, which is dominated by the casino, offers a hyperactive experience you won't soon forget. You'll find just about everything you'll need here, but there isn't much of a beach, except at low tide. The resort now includes the 693-room Riviera Towers, which used to be the Cable Beach Hotel and Casino; it is linked to the Crystal Palace casino by a 20-shop mall. In short, the Crystal Palace is the resort to choose if you need to be in the center of all the action. The rooms are spacious but not particularly sumptuous. A 15th-floor penthouse called Galactic Fantasy, which is robot-controlled, costs an unbelievable $25,000 a night. *Box N 8306, Nassau, tel. 809/ 327–6200 or 800/222–7466. 1,550 rooms. Facilities: 10 tennis courts, water sports, health club, water theme park, 12 restaurants, 6 lounges, discos, Las Vegas–style revue. AE, CB, DC, MC, V.*

Guanahani Village Time Sharing Resort. This accommodation is a bit expensive considering its lack of facilities: There's no restaurant, for example, and it does not take credit cards. However, the Cable Beach location and nicely landscaped set-

Cable Beach Manor, **4**

Carnival's Crystal
Palace Resort &
Casino, **8**

Casuarinas Hotel &
Villas, **3**

Guanahani Village
Time Sharing
Resort, **2**

Henrea Carlette
Hotel, **5**

Le Meridien Royal
Bahamian Hotel, **6**

Nassau Beach Hotel, **9**

Orange Hill Beach
Inn, **1**

West Wind, **7**

Wyndham
Ambassador Beach
Hotel, **10**

88
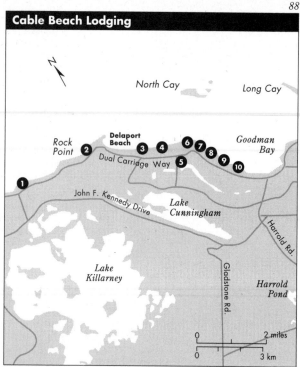

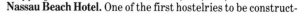

ting surrounding its well-furnished, three-bedroom townhouses and luxury villas may make the resort worth the price
to some travelers. *Box N 3223, Nassau, tel. 809/327–7962. 26
units with kitchens. Facilities: beach, pool, pool bar, baby-
sitting. No credit cards.*

★ **Le Meridien Royal Bahamian Hotel.** Lampposts line the driveway of this dignified property, where the international
clientele are greeted by a courtyard with a fountain and statues of Greek women. Built in 1946, the resort, which was once a
private club, has just spent $6 million in indoor and outdoor
renovations, with neoclassic furniture in the rooms, some of
which overlook the hotel's own modest beach. For those with a
taste for privacy, pink villas with sugar-white roofs are also
available; a few of these villas are individual townhouses, each
boasting three bedrooms, a private pool, a sun room, and a
whirlpool in the master suite. The hotel provides a quiet, elegant atmosphere on a smaller scale than the larger resorts in
the area. The lobby of the main building, the six-story Manor
House—where tea is served from 4 PM to 6 PM during the winter
season—is decorated with marble. The hotel also features a modern health spa, complete with an aerobics room, Universal machines, a steam room and a sauna, a whirlpool, facials, masseurs,
and mud baths. *Box N 7528, Nassau, tel. 809/327–6400 or 800/
543–5400. 145 rooms and 25 villas, on the beach. Facilities:
concierge service, large pool terrace, 2 tennis courts, ballroom,
billiard room, health spa, Café de Paris restaurant. Small
shopping center across the street. AE, DC, MC, V.*

★ **Nassau Beach Hotel.** One of the first hostelries to be constructed on Cable Beach in the '40s, this resort, now the property of the Trusthouse Forte chain, retains a serene graciousness in glaring contrast to its next-door neighbor, Carnival's Crystal Palace. It's especially popular with more conservative guests in their forties and older. The hotel—whose Frilsham House restaurant is second only to Graycliff in its quintessential fine cuisine—is composed of three wings set amid tropical gardens, fountains, and scenic walkways. The rooms were recently redecorated with warm pink-and-orange tropical furnishings. *Box N 7756, Nassau, tel. 809/327-7711 or 800/223-5672. 411 rooms. Facilities: 6 tennis courts, heated pool, health spa, sailing, snorkeling, windsurfing (the hotel is home to the annual International Windsurfing Regatta, held in January), parasailing, deep-sea fishing, 6 restaurants, 4 bars. AE, CB, DC, MC, V.*

Moderate **Cable Beach Manor.** This two-story hotel boasts a beautiful stretch of white sandy beach, and perhaps because of its small size, it enjoys a reputation for congeniality among its guests. The one- and two-bedroom apartments overlook either the pool or the ocean. A shady courtyard, with lounge chairs, a breakfast area, and a garden of coconut trees and flowered plants, provides a respite from the sun. The resort also offers long-term rentals for visitors who would like to extend their stay. The hotel is located about a 15-minute drive from the airport and downtown Nassau. *Box N 8333, Nassau, tel. 809/327-7785. 34 suites and studios. Facilities: beach, kitchens, pool, nearby stores. No restaurant. AE, DC, MC, V.*

★ **Casuarinas Hotel & Villas.** In 1977, Eleutheran native Nettie Symonette, who had previously worked for Paradise Island developer Dr. Axel Wenner-Gren and in Nassau hotel management, bought 1½ acres of land on Cable Beach. The land contained only a guardhouse and an abandoned residence, but she parlayed her original investment into a seven-building, 80-unit hotel/restaurant that she named after the casuarina trees dotting the property. The hotel is now considered one of Nassau's most profitable, thanks to Nettie and the impeccable commitment to service she instilled in her help. Casuarinas has two excellent restaurants: Albrion's, which specializes in Bahamian and American cuisine, and the upscale Round House (the rehabilitated guardhouse). Yellow drapes and bedspreads lighten the rooms, while hanging baskets of plants adorn the lounge. *Box N 4016, Nassau, tel. 809/327-8153. 80 rooms, some with kitchens. Facilities: private beach, 2 restaurants, lounge, laundry, baby-sitting service, complimentary bus service to casino and downtown. AE, DC, MC, V.*

Henrea Carlette Hotel. You have to walk across West Bay Street to get to the beach, but, otherwise, this small apartment resort is close to the nightlife, water sports, and tennis available on Cable Beach. The rooms all have kitchens and balconies overlooking the pool courtyard. *Box N 4227, Nassau, tel. 809/327-7801. 18 rooms. Facilities: scooters on premises, pool, restaurant, bar. AE, MC, V.*

★ **Wyndham Ambassador Beach Hotel.** This amiable establishment offers good value for the money; it recently underwent room and lobby renovations to the tune of $3 million. The lobby has attractive blue-and-cream walls and tropical-style wicker furniture. The balconied rooms with sea-green decor overlook either the garden, the pool, or the ocean. A plethora of activities are available, many of them on the 1,800-foot beach, where there is also a good boutique. Excellent Italian food may be sampled at the intimate Pasta Kitchen. *Box N 3026, Nassau, tel. 809/327–8231. 400 rooms. Facilities: 8 tennis courts, squash, racquetball, waterskiing, windsurfing, parasailing, snorkeling, Cable Beach Golf Course across the street, 3 restaurants, 4 bars. AE, DC, MC, V.*

Inexpensive   **Orange Hill Beach Inn.** Just west of the main Cable Beach hotels, this charming family-run establishment set in a former orange orchard (hence the name) is just a hundred yards from a private beach. The property has large lawns, tropical fruit trees, and flowers. Owners Danny and Judy Lowe go out of their way to ensure personal service. Sports-club groups that stay there are offered special programs. *Box N 8583, Nassau, tel. 809/327–7157. 18 rooms. Facilities: kitchens, restaurant, bar, baby-sitting, game room. AE, MC, V.*

West Wind. Sailing and boating facilities are the lure for this resort of cozy townhouses with deeply slanted roofs on the west end of Cable Beach, 6 miles from downtown. The townhouses have kitchens, but there is no central restaurant. *Box 10481, Nassau, tel. 809/327–7680. 21 rooms. No credit cards.*

Southwestern New Providence

Expensive   **Divi Bahamas Beach Resort and Country Club.** Tropical birds in cages greet you at this secluded 180-acre resort (including a top-rated 18-hole golf course) in the southern part of New Providence. Its colonial-style architecture features white pillars at the entrance and ornate balconies. Hallways leading to the rooms tend to be rather dark, but the rooms themselves are light and cheerful; they have ceiling fans, wicker chairs, and paintings with island themes. The rooms look onto the gardens or the pool, which is a busy area; guests drive to the beach in golf carts. *Box N 8191, Nassau, tel. 809/362–4391 or 800/367–3484. 339 rooms. Facilities: golf course, pool, 4 tennis courts, dive operation, water sports, small straw market, 3 restaurants, 3 bars. AE, DC, MC, V.*

The Arts and Nightlife

Performing Arts

Nassauvians occasionally produce their own plays, musicals and ballets at the **Dundas Centre for the Performing Arts,** on Mackey Street. For information, call 809/393–3728.

Nightlife

Once upon a time a couple of decades ago, before Nassau burgeoned as a tourist mecca, there was really only Peanuts Taylor's native nightclub on Bay Street for after-dark frolicking with the locals. Now the Cable Beach and Paradise Island hotels have their own flashy clubs, bistros, and discos, and there's a variety of late-night entertainment. The attire for attending these soirees is as casual as the atmosphere. What's good enough for Peanuts Taylor is good enough for Paradise.

Nassau/Cable   **Club Waterloo** (tel. 809/398–1108) on East Bay Street is a popu-
Beach   lar club, with nonstop dancing Monday–Saturday till 4 AM (no live band on Mondays).

Drumbeat Club (tel. 809/322–4233) on West Bay Street, just up from the British Colonial Hotel, features the legendary Peanuts Taylor, still alive and well and beating away at those tom-toms; his band and gyrating dancers put on two shows nightly, at 8:30 and 10:30.

Flamingo Club (tel. 809/362–4391), at the Divi Bahamas Beach Resort and Country Club on South West Bay Road, provides nightly cabaret entertainment at 9 and 11.

Jokers Wild (tel. 809/323–7860), off Nassau Street, features jazz and comedy acts Tuesday–Saturday from 8 PM; Sunday from 4 PM. The $15-per-person charge includes one drink.

Le Paon (tel. 809/363–2011), in the Sheraton Grand Hotel, has four separate areas for evening dancing and socializing.

Out Island Bar (tel. 809/327–7711), at the Nassau Beach Hotel, features calypso dancing nightly Sunday–Wednesday 8 PM–2 AM; Thursday–Saturday 8 PM–3 AM.

Palace Theater (tel. 809/327–6200), at Carnival's Crystal Palace Resort & Casino on Cable Beach, always presents lavish Las Vegas–style productions with state-of-the-art special effects and two-color lasers. Open nightly except Mondays.

Shooter's Bar & Grill (tel. 809/393–3771) on East Bay Street, on the lower floor of the Harbour Club, offers the latest sounds from an original Wurlitzer jukebox.

Paradise Island **Blue Lagoon Lounge** (tel. 809/363–2400), at Club Land'Or on Paradise Island, serves up calypso music nightly 5 PM–1 AM in a romantic setting overlooking the lake.

Club Pastiche (tel. 809/363–3000), at the Paradise Island Resort & Casino complex, is a popular disco with light shows.

Le Cabaret (tel. 809/363–3000), also at the Paradise Island Resort, offers a late-night revue (show times vary) with magic acts, acrobats, and an international cast.

Trade Winds Calypso Shore Lounge (tel. 809/363–3000) stages an evening native show with live Bahamian music at the casino complex.

Casinos

New Providence has two mammoth casinos, the **Paradise Island Resort & Casino** (tel. 809/363–3000) and **Carnival's Crystal Palace Resort & Casino** (tel. 809/327–6459) on Cable Beach, which cater to everyone from the high roller to the lady from Dubuque who sits at the slot machines with a mound of quarters in her lap. (Paradise Island even has a "salon privé" set aside to cater to the especially well heeled.)

Each complex has similar facilities—more than 700 slot machines and blackjack, craps, roulette, and baccarat tables. One-armed-bandit addicts can even sneak out of their rooms in the middle of the night, for the machines are always open for play. Tables are open at 10 AM until the wee hours. As for dress, you may leave your black tie at home, for these are hardly your intimate European gaming houses. Dress suits the casual atmosphere. You have to be 21 years old to gamble; Bahamians and permanent residents are not permitted to indulge.

For neophytes walking into a casino to gamble for the first time, here's some advice that may make the inevitable conclusion a little less painful:

- Start by playing the roulette wheels. The game is fun, yet it requires little skill.
- Always put in the maximum amount of coins while playing the slot machine. The machines are designed to provide a bigger payoff when the maximum amount is played.

- While playing blackjack, it is wise to split aces and 8's; this gives the player "double hands" and increases the odds of winning.

4 Grand Bahama Island

Introduction

Grand Bahama, the fourth-largest island in the country (after Andros, Eleuthera, and Great Abaco), lies only 55 miles offshore from Palm Beach, Florida. The ever-warm waters of the Gulf Stream lap its shores from the west, and the Great Bahama Bank protects it on the east. Until four decades ago, the island was largely undeveloped. Then a sudden boom transformed it into the most economically successful of the Bahamas' destinations, except Nassau.

Most of Grand Bahama's commercial activity is concentrated in Freeport, the second-largest city in the Bahamas. If you're planning a vacation to get away from it all, this is not the place for you. In 1989, about one third of the nearly 3.4 million people who came to the Bahamas visited Freeport and the adjacent suburb of Lucaya; they were drawn by two bustling casinos, a row of plush hotels offering close to 2,900 rooms, two large shopping complexes, and a variety of sports activities on land and sea. Each day the city's port welcomes several thousand cruise-ship passengers from the Florida ports of Miami, Fort Lauderdale, and Palm Beach, half of them staying over on the island for one to seven days. Indeed, Freeport's harbor underwent extensive dredging last year to accommodate more ships in the future.

Three sights fairly close to Freeport are worth visiting: the 100-acre Rand Nature Centre; the Garden of the Groves; and the Lucayan National Park, with underwater caves, forest trails, and a secluded beach. Outside of the ever-expanding Freeport region, however, most of the eastern and western parts of the 96-mile-long island still remain comparatively untouched, a world of casuarina, palmetto, and pine trees, blessed with long stretches of open beach, broken only by inlets and charming little fishing villages.

In 1492, when Columbus set foot on the Bahamian island of San Salvador, the population of Grand Bahama was made up of Indians. Skulls found in caves on Grand Bahama—and now on view at the Grand Bahama Museum, near the Garden of the Groves—attest to the existence of the Lucayans, a friendly tribe, who were constantly fleeing from the predatory Caribs. The skulls show that the Lucayans were flatheaded; anthropologists say the Lucayans flattened their babies' foreheads with boards to strengthen them, the object of this particularly gruesome exercise being to make them less vulnerable to the cudgels of the Caribs, who were cannibals.

In the 18th century, the first white settlers on Grand Bahama were Loyalists escaping the wrath of American revolutionaries who had just won the War of Independence. (The Spanish visited the island briefly in the early 16th century, but they dismissed it as having no commercial value and went on their way.) When Britain abolished the slave trade early in the 19th century, many of the Loyalists' slaves settled here as farmers and fishermen.

Grand Bahama next jumped into a kind of prominence in the Roaring Twenties, when the west end of the island, along with its neighbor Bimini, became a convenient jumping-off place for rumrunners ferrying booze to Florida during Prohibition. But it was not until the '50s that American settler Wallace Groves envisioned the grandiose future of Grand Bahama. Groves had been involved earlier in the lumber business on Grand Bahama and Abaco. In fact, until the '50s, the harvesting of pine trees was the major occupation on Grand Bahama, employing some 1,700 workers. Groves's dream was to establish a tax-free port for the shipment of goods to the United States, a plan that would also involve the building of a city.

In 1955, largely due to Groves's efforts and those of British industrialist Sir Charles Hayward, the government signed what was known as the Hawksbill Creek Agreement (named after a body of water on the island), which set in motion the development of a planned city. Settlers were allowed to take control of 200 square miles near the center of the island; they were given tax concessions and other benefits. In return, the developers would build a port, an airport, a power plant, roads, waterways, and utilities. They would also promote tourism and industrial development.

Today the island's centers have become Freeport and Lucaya; they are separated by a 5-mile stretch of East Sunrise Highway, though no one is quite sure where one community ends and the other begins. A modern industrial park has developed west of Freeport and close to the seaport. Companies such as Syntex Pharmaceuticals, Chevron Oil, and Smith Kline Beckman have been attracted here because there is no corporate, property, or income tax, and no customs duties or excise taxes on materials for export manufacturing. In return, these companies have become involved in community activities and charities.

Over the years, Grand Bahama has become the setting for numerous international events, such as the Grand Bahama Vintage Grand Prix, the Michelin National Long Driving Championship, the Grand Bahama 10K Road Run, and the Grand Bahama Conchman Triathlon. The island's five golf courses play host to tournaments throughout the year, and the surrounding waters bring in anglers from around the world to participate in deep-water fishing tournaments. The island is also a popular destination for scuba divers, particularly because it serves as the home for the world-famous diving school, UNEXSO.

Essential Information

Arriving and Departing by Plane

Airport and Airlines   **TWA** (tel. 800/221–2000) flies in regularly to **Freeport International Airport** (tel. 809/352–6020) from Boston, New York City, St. Louis, and Chicago. **Bahamasair** (tel. 800/222–4262) flies from Newark, and **Pan Am** (tel. 800/221–1111) has service from New York City. **Delta** (tel. 800/221–1212) offers flights from Fort Lauderdale. **Comair** (tel. 800/354–9822) has service from Orlando. Comair and **Aero Coach** (tel. 800/432–5034) have direct service from Fort Lauderdale, Tampa, and West Palm Beach. Bahamasair, **Eastern** (tel. 800/327–8376), and Pan Am fly in from Miami.

Air Canada (tel. 800/422–6232) has service from Montreal. **Conquest** (tel. 800/722–0860) offers flights three times a week from Toronto.

For charter flights, try **Airlift International** (tel. 305/871–1750) from Fort Lauderdale and West Palm Beach.

Between the Airport and Hotels
By Taxi
No bus service is available from the airport to your hotel. Metered taxis meet all incoming flights, and the driver will charge you around $10 to take you to Freeport or Lucaya. There are several taxi companies in Freeport (*see* Getting Around, below).

Arriving and Departing by Ship

Several cruise lines serve Freeport (*see* From North America by Ship in Chapter 1).

Getting Around

By Car If you plan to drive around the island, you'll find it more economical to rent a car than to hire a taxi. Automobiles may be rented at the Freeport International Airport and at individual hotels at a cost of $45 a day and up. Local car-rental companies include **Avis Rent-A-Car** in Freeport (tel. 809/352–7666), in Lucaya (tel. 809/373–1102), and at the airport (tel. 809/352–7675); **Budget Rent-A-Car** at the Atlantik Beach Hotel (tel. 809/373–4938) and the airport (tel. 809/352–8843); **National Rent-A-Car** at Holiday Inn (tel. 809/373–4957) and the airport (tel. 809/352–9308); **Eddie's Auto Sales and Service** at the airport (tel. 809/352–3165); **Dollar Rent-A-Car** at the Princess Country Club/Princess Tower (tel. 809/352–3716) and the airport (tel. 809/352–3714); and **Welcome Rent-A-Car** at Holiday Inn (tel. 809/373–3334, ext. 5500).

By Taxi Taxi fares are fixed by the government at $1.20 for the first ¼ mile, 20¢ for each additional ¼ mile. Taxi companies in Freeport include **Freeport Taxi Co., Ltd.** (Old Airport Rd., tel. 809/352–6666) and **Austin and Sons** (Queen's Hwy., tel. 809/352–5700).

By Bus Many privately owned buses travel around downtown Freeport and Lucaya, with a fare of 75¢. For the 30-minute trip to West End, catch **Franco's People Express,** which leaves twice daily from the International Bazaar and the Holiday Inn. The fare is $8 round-trip.

By Bicycle Bicycle rentals start at about $10 a day. Try **Castaways Resort** (E. Mall Dr. and W. Mall, tel. 809/352–6682), **Princess Country Club** (W. Sunrise Hwy. and S. Mall, tel. 809/352–6721), **Freeport Inn** (E. Mall and Explorer's Way, tel. 809/352–6648), **Holiday Inn** (Royal Palm Way, tel. 809/373–1333), **Princess Tower Hotel** (W. Sunrise Hwy., tel. 809/352–9661), and **Windward Palms Hotel** (E. Mall and Settlers Way, tel. 809/352–8821).

By Scooter Motor-scooter rentals start at about $25 a day. Contact **Bahamas Princess Resort & Casino** (W. Sunrise Hwy. and S. Mall, tel. 809/352–6721), **Curtis Enterprises Ltd.** (Ranfurly Circle on the Mall, tel. 809/352–7035), **Holiday Inn** (Royal Palm Way, tel. 809/373–1333), **Princess Tower Hotel** (W. Sunrise Hwy., tel. 809/352–9661), and **Sun Club Resort** (E. Mall and Settlers Way,

tel. 809/352–3462). Cruise-ship passengers may also rent motor scooters in the Freeport harbor area.

By Boat **Swashbuckler** (Box F 318, Midshipman Rd., tel. 809/373–2909)
will rent you an unsinkable and simple-to-operate Boston
Whaler for $100–$150 a day. You can do your own fishing or
snorkeling, or find your own beach.

Important Addresses and Numbers

Tourist The main **Ministry of Tourism** office is located at the Sir Charles
Information Hayward Library (E. Mall, tel. 809/352–8044). The Ministry of
Tourism also operates information booths at the Freeport In-
ternational Airport (tel. 809/352–2052), the Harbour Cruise-
ship Port (tel. 809/352–7888), the International Bazaar, and
Port Lucaya (tel. 809/373–8988).

The **Grand Bahama Island Promotion Board** has an office at the
International Bazaar (tel. 809/352–7848 or 809/352–8356). You
can pick up brochures and maps, and tips on what to do on the
island. Ask also about Bahamahosts, specially trained tour
guides who will talk to you about their islands' history and culture, and pass on their individual and imaginative knowledge of
Bahamian folklore.

Emergencies **Police** (tel. 911).
Ambulance (tel. 809/352–2689 or 809/352–6735).
Fire Department (tel. 809/352–8888).
Hospital: The government-operated **Rand Memorial Hospital**
(E. Atlantic Dr., tel. 809/352–6735) has 74 beds.
Sea Rescue (tel. 809/352–2628).
American Express (tel. 809/352–4444) is located in the Kipling
Building downtown. Open weekdays 9–1 and 2–5.

Opening and Closing Times

Banks on Grand Bahama are generally open Monday–Thursday 9:30–3; Friday 9:30–5. Some of the major banks on the island include Bank of Montreal, Bank of Nova Scotia, Barclays
Bank, and Chase Manhattan Bank.

Shops are usually open Monday–Saturday 10–6.

Guided Tours

Grand Bahama Island has many attractions worth visiting,
both natural and man-made, including beaches, museums,
shopping plazas, parks, and gardens. Most tours can be booked
through the tour desk in your hotel lobby, at tourist information booths, or by calling one of tour operators listed below.

Types of Tours A Grand Bahama day trip will take you to the major attractions
on the island at a cost of $25 adults, $12 children under 12. A
glass-bottom boat tour, which visits offshore reefs and sea gardens, starts at $10; $5 children under 12. If you're interested in
a trip to the Garden of the Groves, expect to pay about $10 ad-
ults, $8 children under 12. A tour of the historic West End costs
$16 adults, $12 children under 12.

For evening entertainment, a dinner cruise will cost around $40
adults, $30 children under 12. Nightclub tours are about $20.

You can even take a day trip to Nassau, on New Providence Island, that includes round-trip transportation, a sightseeing tour of Nassau, a visit to Paradise Island, and shopping on Bay Street. Such a package will cost about $145 adults, $125 children under 12.

Tour Operators   The following tour operators on Grand Bahama offer a combination of the tours described above, and several of them have desks in major hotels: **Executive Tours** (Box F 2509, Mercantile Bldg., tel. 809/352–8858; at the airport, tel. 809/352–5401), **Forbes Charter** (Box F 3273, tel. 809/352–7142), **Freeport Lucaya Tours** (Box F 358, Old Airport Rd., tel. 809/352–7082), **Fun Tours Ltd.** (Box F 159, Milton St., tel. 809/352–7016), **Grand Bahama Tour Ltd.** (Box F 453, 10 Savoy Bldg., tel. 809/352–7234; at the airport, tel. 809/352–7347), **Greenline Tours** (Box F 2631, 30D Kipling Bldg., tel. 809/352–3465), **International Travel & Tours** (Box F 850, tel. 809/352–9311), **Sun Island Tours** (Box F 2585, tel. 809/352–4811), and **Reef Tours Ltd.** (Box F 2510, Lucayan Bay Hotel Dock, tel. 809/373–5880).

Air Tours   You can take short airplane flights around Grand Bahama, to Nassau, or to some of the nearby Family Islands on **Helda Air Holdings Ltd.** (Box F 3335, Freeport, tel. 809/352–8832) and **Taino Air** (Box F 7-4006, Freeport, tel. 809/352–8885).

Exploring Grand Bahama Island

Highlights for First-time Visitors

Garden of the Groves (Tour 3: East End)
Grand Bahama Museum (Tour 3: East End)
International Bazaar (Tour 1: Freeport and Lucaya)
Lucayan Beach Casino (Tour 1: Freeport and Lucaya)
Lucayan National Park (Tour 3: East End)
Port Lucaya (Tour 1: Freeport and Lucaya)
Princess Casino (Tour 1: Freeport and Lucaya)
Rand Memorial Nature Centre (Tour 2: West of Freeport and Lucaya)
UNEXSO (Underwater Explorers Society) and the **Dolphin Experience** (Tour 1: Freeport and Lucaya)
West End (Tour 2: West of Freeport and Lucaya)

Tour 1: Freeport and Lucaya

Numbers in the margin correspond with points of interest on the Freeport and Lucaya map.

❶
❷
This tour begins on foot at the center of Freeport at two adjacent attractions, the **Bahamas Princess Resort & Casino** (tel. 809/352–9661; *see* Lodging, below) and the exotic **International Bazaar,** which is a kind of miniature world's fair located at the intersection of West Sunrise Highway and Mall Drive. Beware: These places attract cruise-ship passengers in droves. In the days before enlightened egalitarianism of the sexes, it was said that the men gambled or golfed while the women shopped (and indeed, the bazaar was originally conceived as a distraction for wives), but nowadays women and men can be seen in equal numbers in both places.

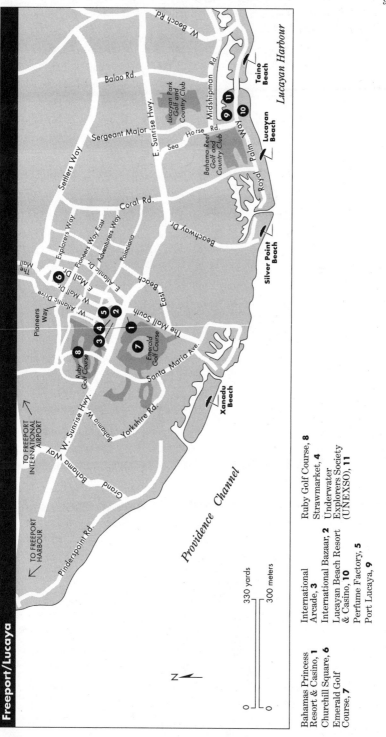

Freeport/Lucaya

Bahamas Princess Resort & Casino, **1**

Churchill Square, **6**

Emerald Golf Course, **7**

International Arcade, **3**

International Bazaar; **2**

Lucayan Beach Resort & Casino, **10**

Perfume Factory, **5**

Port Lucaya, **9**

Ruby Golf Course, **8**

Strawmarket, **4**

Underwater Explorers Society (UNEXSO), **11**

The Princess Casino, with its 450 slot machines, 40 blackjack tables, and other gambling temptations, has a distinctive Moorish-style dome. (For more information on the casino, *see* Arts and Nightlife, below.) At the entrance to the 10-acre International Bazaar stands a 35-foot red-lacquered torii, the traditional gate that is a symbol of welcome in Japan. Between the casino and the bazaar is the **International Arcade,** with its own array of smart shops.

If the International Bazaar, which was built in 1967, looks like something from a Hollywood soundstage, that's not surprising; the complex was designed by a special-effects artist named Charles Perrin. Some 90 shops, lounges, and restaurants representing 25 countries may be found along its narrow walkways. Here, you can purchase—at 20%–40% below U.S. prices —silver and emeralds from South America, French perfumes, Spanish leather, brass from India, Chinese jade, African carvings, tailored clothes from Hong Kong, Thai silks, Irish linens, English china, and hookahs from Turkey. The choice of ethnic restaurants in the complex is almost as varied as the shops.

Colombian Emeralds International, in the South American section of the bazaar, offers a free tour of its jewelry factory. You can watch its craftsmen fashion gold, silver, and gemstones into rings, bracelets, and pendants. Freeport is home base for this company, though you'll find its shops scattered throughout the Caribbean. You may pay less than $100 for an emerald set in a 14k ring, but most pieces start at $300. *Tel. 809/352–5464. Free tours Mon.–Sat. 10–1 and 2–5.*

Time Out   Across East Mall Drive from the bazaar is the **Sir Winston Churchill Pub** (tel. 809/352–8866), a brass-railed tavern where you can rest for a few minutes and quaff a refreshing pint of Watney's beer or Courage ale. The adjoining Chartwell Room (the great statesman's home in Kent was named Chartwell) evokes an English atmosphere with blackened beams in a country-inn ambience; the menu includes the mandatory roast-beef and Yorkshire-pudding dishes.

Next, drop by the local **Strawmarket,** to the right of the bazaar entrance. Dozens of stalls display a seemingly endless selection of straw goods such as handbags, place mats, hats, and baskets; you'll also find T-shirts, wood carvings of mahogany and native pine, and handcrafted jewelry. In this colorful, boisterous world, don't be shy about haggling over prices. The Bahamian vendors will be surprised if you don't.

You'll also want to visit the **Perfume Factory** (Box F 770, tel. 809/352–9391), at the rear of the bazaar. Housed in a pink-and-white replica of an old Bahamian mansion, the kind built by Loyalists transplanted to the Bahamas after the American Revolution, the quiet and elegant Perfume Factory has an interior that resembles a tasteful drawing room. This is the home of Fragrance of the Bahamas, a company that produces some of the most popular perfumes, colognes, and lotions in the islands, using the scents of jasmine, cinnamon, gardenia, spice, and ginger. Bahamian women conduct free tours of the mixology laboratory, where customers are invited to create their own blend, choosing from 140 different fragrances. They can sniff mixtures until they hit on the right combination; then they can bottle, name, and take their new perfumes home for a $15 charge.

A short distance away from the bazaar, along East Mall Drive, **⑥** is **Churchill Square,** where many of Freeport's businesses and banks are located. The 74-bed **Rand Memorial Hospital** is on East Mall Drive, and the **Court House** is just west on Pioneers Way. In fact, between Explorers Way in the north and Pioneers Way in the south, you'll find most of Freeport's commercial buildings, as well as two supermarkets, **Pantry Pride** and **Winn Dixie.**

Just west of the bazaar, on either side of West Sunrise High- **⑦** way, lie two of the island's five golf courses, the **Emerald** and **⑧** the **Ruby** (tel. 809/352–6721), both of them owned by the people who run the Princess Resort.

For the next part of this tour, you'll need to drive or take a taxi. Head east from the bazaar along East Sunrise Highway, and turn south down Seahorse Road; you'll come to Lucaya's capa- **⑨** cious shopping complex, the festive **Port Lucaya,** on the water-front across from several major hotels. The complex consists of 12 low-rise, pastel-painted buildings whose tropical-colonial style architecture has been influenced by that of traditional island homes. Here you can choose from about 75 stores, including restaurants, bars, and shops that sell clothes, crystal and china, watches, jewelry, and perfumes. The protected walkways have small, well-kept gardens of hibiscus and croton.

The centerpiece of the complex is **Count Basie Square** (the Count had a home on Grand Bahama), with a vine-covered bandstand where a live band plays dance music. Small musical groups, steel bands, and gospel singers also contribute free entertainment. Port Lucaya overlooks a 50-slip marina, where a replica of the 16th-century Spanish ship *El Galleon I* (tel. 809/373–7863) is host to dinner cruises and trips to nearby islands. If you happen to have your own boat, you're permitted courtesy docking at the marina while you shop or dine at the complex.

Just outside of Port Lucaya is a sight that isn't someone's week-ly wash hanging out to dry—instead, it's yet another straw-market, this one festooned mainly with T-shirts. Across from Port Lucaya on Seahorse Road, you'll find the wooden, winding **Lucayan Beachwalk,** which takes you to the beach at the lavish, **⑩** 16-acre **Lucayan Beach Resort & Casino** (tel. 809/373–7777; *see* Lodging, below).

Adjacent to Port Lucaya is one of the world's best-known div- **⑪** ing schools, the **Underwater Explorers Society (UNEXSO),** which serves more than 12,000 customers a year from around the world and trains more than 2,500 of them in scuba diving. Near-by Treasure Reef, where more than $2 million in Spanish treasure was discovered in the '60s, is one of the school's favor-ite dive sites. UNEXSO has an extensive dive shop, where you can talk to instructors, pick up brochures, and meet other div-ers. *Tel. 809/373–1250. A learn-to-dive course and two dives costs $99; a snorkeling trip, which includes all equipment, costs $15. Open daily 8–6.*

UNEXSO is also the home of what is called the **Dolphin Experi-ence.** If you would like to spy on the underwater conversations of these intelligent mammals, you may sit in a booth with a headset and listen. The experience costs $10. Afterward, go

down to the dock and sit near the edge; one of the friendly creatures will come up for a pat on the head. The dolphin exper-
iment started in 1987, when five wild bottle-nosed creatures
were brought in and trained to interact with people in a large,
open-water pool; later, they were trained to go out into the sea
and swim with scuba divers on the open reef. Now for $45, you
can get into the pool at 10 AM and 3 PM and cavort with the dolphins for about 20 minutes. If you really get hooked on these
affectionate and docile animals (once thought to be the mermaids
of ancient lore), you can also enroll as an assistant trainer and
work with the trainers for a day in different aspects of the dolphin
program. *Tel. 809/373–1250. Closed Sat.*

Tour 2: West of Freeport and Lucaya

*Numbers in the margin correspond with points of interest on
the Grand Bahama Island map.*

Start this tour from your Freeport or Lucaya hotel by driving
along East Sunrise Highway in a westerly direction to the International Bazaar, where the road becomes West Sunrise
Highway. After you pass industrial complexes such as Syntex
and the Bahamas Oil Refining Co. on your left, you'll come to
the junction of Queen's Highway, which runs all the way to
West End, about 30 miles from the main hotel and shopping
area of Freeport.

Turn left (west) past the Freeport Harbour, where cruise ships
are docked and a seemingly endless line of taxis inches up to
take the passengers to the casinos or the malls. Just to the east
❶ of the harbor is **Hawksbill Creek,** which has a charming fish
market. From here, on either side of the road, you'll pass little
seaside villages, many of them more than 100 years old, with
houses painted in bright blue and yellow pastels. Settlements
like these around the island, such as Smith's Point, Pinder's
Point, William's Town, and Cooperstown, have names derived
from the surnames of the original homesteaders and are populated by descendants of these founders. Turn west again at the
long, narrow hamlet of Eight Mile Rock, where you'll pass a
tiny restaurant/bar named Henry's Place, a grocery store, a
playing field, a church, and small settlements such as Bartlett
Hill and Martin's Town (ask for Mr. Bartlett or Mr. Martin if
you would like any more information about their abodes).

Time Out Just past the village of Holmes Rock and Deadman's Reef are
two popular unpretentious restaurant/bars, **Harry's American
Bar** (tel. 809/348–2660) and the **Buccaneer Club** (tel. 809/348–
3794). During the day, you can have drinks and barbecued
snacks at Harry's, though the place closes between Labor Day
and mid-December. The Buccaneer Club serves more substantial local and U.S. cuisine with a Continental flair during the
evening hours only. It's also a superb place to lie on the beach
with a rum concoction and watch the sun set.

After you pass Bootle Bay village, the road swings north briefly, then west again; you know you're getting close to West End
as the island becomes narrower, with the sea suddenly on your
right. Fishermen tie their boats up offshore, opposite their little houses on the other side of the road. Residents of Grand
Bahama come here to buy fresh fish, and if they fancy a conch
salad, one of the fishermen will be sure to pop into his house for

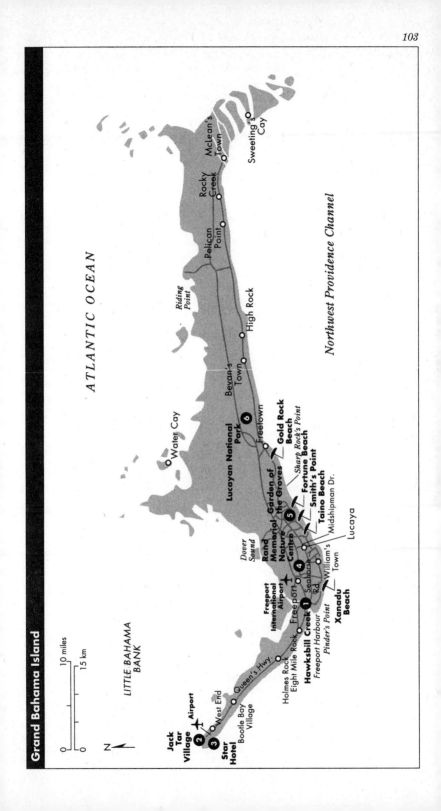

the necessary ingredients. Locals at little booths also offer fried grouper and peas 'n' rice.

On the left, just before you get to the sight of the West End's ❷ mammoth Club Med-style, all-inclusive tourist resort, **Jack Tar Village,** you'll see on your left a dilapidated, two-story wooden building, looking for all the world like part of a ghost town. This is ❸ the **Star Hotel,** one of the oldest buildings on the island (and thought to be the oldest hotel), which saw lots of furtive action during the rumrunning days of Prohibition. The place hasn't had a stay-over guest in years, but you can still get a drink there and eat grouper fingers at its little restaurant. If you want music and dancing, however, look in at **Austin's Calypso Bar** next door. You may also see some sumptuous yachts anchored offshore or at the Jack Tar marina, because this is a favorite, easily accessible port of entry for American sailing enthusiasts. (At press time, Jack Tar Village had closed for renovations in spring 1990 but the marina remained open.)

Time Out   On your way back from West End, you'll come across the 11-room **Harbour Hotel** (tel. 809/346–6432) on your left. Freeporters who visit West End like to stop off here for a bite of native grouper and a swig of Kalik beer. You can also enjoy a disco during the evening. The place offers a delightful watery vista and recently completed a new marina.

Return by Queen's Highway, turn south (right) at the airport onto The Mall (a short road), and then go immediately right ❹ onto Settlers Way, until you come to the **Rand Memorial Nature Centre.** The hundred woodland acres here are named after the former president of Remington Rand, philanthropist James H. Rand, who donated a hospital and library to the island. The reserve includes a half-mile of winding trails conveniently designed to show off the 130 native plants, including 20 species of wild orchids.

You may observe a Cuban emerald hummingbird sipping the nectar of a hibiscus, or a Bahama woodstar, which is even tinier. You may even see a raccoon, the only large native mammal living in the area, or what is believed to be the smallest snake in the world, the harmless five-inch-long worm snake. *Tel. 809/ 352–5438. Admission: $2 adults and children (only 8 years and older admitted). Guided tours weekdays 10, 2, and 3; Sun. 2 and 3. Closed Sat.*

Tour 3: East End

Begin this tour by getting on to Seahorse Road, which runs east along the channel opposite Port Lucaya (this road is south from East Sunrise Highway if you're coming from Freeport, north if you're coming from Lucaya) on to Midshipman Road. ❺ This route will take you to the **Garden of the Groves,** the halcyon spot dedicated to pioneer developers Wallace Groves and his wife. Groves came up with the idea for this prizewinning natureland and contributed it to the island. The park, which covers 11 acres, features some 5,000 rare varieties of trees, flowers, and shrubs. The various plant species are identified with signs. You can walk past streams, ponds, waterfalls, and a gully. Perhaps the most photographed attraction in the gardens is a grotto, a favorite venue for weddings. *Tel. 809/ 352–4045. Admission free. Open 10–5. Closed Wed.*

If you would like to learn more about the role Grand Bahama played in the history of the country, the Garden of the Groves adjoins the **Grand Bahama Museum,** which has artifacts of the Lucayan Indians. *Tel. 809/352–4045. Admission: $2 adults, $1 children under 12. Open 10–5. Closed Wed.*

Continue eastward along Midshipman Road and past Sharp Rock's Point and Gold Rock. A dozen miles from Lucaya, you'll drive into the 40-acre **Lucayan National Park.** This land preserve by the sea contains trails and elevated walkways through a natural forest of wild tamarind and gumbo limbo trees, an observation platform, a mangrove swamp, what is believed to be the largest explored underwater cave system in the world (it's 7 miles long), and sheltered pools containing rare marine species. In Ben's Cave and Burial Mound Cave, bones of the early Lucayan Indians were found. A boardwalk pathway will take you through forest and swamp and over high dunes to Gold Rock Beach, a perfect place to relax after your half-hour tour.

At press time, you still had to find your own way around the park with the help of a large map detailing its distinctive features. The Bahamas National Trust hopes to soon have local guides to take visitors around. *For information about the park, which is always open at no charge, contact the National Trust: South Riding Holdings Ltd., Box F 2530, Freeport, tel. 809/ 348–3475.*

It's a lonely drive if you want to continue your journey to the eastern end of the island; the road is broken only by the USAF Missile Tracking Base, which tracked the early stages of the Cape Canaveral launches, just off Free Town, and the nearby Burmah oil refinery at High Rock, which is on a bluff overlooking the sea where tankers unload their crude oil.

At Bevin Town, you'll find the Three Sisters restaurant, the Star Club bar, and a general-repair shop, the only one on this end of the island. You'll pass through the little settlements of Pelican Point and Rocky Creek, with the Atlantic Ocean lapping the pristine white beaches on your right, until the road ends at McLean's Town.

On your return, you can turn right (north) at Midshipman Road by the Garden of the Groves, curve round onto East Sunrise Highway, and then drive back to Freeport.

Shopping

In the hundreds of stores, shops, and boutiques of Freeport and Lucaya, you'll find bargain goods that may cost 40% less than what you would pay back home. Be aware, however, of what you're buying; if you're in the market, say, for a watch, china, crystal, or perfume, check prices before you leave home so that you can know if you're getting a real bargain on Grand Bahama. You'll have to use your own judgment in considering more precious items such as Mexican silver or Chinese jade. Don't try to haggle with shopkeepers, except at the straw-markets. Although there is no sales tax in the Bahamas, don't take the name Freeport too literally. Unlike St. Thomas, this is not a duty-free land.

Shops in Freeport and Lucaya are open Monday through Saturday from 10 to 6. Stores may stay open later in Port Lucaya.

Shopping Centers

For the best bargains on fine imported goods, exotic items, and European fashions, make your first stop at the **International Bazaar,** located at the intersection of West Side Highway and Mall Drive. This 10-acre complex features a seemingly endless array of shops representing imports from nearly a dozen different countries. Right next to the bazaar, you'll also have fun browsing and bargaining at the **Strawmarket,** with its bountiful selection of souvenirs and gift items woven by hand from straw, raffia, and palm fronds. The **Perfume Factory** (tel. 809/352–9391), which adjoins the bazaar, offers an excellent selection of perfumes, colognes, and lotions in a variety of fragrances; you can also create your own perfume.

For more bargains, head for the attractive harbor-side setting of **Port Lucaya,** near the UNEXSO dock, with 75 boutiques and restaurants housed in 12 pastel-colored buildings. You can also take a break with entertainment provided by local musicians, who often perform at the bandstand. If you still have shopping fever, you can try the 60 stores at the new **Regent Centre,** which is located downtown (north of the International Bazaar) at The Mall and Explorers Way.

Specialty Shops

The following stores may be found in the International Bazaar, unless otherwise noted. Many of them have branches at Port Lucaya and the Regent Centre.

Antiques   The **Old Curiosity Shop** (tel. 809/352–8008) carries old English clocks, coins, and art. For Spanish antiques, stop off at **El Galleon** (tel. 809/352–5380), which also carries watches and jewelry.

China and Crystal   **Casa Miro** (tel. 809/352–2660) specializes in high-quality Spanish porcelain but also stocks jewelry, fans, and leather purses and wallets. At **Island Galleria** (tel. 809/352–8194), you'll find such china and crystal by Waterford, Wedgwood, Aynsley, Orrefors Sweden, and Coalport. **Midnight Sun** (tel. 809/352–9510) is the place to go for gift items by Royal Worcester, Stratton, Daum, and Lalique; you can also purchase Hummel figurines.

Fashion   The **London Pacesetter Boutique** (tel. 809/352–2929) has a good selection of swimwear. Drop by **Gemini II** (tel. 809/352–2377) for swimwear by Charles Jourdan and sportswear by Esprit. If you are willing to go a bit out of the way, you can go and meet the Bahamian artists who work on the brilliantly colored Androsia batik fabrics at the **Androsia Harbour Outlet** (tel. 809/352–2255) at Freeport Harbour.

Jewelry   If you're searching for fine diamonds, rubies, sapphires, and gold and silver jewelry, you'll want to visit **Colombian Emeralds International** (tel. 809/352–5464), which also carries the best brands in watches, such as Tissot, Omega, and Citizen. Another store called the **Colombian** (tel. 809/352–5380) features a line of Colombia's famed emeralds. For more good buys in elegant watches, check out **La Sandale** (tel. 809/352–5380), which stocks Cartier and Chopard; the **Old Curiosity Shop** (tel. 809/352–8008); the **Ginza** (tel. 809/352–7515); **Little Switzerland**

(tel. 809/352–7273); **Island Galleria** (tel. 809/352–8194); and **El Fendi** (tel. 809/352–7908).

Leather Goods   The **Leather Shop** (tel. 809/352–5491) at the Oasis section of the International Bazaar features Gucci, MCM, and Fendi handbags and briefcases. You'll find eel-skin leather goods at the **Unusual Centre** (tel. 809/352–3994) in the Spanish section of the bazaar. **El Fendi** (tel. 809/352–7908) specializes in Italian leather goods.

Perfumes   Perfumes often can be purchased at a sweet-smelling price of 30% below U.S. prices. **Casablanca Perfumes** (tel. 809/352–5380), in the Moroccan section of the Bazaar, stocks Giorgio products and the latest scents from Paris. **Oasis** (tel. 809/352–5923) is a complete pharmacy where you can choose from a selection of French perfumes; it also sells cosmetics, jewelry, and leather goods. The **Perfume Factory** (tel. 809/325–9391) sells a large variety of perfumes, lotions, and colognes by Fragrance of the Bahamas; here you can find a product called Pink Pearl, which actually contains conch pearls, and Sand cologne, which has a sample of the island's sand at the bottom of the bottle. For more perfume bargains, visit **Parfum de Paris** (tel. 809/352–8164) and **Prestige Perfumes** (tel. 809/373–8633).

Sports

Bowling

Sea Surf Lanes has eight lanes and a snack shop. *Queen's Hwy., Box F 3245, tel. 809/352–5784. Cost: adults $1.75 per game, children $1.50; shoe rental 55¢.*

Fitness Centers

ABC Rainbow Spa and Culture Club (Pioneers Way, Box F 747, tel. 809/352–5683), which is owned and managed by a doctor and his wife, features a Universal gym, free weights, two hot tubs, a large swimming pool, and a 400-meter jogging track.

Bahamas Princess Resort & Casino (W. Sunrise Hwy., Box F 207, tel. 809/352–6721) offers a small fitness area open to guests and nonguests, with a Universal gym, bicycles, aerobics and jazz classes, a sauna, massages, and facials.

Golf

Bahamas Princess Hotel & Golf Club has two courses, the 7,005-yard Ruby and the 6,420-yard Emerald, both par-72. A pro shop is also available to visitors. *West Side Hwy., Box F 207, tel. 809/352–6721. Cost: greens fees $10; mandatory electric carts $24; clubs $10.*

Fortune Hills Golf & Country Club is a nine-hole, par-36, 3,453-yard course. The club also features a restaurant, bar, and pro shop. *E. Sunrise Hwy., Box F 2619, tel. 809/373–4500. Cost: $7 for 9 holes, $12 for 18; electric carts $11 for 9 holes, $20 for 18; clubs $5 for 9 holes, $8 for 18.*

Lucayan Golf & Country Club offers a 6,800-yard, par-72 course, as well as a cocktail lounge, pro shop, and restaurant.

Lucaya Beach, Box F 333, tel. 809/373–1066. Cost: $15 for 9 holes, $22 all day; electric carts $14 for 9 holes, $24 for 18.

Horseback Riding

Pinetree Stables has trail and beach rides three times a day (except Mondays); all trail rides are accompanied by an experienced guide. Visitors have a choice of English or Western saddles. *Beachway Dr., tel. 809/373–3600. Cost: $20 for 1½ hrs., stables or arena rides $15 per hr. Private lessons: $25 per hr.*

Tennis

Holiday Inn has four courts. *Royal Palm Way, Box F 760, tel. 809/373–1333. Cost: $5 per hr.*

Princess Country Club has 12 courts, with eight of them lighted for night play. *W. Sunrise Hwy., Box F 207, tel. 809/352–6721. Cost: $5 per hr., $10 night play.*

Silver Sands Sea Lodge features two courts. *Royal Palm Way, Box F 2385, tel. 809/373–5700. Cost: guests free, nonguests $5 per hr.*

Xanadu Beach Hotel has three courts. *Sunken Treasure Dr., Box F 2438, tel. 809/352–6782. Cost: guests free, nonguests $5 per hr. during the day; guests and nonguests $10 per hr. for night play.*

Water Sports

Boating and Fishing Grand Bahama Island offers a wide variety of boating opportunities. Xanadu Beach Marina in Freeport offers 400 feet of dockage plus 77 slips and provides dockside valet service. The Running Mon Marina, a half-mile to the east, has 66 slips and serves as the base for a deep-sea fishing fleet. Inside Bell Channel at Lucaya, the 150-slip Lucayan Marina features complimentary ferry service to the Lucayan Beach Resort. The 15-slip Port Lucaya Marina features a broad range of water sports. Powerboats can explore the Grand Lucayan Waterway, a man-made channel that goes through the island to Dover Sound on the north side. At the east end of Grand Bahama, the Deep Water Cay Club offers a few slips for boats.

Boat charter rentals cost about $300 a half-day, $600 all day. Bahamian law limits the catching of game fish to six dolphin, kingfish, or wahoo per person per day. For boat rentals, contact **Lucayan Harbour Inn** (Midshipman Rd., Box F 336, tel. 809/373–8888), **Running Mon Marina** (North Blvd., Box F 2663, tel. 809/352–6834), and **Xanadu Beach Hotel** (Sunken Treasure Dr., Box F 2438, tel. 809/352–6780).

Diving Grand Bahama Island has some fascinating dive sites near the West End. An extensive reef system runs along the edge of the Little Bahama Bank from Mantinilla Shoals down through Memory Rock, Wood Cay, Rock Cay, and Indian Cay. Sea gardens, caves, and colorful reefs rim the bank all the way from the West End to Freeport/Lucaya and beyond. Some of the main dive sites around the island include Theo's Wreck, a 230-foot steel freighter that was sunk in 1982 near Freeport; Angel's Camp, a reef about a mile and a quarter off Lucayan Beach, offering a scattering of small coral heads surrounding one large head; Pygmy Caves (in the same area as Angel's Camp), which are formed by overgrown ledges and cut in the reef; Zoo Hole, west of Lucaya, with huge caverns at 75 feet containing various marine life; and Indian Cay Light, on the West End, featuring several reefs that form a vast sea garden.

Sunn Odyssey Divers (Atlantik Beach Hotel, tel. 809/373–1444) runs three daily reef trips and handles the resort diving for most of the hotels in Freeport/Lucaya. **UNEXSO (Underwater Explorers Society,** Box F 2433, tel. 809/373–1244, 305/359–2730, or 800/992–DIVE), a world-renowned scuba-diving school, provides full equipment for rental, 12 guides, and three boats, as well as NAUI and PADI certification. **West End Diving Centre,** which may be reached through UNEXSO, has full equipment for rental, four guides, and one boat; it offers coral-reef, wall, night-drift, and cave diving. Diving instruction for beginners, including all equipment, is available for $99; a snorkeling trip costs $15. Experienced divers can participate in coral-reef, wall, drift, cave, and blue-hole dives. A six-dive package costs $132; an unlimited package for seven days is offered for $295.

Parasailing **Atlantik Beach Hotel** (Royal Palm Way, Box F 531, tel. 809/373–1444) charges $15 for seven minutes. **Holiday Inn** (Royal Palm Way, Box F 760, tel. 809/373–1333) charges $20 for five to seven minutes.

Waterskiing **Holiday Inn** (Royal Palm Way, Box F 760, tel. 809/373–1333) offers waterskiing at $10 for 3 miles.

Windsurfing **Atlantik Beach Hotel** (Royal Palm Way, Box F 531, tel. 809/373–1444) carries 18 boards. Cost: $150 per week, $10 per hour, private lesson $25.

Beaches

Some 60 miles of uncluttered beaches extend between Freeport/Lucaya and the isolated eastern end of the island, McLean's Town, most of them enjoyed only by the people who live in the settlements along the way. The Lucaya hotels are lucky to have their own beaches, with the accompanying water sports; guests at Freeport hotels are shuttled free to places like **Xanadu Beach,** which has a mile-long stretch of white sand.

Local residents have their own particular favorites. Off East Sunrise Highway, go down Beachway Drive south of Freeport until you come to **Williams Town.** Here, just east of Xanadu Beach, a few native houses are perched over the water, their owners' fishing boats tied up offshore. Your sandy solitude will be broken only by the occasional intrusion of horseback riders from the nearby Pinetree Stables clip-clopping along the water's edge.

East of Freeport, three delightful beaches run into one another—**Taino Beach,** which has the advantage of easy access to the Stoned Crab restaurant (tel. 809/373–1442) for seafood dishes; **Smith's Point;** and **Fortune Beach.** Farther east on the island, at the end of the trail from the Lucayan National Park, you'll find **Gold Rock Beach,** which is only a 20-minute drive from the Lucaya hotels. Locals drive here during the weekends for picnics. Tables are available, but there are no rest rooms.

Dining

By Laurie Senz
and Ian Glass

You'll find hundreds of dining alternatives in Freeport and Lucaya, including elegant dining rooms at large hotels, charming cafés by the water, poolside snack bars, local hangouts, and fast-food joints. Many of the better restaurants may be found at hotels and resorts. The choices of cuisine are about as varied as what you'll find in Nassau, Cable Beach, and Paradise Island, with menus often combining Continental, American, and Bahamian fare; Freeport's International Bazaar is worth exploring for more exotic cuisines, such as Indian or Japanese.

In general, the restaurants on Grand Bahama Island cannot be rated as highly as those on New Providence Island; only a handful of establishments in Freeport and Lucaya could be considered fine dining. However, a meal in Freeport usually costs a visitor less than a comparative one in Nassau. Prices on menus often include three courses—an appetizer or salad, an entrée, and a dessert.

Highly recommended restaurants in each price category are indicated by a star ★.

Category	Cost*
Expensive	over $30
Moderate	$20–$30
Inexpensive	under $20

per person, drinks and including 15% gratuity

Freeport

Expensive   **Crown Room.** In the far left corner of the Bahamas Princess Casino, you'll find this French-Continental restaurant tucked away from the bustle of the gaming tables. The intimately lighted dining room features rose-colored beveled mirrors alternating with coral panels along the walls, high-back French colonial chairs, and white Italian smoked-glass chandeliers in the shape of leaves. Light jazz music plays in the background. This is a pleasant place for celebrating a casino win, but the tables are placed a bit too close together to enjoy a truly romantic tête-à-tête. The specialties include escargots in basil sauce, a Caesar salad prepared tableside, and *lobster casino* (chunks of lobster sautéed with a cream and cognac sauce), which is worth the splurge. The Crown's rack of lamb is a wise choice for meat lovers. *Bahamas Princess Casino, tel. 809/352–7811 or 352–6721, ext. 54. Reservations required. Jacket required. AE, V. Dinner only. Closed Mon.*

Ruby Swiss. This four-year-old establishment, which is popular with both locals and tourists, offers generous portions, excellent service, and musical entertainment. Artificial potted ficus trees, lighted with twinkling lights, add to the festive mood, and burgundy drapes contribute a touch of elegance to the large dining room. Although you can have a nice evening out here, the ambience isn't conducive to a romantic evening. The extensive Continental menu features 14 different seafood dishes and more than 17 beef offerings; the wine list includes more than 48 varieties from six countries. The specialties in-

Freeport/Lucaya Dining

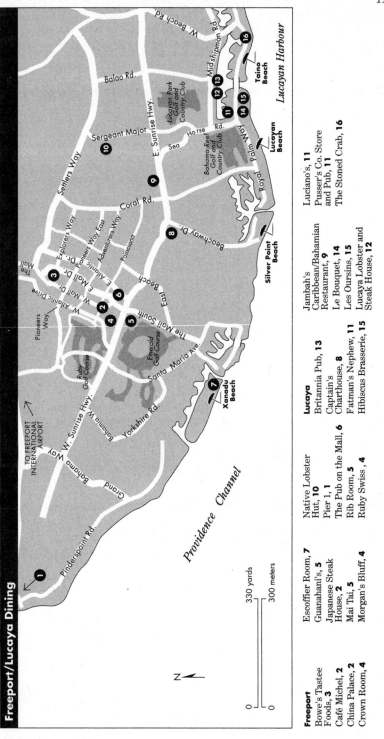

Freeport
Bowe's Tastee Foods, **3**
Café Michel, **2**
China Palace, **2**
Crown Room, **4**
Escoffier Room, **7**
Guanahani's, **5**
Japanese Steak House, **2**
Mai Tai, **5**
Morgan's Bluff, **4**

Native Lobster Hut, **10**
Pier 1, **1**
The Pub on the Mall, **6**
Rib Room, **5**
Ruby Swiss, **4**

Lucaya
Britannia Pub, **13**
Captain's Charthouse, **8**
Fatman's Nephew, **11**
Hibiscus Brasserie, **15**

Jambah's Caribbean/Bahamian Restaurant, **9**
Le Bouquet, **14**
Les Oursins, **15**
Lucaya Lobster and Steak House, **12**

Luciano's, **11**
Pusser's Co. Store and Pub, **11**
The Stoned Crab, **16**

clude *steak Diane* (thinly sliced steak flavored with cognac), *fondue bourguignonne* (prepared with filet mignon), and desserts flambéed at the table. Snacks are served until 5 AM, so this is a good place to come after gambling. The Swiss owner of the restaurant can often be found enjoying a late supper at a corner table. *Adjacent to the Bahamas Princess Tower, Bahamas Princess Resort, tel. 809/352–8507. Reservations required for dinner. Dress: casual. AE, CB, DC, MC, V.*

Moderate– **Escoffier Room.** Formerly the private dining room of reclusive
Expensive billionaire Howard Hughes, this restaurant, which has only 18 well-spaced tables, is appropriately named after a 19th-century culinary artist who became known as "the king of chefs and the chef of kings." The wood-paneled dining room features smoked-glass French mirrors and provides the perfect setting for a romantic evening. If you're looking for something special, order either the roast duck *à l'orange* or the veal *sirena* (sautéed in marsala wine, cream, and mushrooms), which are both dramatically prepared next to your table. *Xanadu Beach Hotel, tel. 809/352–6782. Reservations required. Jacket required. AE, DC, MC, V.*

Rib Room. This establishment resembles an English hunting lodge with its long narrow rooms, rough hewed timber ceiling, wood and brick walls, red leather chairs, and scotch-plaid carpet. Come here when you're in the mood for a generous portion of prime rib, steak, or surf and turf. Some of the prices can be high, but a good deal is the special three-course meal, served from 6 to 7 PM, which includes appetizer, entrée, dessert, and coffee for only $21.50 per person. *Princess Country Club, Bahamas Princess Resort, tel. 809/352–6721, ext. 59. Reservations required. Jacket required. AE, DC, MC, V. Dinner only. Closed Tues.–Wed.*

Moderate **Guanahani's.** Named after the Lucayan Indian word for the is-
★ land of San Salvador, this dining spot has three main dining rooms that are separated by two sets of Moorish arches; the rest of the decor is predominantly Bahamian, featuring a high cedar-and-cypress-wood ceiling, potted palms, laminated wood tables, and high-back rattan chairs. Couples will enjoy a window seat with a view of the romantically lighted rock-garden waterfall. The menu includes steak, ribs, chicken, fish, lobster tail, and shrimps—for the most part either grilled, blackened, or barbecued. All à la carte dinners come with a dessert of hot fudge fondue, served with a large plate of sliced fresh fruits. The Bahamian chef also makes a good conch chowder, an island favorite. If you can dine before 6:30 PM, you can take advantage of the special, which features a choice of six main courses for only $12.50 per person. *Princess Country Club, Bahamas Princess Resort, tel. 809/352–6721, ext. 56. Reservations advised. Dress: casual. AE, DC, MC, V. Dinner only. Closed Sat.*

Mai Tai. Just the place for an exotic drink and dinner after 18 holes, this Polynesian and Szechuan restaurant can be found in the Emerald Golf Course's clubhouse, which overlooks the 10th fairway. Straw and bamboo decorations, Hawaiian paintings, and wooden masks grace the walls of the large dining room. Four Hong Kong chefs expertly prepare standard Polynesian and Chinese favorites such as the combination *pupu* platter (egg rolls, teriyaki beef, and chicken wings). *Princess Country Club, Bahamas Princess Resort, tel. 809/352–7277. Reservations advised. Dress: casual. AE, MC, V.*

Morgan's Bluff. The cheerful, relaxed ambience of this family-style seafood restaurant, named after 17th-century pirate Sir Henry Morgan, is enhanced by the eclectic nautical decor that centers on a collage of colorful sails suspended from the ceiling. A row of red neon "portholes" decorates one of the walls. The menu features an array of tasty island specialties such as conch chowder, conch fritters, Bahamian lobster tail, blackened red fish, and fresh grouper sautéed in lemon, butter, and spices. *Princess Tower, Bahamas Princess Resort, tel. 809/352-6721, ext. 59. Reservations advised. Dress: casual. AE, MC, V. Dinner only. Closed Wed.*

Native Lobster Hut. This is the place to sample true Bahamian dining, with different specials each day, such as steamed conch, okra soup, native mutton, corned beef brisket-turtle, and pea soup and dumplings. The 60-seat dining room is part of a busy complex that includes a long bar, pool table, and disco, so you can dance between courses if you wish. The restaurant is located near the International Bazaar. *Sgt. Major Dr., tel. 809/373-1799. Reservations advised. Dress: casual. AE, MC, V.*

Pier 1. You actually do walk the plank to get to this rustic, windswept eatery on stilts, where you can observe the cruise-ship activity of Freeport Harbour or watch the sunset while sipping cocktails. Not surprisingly, the pleasant dining area can become crowded with cruise passengers who seek a scrumptious sample of island seafood (including fresh oysters) and Bahamian cooking before returning to shipboard dining. Lower-priced specials are served between 5 and 7 PM. *Freeport Harbour, tel. 809/352-6674. Reservations required. Dress: casual. AE, MC, V.*

Inexpensive **Bowe's Tastee Foods.** This simple restaurant, a short walk from the International Bazaar, seats only 16; locals like to eat at the counter. Here you can sample real Bahamian fare, choosing from such delectable dishes as cracked conch, boiled fish, steamed grouper, crab soup and dumplings, and chicken in the bag. The sandwiches here are satisfying as well; they're elaborate enough to make Dagwood drool. The place is conveniently open from early morning until midnight (and sometimes later); delivery to your hotel room is also available. *Explorer's Way, tel. 809/352-5130. No reservations. Dress: casual. No credit cards.*

International Bazaar (Freeport)

Moderate **The Pub on the Mall.** Diners here have three options. The Prince of Wales Lounge, an English-style pub, serves fish and chips, kidney pie, and three different types of ale. The Baron's Hall Grill Room offers a medieval setting: Banners, coats of arms, and a tapestry of King Richard the Lionhearted cover the walls. The diverse menu includes a satisfying Angus beef or *coquille St. Jacques.* A third restaurant, Silvano's, serves fine homemade canneloni and fettuccine in a circular dining room with a striking red ceiling and paintings of Italian cities. *Ranfurly Circus opposite International Bazaar, tel. 809/352-5109 (Prince of Wales Lounge and Baron's Hall); tel. 809/352-5111 (Silvano's). Reservations advised. Dress: casual. AE, MC, V.*

Inexpensive– **Japanese Steak House.** Experience an authentic taste of Japan
Moderate in a tropical climate as the chefs here prepare chicken, seafood, and Kobe steaks in a fast-paced sizzling show right on the hibachi at your table. The two rooms, separated by sliding rice-paper

doors, are gracefully decorated with umbrellas, fans, and red and gold lanterns. In the geisha room at the back, diners can sit on the floor Japanese style. The front room features long tables set for groups of 10 or more, which means you sit with other diners. All of the hibachi meals include soup, salad, vegetables, and rice with the entrée. The à la carte menu is more expensive, but you can save money by ordering the early-bird dinner special; it costs only $14.95 per person and features four different complete hibachi meals. (A sister restaurant, the Big Buddha, is located on the waterfront at the Port Lucaya Marketplace.) *International Bazaar, tel. 809/352–9521 or 809/373–8499. Reservations not necessary. Dress: casual. AE, MC, V. Closed Sun.*

Inexpensive **Café Michel.** This unpretentious spot provides a relaxed place to snack if you're not interested in dressing up. Outside this café, you can munch on a sandwich and people-watch at one of the 20-odd umbrella-shaded tables right off the International Bazaar's main promenade. The small, indoor restaurant offers a no-frills, coffee-shop atmosphere with only 11 tables. The menu includes both American and Bahamian dishes; the $10.95 dinner special is a tasty and filling bargain. *International Bazaar, tel. 809/352–2191. Reservations not necessary. Dress: casual. AE, MC, V.*

China Palace. Good Cantonese and Szechuan cuisine, alongside some American offerings, can be sampled at this lively restaurant with a striking red-and-green exterior that resembles a mandarin's palace. You enter by walking up a flight of stairs decorated with dragons and Chinese characters. The tastefully designed dining room features Chinese screens artfully placed to hide the kitchen doors and delicate statues placed in a recessed wall. The Chinese Happy Hour is 4–6 PM; tropical drinks are served with names like Bahamian Scorpion and Bali Daiquiri. A special dinner (soup, appetizer, entrée, and dessert) is available for only $13.75 per person. *International Bazaar, tel. 809/352–7661. Reservations not necessary. Dress: casual. AE, MC, V. Closed Sat.*

Lucaya

Expensive **Le Bouquet.** A relatively new addition to the local dining scene, this charming, intimate French restaurant with its rose-and-green country-manor decor could be a setting in an oldfashioned romantic novel. Fresh flowers adorn the well-spaced tables. The extensive menu concentrates on seafood, beef, and fowl prepared in the traditional French manner; some dishes reflect a Bahamian influence. Recommended specialties include *la tortue claire "Lady Curzon"* (turtle soup with curry cream and cheese straws) and *le carré d'agneau roti aux aromes de Provence* (a tender rack of lamb for two). A tuxedoed waiter will skillfully flambé your dessert alongside the table. *Holiday Inn, tel. 809/373–1333. Reservations advised. Jacket required. AE, CB, DC, MC, V. Dinner only. Closed Tues.*

Captain's Charthouse. In the oldest restaurant in Lucaya, you can enjoy an attractive view of the treetops and also watch the chef prepare the house specialties—lobster tail, pepper and sirloin steak, and prime rib—in the middle of a low-key dining room. Portions tend to be generous, and a large salad bar is also available. Old sea charts and marine-life paintings on the walls contribute to the nautical ambience. The Mates Lounge has long been a gathering place for local residents. The owner will be happy to pick up diners at their hotels in his van and return them afterward. *E. Sunrise Hwy. and Beachway Dr., tel. 809/ 373–3900. Reservations advised. Dress: casual. AE, MC, V.*

★ **Luciano's.** One of the best places for fine dining on the island, this sophisticated Port Lucaya restaurant specializes in Italian and French cuisine, served under the expert eye of owner Luciano Guindani, who formerly ran the Arawak dining room at the Lucaya Country Club. The large dining room, which overlooks the waterway, offers a modern decor of halogen lamps and abstract paintings. You can't go wrong with the house specialty, veal Luciano, which is topped with shrimp, lobster, and a spicy cream sauce. *Port Lucaya Marketplace, tel. 809/373–9100. Reservations required. Jacket required. AE, MC, V.*

★ **Les Oursins.** The pride and joy of the Lucayan Beach Resort, this distinguished establishment offers gracious Continental cuisine with a Gallic accent in a refined, burgundy-and-white dining room. The name of this restaurant means "sea urchins," and sea-urchin shells have been cleverly modeled into the light fixtures; elegant floral prints grace the walls. Some of the recommended dishes include grilled frogs' legs with Malaysian rice, stuffed lobster Thermidor, fillet of sole in champagne sauce, and black Angus sirloin steak with a green peppercorn sauce. *Lucayan Beach Resort & Casino, tel. 809/373–7777. Reservations required. Jacket required. AE, MC, V.*

Moderate **Britannia Pub.** This jovial, British-style bar/restaurant, founded in 1968, features mock-Tudor decor, a beamed ceiling, and the inevitable dart boards. Locals and tourists enjoy English beer at the bronze-surfaced bar. Because one of the owners, Takis Telecano, is Greek, the menu features, alongside the Bahamian seafood and traditional English fare, such Greek dishes as shish kebab and moussaka. *King's Rd., Bell Channel, tel. 809/373–5919. Reservations advised. Dress: casual. AE, MC, V.*

Jambah's Caribbean/Bahamian Restaurant, Jerk Pit and Lounge. A Jamaican touch pervades this unusual, upbeat dining spot decorated with tropical paintings and potted flowers. Reggae music plays jauntily in the background. The menu features Jamaican jerk pork, chicken, and fish (covered in herbs and cooked slowly over a coal fire), Bahamian dishes, and Caribbean-style drinks. You can bet the bread will be fresh, because the restaurant has its own bakery. Ice cream provides the basis for irresistible high-calorie desserts. *E. Sunrise Hwy., tel. 809/373–1240. No reservations. Dress: casual. AE, MC, V.*

Lucaya Lobster and Steak House. Diners can choose from a half-dozen meat selections (including center-cut pork chops, prime ribs, and New York strip steak) and eight seafood combinations in this large, rustic restaurant with an open grill. Both locals and tourists appreciate the economical early-bird specials (served 4–6:30 PM) featuring steak and lobster paired with peas 'n' rice and salad. For families, this place is one of the best buys around. *Midshipman and King's rds., tel. 809/373–5101. No reservations. Dress: casual. AE, MC, V.*

The Stoned Crab. This comfortable, informal local favorite, with its 14-story, pyramid-roof, faces one of the island's loveliest stretches of sand, Taino Beach. The scrumptiously sweet, fist-sized stone crabs are locally caught, and so are the lobsters. The Delmonico and pepper steaks are also well prepared. In fair weather, diners can enjoy the delightful ocean view from the outdoor patio. *Taino Beach, tel. 809/373-1442. Reservations advised. Dress: casual. AE, MC, V. Dinner only.*

Inexpensive–
Moderate
Hibiscus Brasserie. Located in the Lucayan Beach Resort close to the casino, this simple coffee shop serves reliable, good food at reasonable prices. The breakfast and lunch menu combines standard American and island fare. For dinner, try one of the Bahamian creations; these include pumpkin soup served with minced lobster, and red pea soup paired with strips of veal and shrimp. The service is both friendly and efficient, so this is a good place to stop for a quick cup of coffee or a three-course meal. *Lucayan Beach Resort & Casino, tel. 809/373-7777. Reservations advised for dinner. Dress: casual. AE, DC, MC, V.*

Inexpensive
Fatman's Nephew. Owner Stanley Simmons named his restaurant for his two rotund uncles who taught him the restaurant trade. One of the better spots to dine in Port Lucaya, this relaxed place serves substantial Bahamian fare. The best area to sit is on the L-shaped alfresco terrace overlooking the waterway and marina. The menu is somewhat limited, but the value for the price can't be beat. Try the Southern-style ham hocks, cracked conch, or curried beef. For the less adventurous, the menu also includes good old American hamburgers. *Port Lucaya Marketplace, tel. 809/373-8520. Reservations not necessary. Dress: casual. AE, MC.*

Pusser's Co. Store and Pub. Fashioned after an old Welsh pub, this amiable establishment overlooking Port Lucaya is part bar, part restaurant, and part maritime museum. Its name derives from the term applied to the daily rum ration that used to be issued by the "Pusser" (navy slang for "Purser") to British sailors. The nautical-theme decor also incorporates antique copper measuring cups and Tiffany lamps suspended from the wood-beam ceiling. A mechanical furry creature called Mr. Pusser plays honky-tonk music on a computerized piano. Locals swap tall tales and island gossip with tourists as they people-watch and drink the rum-based Pusser's Painkillers. The outside terrace is the most popular area in which to dine. Solid English fare is favored, such as shepherd's pie, fisherman's pie, and steak and ale pie. Other recommended dishes include double-cut lamb chops, Bahamian lobster tail, and strip sirloin. *Port Lucaya Marketplace, tel. 809/373-8450. Reservations not necessary. Dress: casual. AE, MC, V.*

Outside Freeport

Expensive
Buccaneer Club. The oldest restaurant on the island, this festive place on the way to the West End, a 20-minute drive from Freeport, features good Bahamian and Swiss cuisine in a rustic chalet setting. Barbecued dishes are also served at lunch. You may wish to time your arrival to toast the sunset from the uncluttered mile-long beach nearby. (The restaurant will pick you up if you're without a car.) *Deadman's Reef, tel. 809/348-3794. Reservations required. Dress: casual. AE, MC, V.*

Moderate
Club Caribe. This attractive, small eatery on the beach provides the ideal spot in which to unwind. Relax with a Bahama Mama drink, or dine on the local fare, such as minced Bahamian lobster, grouper, or steamed pork chops. (Free transportation will be provided from your hotel if you're carless.) *Mather's*

Town, off Midshipman Rd., tel. 809/373-6866. Reservations required. Dress: casual. AE, MC, V.

Inexpensive **Harry's American Bar.** This rustic neighbor of the Buccaneer Club (*see* above) is one of those simple pop-in-for-lunch places on the way to or from the West End. The unadorned menu includes hamburgers and fish and chips. *Deadman's Reef, tel. 809/348-6263. No reservations. Dress: casual. No credit cards.*

Lodging

By Laurie Senz   On Grand Bahama Island, visitors can choose among approximately 2,900 rooms and suites, ranging from attractive one- and two-bedroom units in sprawling resort complexes to practical apartments with kitchenettes to comfortable rooms in economy-oriented establishments. Most of the higher-priced hotels in Freeport and Lucaya were built within the last three decades and have managed to maintain their appeal to customers through continual renovation over the years. Those visitors who enjoy lying on the beach will probably opt for Lucaya; their incidental wants, such as gambling and shopping, are close at hand. Travelers whose priorities focus on gambling and shopping will more likely enjoy Freeport; if they want to go to the beach, their hotels will provide complimentary transportation. Small apartment complexes and time-sharing rentals are also popular alternatives, especially if you're planning to stay for more than a few days.

All of the larger hotels offer honeymoon packages, and several of them also offer special deals in three-, four-, or seven-day money-saving packages to golfers, gamblers, and other vacationers. Families will find that almost every hotel, even the small economy ones, offers baby-sitting services. Some also allow children under 12 to stay in a room for free and will even provide a crib or rollaway bed at no extra charge. Hotel rates tend to be lower than in Nassau, Cable Beach, and Paradise Island.

Highly recommended hotels in each price category are indicated by a star ★.

An 8% tax is added to your hotel bill, representing resort and government levies. Some hotels may add a $2–$3 for maid service and use of pool. Rates for stays between April 15 and December 14 tend to be 25%–30% lower than those during the rest of the year.

Category	Cost*
Expensive	over $125
Moderate	$85–$125
Inexpensive	under $85

Prices are for a standard double room, excluding tax and service charges.

Freeport

Expensive **Bahamas Princess Resort & Casino.** This complex consists of
★   two sister resorts separated by a roadway, two 18-hole champi-

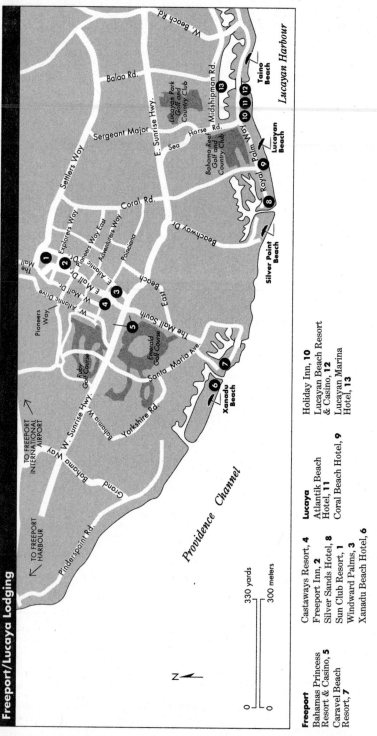

Freeport/Lucaya Lodging

118

Freeport
Bahamas Princess Resort & Casino, **5**
Caravel Beach Resort, **7**
Castaways Resort, **4**
Freeport Inn, **2**
Silver Sands Hotel, **8**
Sun Club Resort, **1**
Windward Palms, **3**
Xanadu Beach Hotel, **6**

Lucaya
Atlantik Beach Hotel, **11**
Coral Beach Hotel, **9**
Holiday Inn, **10**
Lucayan Beach Resort & Casino, **12**
Lucayan Marina Hotel, **13**

onship golf courses, a beach club, and a 20,000-square-foot Moorish-style domed casino. As a whole, the complex offers good service, with an activities hostess who coordinates a daily schedule of events and games for both children and adults. The International Bazaar is located nearby for serious shoppers. Those who prefer a beach over a pool, however, must take a free bus shuttle (which runs every half hour) over to the resort's beach club, which is also used by several other hotels. Guests may also take advantage of a dining plan at eight restaurants and special packages for golfers and honeymooners.

Princess Tower. Located next door to the casino, this 10-story building is the quieter of the two properties because most of its guests are usually gambling. Its dramatic, Moorish-style design features turrets, arches, and a dazzling white dome. When you enter the oversize, octagonal lobby, you may feel like you've been transported to a sultan's palace; the lobby has Portuguese emerald and royal-blue floor tiles, a soaring colonnade of ash-white arabesque arches, green-and-gold wallpaper, and a 28-foot-high domed center. The large rooms, however, are strictly contemporary, offering soft mauve decor, mirrored closets, framed watercolor prints, and oakwash wood furniture.

Princess Country Club. This 565-room, tropically landscaped property, which is across the street from the Princess Tower, attracts a lively, mixed crowd of serious golfers, families, and couples who enjoy sports. Everything here is designed on a gargantuan scale, except for the rooms, which are average size. The resort features tiered waterfalls cascading down from a man-made rock formation that rises from the center of an enormous pool. Eight two- and three-story guest-room wings radiate outward like the spokes of a wheel from the circular deck around the pool area. The comfortable rooms in wings 2, 4, and 7 were refurbished two years ago with modern vanities and baths, emerald-green carpets, muted floral-print bedspreads and drapes, beige wallpaper, and oakwash wood furniture. Wings 1, 3, and 8 offer rooms with plain wood furniture and tile floors instead of carpeting. Two full wings have been converted to time-sharing kitchen apartments under the name Princess Vacation Club International. *Address for Princess Tower and Princess Country Club: Box F 2623, Freeport, tel. 809/352–9661 or 800/223–1818 in the United States. 965 rooms (including 35 suites). Facilities: 2 pools (one with a swim-up bar), 8 restaurants, 6 bars and lounges, 12 tennis courts, 10K jogging trail, fitness center, sauna, 2 hot tubs, 2 beauty parlors, room service, tour desk, the Ruby and the Emerald par-72 golf courses, 2 children's playgrounds, gift shops, Sultan's Tent disco, Casino Royale theater. AE, DC, MC, V.*

Moderate–Expensive **Xanadu Beach Hotel.** This upscale high-rise hotel, whose recent renovations are expected to be finished by summer 1990, has a new pink exterior and turquoise balconies. The resort is still remembered as one of the final hideaways of eccentric billionaire Howard Hughes; he bequeathed his book collection to a room off the lobby, which has been converted into a library with a tour desk. The hotel consists of two sections, a 13-floor tower and a three-story pool wing. At press time, the tower rooms were all in the process of refurbishing. Each of the cheerful, pool-wing cabana rooms offers blue or burnt-orange carpeting, butterfly-print bedspreads and drapes, a walk-in closet, a large vanity area, and a terrace. A short walk away, guests have access to a wide beach, dotted with coconut palms and tiki huts; it is flanked on both sides by thick Australian pines. The Escoffier restaurant, formerly Howard Hughes's private dining room, is noted for its fine French cuisine. *Box F 2438, Freeport, tel. 809/352–6782, 800/327–0787, or 800/333–3333. 183 rooms. Facilities: complete water-sports center on beach, marina with boat and fishing charters, pool, 3 tennis courts, 3 restaurants, 2 bars/lounges. AE, CB, DC, MC, V.*

Moderate   **Caravel Beach Resort.** Divers, families, or foursomes on tight budgets will enjoy this 12-unit (each with two bedrooms, 1½ baths) bilevel apartment-style hotel, as long as they don't mind being away from just about everything and are oblivious to the rather run-down furnishings. The small rooms have old but fully equipped kitchens. A real plus, though, are the two balconies, one off each upstairs bedroom. Everything here is basic, but the service is helpful and friendly. A cramped front area doubles as a lobby and a small, inexpensive restaurant. The hotel is adjacent to a long, narrow strand of beach. Guests will need a rental car because shops, restaurants, casinos, and sporting activities are not nearby, and taxis can get expensive. *8 Port-of-Call Dr., Bahama Terrace, Freeport, tel. 809/352–4896. 12 units. Facilities: restaurant, kitchens, TV, Laundromat, barbecue pit. MC, V.*

Silver Sands Hotel. If you're looking for a well-designed room with a complete kitchen, a pleasant beach, and a location that's near Freeport or Lucaya, this fairly quiet hotel will suit you perfectly. The three buildings are clustered around two pools with the lobby located in a separate building below the Phoenix restaurant. The recently redone studios situated in two four-story buildings are currently nicer than the one-bedroom suites by the second pool. These studios have soothing, earthtone decor and two double beds facing each other, separated by a butcher-block table. The best rooms may be found on the fourth floor and offer tweed Berber rugs, vaulted ceilings, and large blue-and-white stained-glass skylight windows. The unrenovated kitchens and bathrooms are clean and functional. Every room also has its own balcony or patio. On Monday nights, a free poolside manager's cocktail party is held. The narrow beach, only a 100-yard walk away, features tiki huts for those seeking shade, a dive and snorkel shop, and a beach bar and grill. The hotel is a half-mile from the Port Lucaya Marketplace and the Lucayan Beach Resort & Casino. *Box F 2385, Royal Palm Way, Bahamas Reef, Freeport, tel. 809/327–5700 or 800/327–0787. 164 rooms, including 144 studios and 20 1-bedroom suites. Facilities: color TV, 2 pools, 2 tennis courts, snorkeling and diving, 2 restaurants, 2 bars, shuffleboard courts. AE, MC, V.*

Inexpensive–   **Castaways Resort.** The exterior of this family-run, four-story
Moderate   establishment resembles a wide, unadorned Chinese pagoda and is painted deep coral. About as close to the action as you can get, the hotel is located next door to the International Bazaar and only a short walk away from the Bahamas Princess Casino. The lively lobby offers a boutique, a souvenir shop, four tour operators, and a small video game room. The hotel's two buildings are connected by walkways over garden courtyards filled with royal palms and flowering bushes. The large pool has a sun deck offering some privacy. Beach lovers can take a free shuttle to Xanadu Beach, which the Bahamas Princess guests also use. The average-size, motellike rooms vary in price according to

location; the most expensive rooms, situated near the pool on the ground floor, feature white furniture. Children under 12 can stay in rooms at no additional charge. Every night except Sunday, fire-eaters and limbo dancers perform in a popular show at the hotel's Yellow Bird nightclub. *Box F 2629, Freeport, tel. 809/352–6682 or 800/327–0787. 130 rooms. Facilities: pool, restaurant, bar, video game room, nightclub. AE, DC, MC, V.*

Freeport Inn. This busy 26-year-old budget hotel—clean, simple and centrally located—is popular with guests on short vacations. The four three-story buildings have white balustraded balconies, jalousied windows, and turquoise doors in need of a paint job. The average-size rooms, which were recently renovated, are decorated in earth tones; televisions are available on a rental basis. Because most guests opt for the free shuttle service to Xanadu Beach, which is 2½ miles away, the less inviting small pool and sundeck area tend to be quiet. The noise from the hotel's popular nightclub, which features a live band nightly and a twice-weekly show, may disturb you, depending on the location of your room. The inn is situated only a block from the town center, and it's a mile from the Bahamas Princess Casino and the International Bazaar. *Box F 200, tel. 809/352–6648 or 800/327–0787. 147 rooms (52 with kitchenettes). Facilities: pool with snack bar, restaurant, nightclub, tour desk, bicycle and scooter rentals. AE, MC, V.*

Windward Palms. Business types frequent this quiet, low-rise, coral-colored hotel because of its proximity to the commercial area of downtown. The grounds feature plenty of cabbage palms and green shrubs. The rooms here have been built around a rectangular courtyard with an L-shaped pool in the center; several of them are still in the process of renovation. The ones located in the left wing as you enter the courtyard are recommended; these rooms offer light wood furniture, blue-gray carpeting, and pink-and-blue shell-pattern bedspreads and drapes. Unfortunately, the bathrooms still need overhauling, and the hotel lobby is also a bit run-down. Nevertheless, this is still a pleasant place for the budget-minded, with a small bar patronized by a local crowd. *Box F 2549, Freeport, tel. 809/352–8821 or 800/327–0787. 100 rooms (all with 2 double beds). Facilities: pool, restaurant. AE, MC, V.*

Inexpensive **Sun Club Resort.** Only a few blocks from downtown, this two-story family-run establishment, housed in a white building with brown shutters, is a peaceful spot for economy-minded tourists and an excellent value for those traveling with children. The rooms are clean, comfortable, and functional, with two double beds, a small but complete kitchen, dark wood furniture, vinyl upholstered chairs, and wall-to-wall carpeting. A free shuttle service to the beach runs every hour. Children under age 12 can stay with their parents for free, and rollaway beds are provided at no extra cost. The hotel also offers a pleasant pool area and sundeck, an immaculate lawn where kids can play, a small lounge, and a restaurant open for all meals. *Box F 1808, Freeport, tel. 809/352–3462 or 800/327–0787. 48 rooms (40 with kitchens). Facilities: color TV, pool, restaurant, tennis court, beauty salon, Laundromat, tour desk, bicycle and scooter rentals. AE, MC, V.*

Lucaya

Expensive ★ **Lucayan Beach Resort & Casino.** Since the '60s, this 16-acre, low-rise complex has been considered a class act, but in recent years, unfortunately, it lost a lot of its sparkle. Then the Bahamian government asked a savvy management company to supervise the resort's much-needed multimillion-dollar renovation, which is still in progress. The grounds now have a natural, lush tropical look to replace what was once a wilderness of pine trees and limestone. The resort has stone exterior walls and a white lighthouse on the roof that has become a Lucayan landmark. Its long, narrow stretch of pristine sand, dotted with tiki huts, has kept guests coming back for years. A sundeck and a large pool area, shaded by sea grape and palm trees, are also available. The luxuriously refurbished North Wing rooms boast gray marble bathrooms, silvery-green carpets, white furniture, and wicker chairs. The more expensive Lanai Wing rooms offer king-size beds with half-moon bamboo headboards, minirefrigerators, mauve carpeting, large patios, and superb views of the ocean. Every room in the resort has a water view, either of the sea, the bay, or the wide canal leading into the bay. The staff here is friendly and efficient. A daily activities program for children and adults includes a morning exercise class, Bahamian dance lessons, treasure hunts, and limbo contests. In the evening, guests can dine at the gourmet French restaurant Les Oursins, gamble at the casino, or attend a Las Vegas–style revue at its Flamingo Showcase Theatre. The complex is right near the Port Lucaya Marketplace and UNEXSO, the renowned diving school. *Box F 336, Freeport/ Lucaya, tel. 809/373–7777 or 800/772–1227. 247 rooms (including 10 suites). Facilities: 20,000-square-foot casino, 5 restaurants, 3 lounges/bars, beach, pool, 4 tennis courts, watersports center, nearby golf courses, video game room, small shopping arcade, beauty salon. AE, MC, V.*

Moderate– Expensive **Atlantik Beach Hotel.** The only high-rise in the Lucayan area, this Swiss-owned, 16-story hotel is particularly popular with both the European crowd and couples of all ages. A recently completed four-year renovation overhauled the lobby as well as the arcade, pool, and beach areas. Most of the rooms have been refurbished with remote-control televisions and mauve-and-burgundy carpets, drapes, and bedspreads, but only the 52 suites have brand-new furniture. The best rooms, above the 10th floor, have views of either the bay or the ocean. Honeymooners will enjoy the romantic, island-theme decor of the spacious, one-bedroom bilevel suites. The hotel offers a friendly staff and a relaxed ambience; in high season, the hotel never feels crowded. Outside, lush vegetation and palm trees line a tiled walkway that leads to a large pool, a sundeck, and a Jacuzzi overlooking the private beach. In addition, the only windsurfing school on the island and a complete water-sports facility are located on the premises. Guests get a $10 discount on greens fees at the Lucayan Golf and Country Club. Both the Port Lucaya Marketplace and the Lucayan Beach Resort & Casino are nearby. *Box F 531, Freeport, tel. 809/373–1444 or 800/ 622–6770. 175 rooms (including 52 1- and 2-bedroom suites with refrigerators. Facilities: pool, Jacuzzi, beach, water sports, tennis, golf, shopping arcade, 2 restaurants, Viennese Table snack bar, 2 lounges/bars. AE, DC, MC, V.*

Holiday Inn. Although it still exudes a family atmosphere, this sprawling four-story resort, in the shape of a broad Y, is a lot more elaborate than your average Holiday Inn; it will especially appeal to anyone who loves to party all the time. A number of shops (including a perfumery, a pharmacy, and a jewelry store) line the long lobby, which is unfortunately furnished like the common room of a college dormitory. The best rooms (called Hibiscus) are located in the C wing; they have been sleekly redone in Bahamian decor, featuring thick sea-green carpeting, vivid bedspreads and drapes, and lavender walls and furniture. The majority of the other rooms need to be refurbished. Children and adults have a wide selection of activities, such as sand-castle building, treasure hunts, fashion shows, and Bahamian bingo. At night, you can attend Bahamian luaus at the Beach Pavilion, listen to calypso music at the Poinciana Lounge, or dance at Panache, a popular nightclub. The hotel also offers a wide, immaculate beach and Le Bouquet, a French restaurant. *Box F 2496, Freeport, tel. 809/373–1333 or 800/HOLIDAY. 504 rooms. Facilities: beach, pool, tennis, small exercise room, shopping arcade, beauty parlor, disco, 2 lounges/bars, children's playground, 2 restaurants, poolside snack bar. AE, CB, DC, MC, V.*

Inexpensive **Coral Beach Hotel.** Only 11 units of this large condominium are rented as hotel accommodations. The three seven-story buildings are shaped in a horseshoe with the mouth facing the ocean. The property isn't recommended for families with children or young singles; no entertainment or activities are available on the premises, and there's not much tolerance for noise. However, older, budget-minded travelers who want a quiet, place to stay should find the place adequate. The rather austere rooms, which are spacious and reasonably priced, have old furniture and no phone. Rattan love seats and chairs decorate the cheerful lobby. The pool is large and overlooks a wide, clean beach, marked with tiki huts; there's also a poolside snack bar. Both the Port Lucaya Marketplace and the Lucayan Beach Resort & Casino are a five-minute cab ride away. If you stay one week or longer, you'll get up to 20% off the listed prices. *Box F 2468, Freeport, tel. 809/373–2468. 11 rooms (5 have balconies and complete kitchens). Facilities: pool, beach, 2 restaurants, snack bar, 2 bars, gift shop. AE, MC.*

Lucayan Marina Hotel. This reasonably priced establishment with average-size, comfortable rooms is only a block away from the Lucayan Golf and Country Club. Guests here can use all the facilities available at its big sister, the Lucayan Beach Resort & Casino, for free; every half-hour, free ferry transportation is offered across the channel to the larger resort. This hotel is ideal for divers involved in the UNEXSO program and for yachting enthusiasts; it offers 150 full-service marina slips. *Box F 336, Freeport, tel. 809/373–6916 or 800/772–1227. 142 rooms. Facilities: pool, whirlpool, restaurant, bar. AE, MC, V.*

East End

Moderate **Deep Water Cay Club.** This property offers a chance to get away from it all with a handful of adequately furnished guest cottages scattered along the beach on a private island. Daily activities center on the main lodge, which houses the dining room, a self-service bar, and a tackle shop. Besides lounging on the beach, diving, fishing, and boating are the only diversions here. Guests can participate in some of the best bonefishing in the Bahamas, and there's a 20-mile barrier reef nearby. The resort has its own airstrip, to which guests fly in twice a week (Monday and Friday) from West Palm Beach. *Box 1145, Palm Beach, FL 33480, tel. 407/684–3958. 12 cottages. Facilities: restaurant, bar. AE, MC, V.*

Time Sharing

A number of condominiums in Freeport/Lucaya have become involved in time-sharing operations. Contact any of the following for information about rentals:

Bahama Reef (Box F 2695, Freeport, tel. 809/373–5580). Eleven one-bedroom units and a three-bedroom penthouse are available on a canal 3½ miles from the beach. Visitors have access to bicycles and motor boats.

Dundee Bay Villas (Box F 2690, Freeport, tel. 809/352–4222). These rentals include one-, two-, and three-bedroom units on the beach next to the Xanadu Beach Hotel.

Freeport Resort & Club (Box F 2514, Freeport, tel. 809/352–5371). The apartments here are located in a woodsy setting close to the International Bazaar and the Bahamas Princess Casino.

Lakeview Manor Club (Box F 2699, Freeport, tel. 809/352–2283). One- and two-bedroom apartments are available by the fairway of the fifth hole of the Ruby Golf Course.

Mayfield Beach and Tennis Club (Box F 458, Freeport, tel. 809/352–9776). The rentals here consist of apartments with a pool and tennis court on Port-of-Call Drive at Xanadu Beach.

Ocean Reef Resort and Yacht Club (Box F 898, Freeport, tel. 809/373–4661). These three-bedroom, three-bath apartments are situated close to the International Bazaar, the Bahamas Princess Casino, and golf courses. The resort has a marina and a pool.

For information about other homes, apartments, and condominiums for rent, check with Timesales (Bahamas) Ltd. (Box F 2656, Freeport, tel. 809/352–7039), or with Caribbean International Realty (Box F 2489, Freeport, tel. 809/352–8795).

The Arts and Nightlife

Theater

The **Freeport Players' Guild** (tel. 809/352–5165), a nonprofit repertory company, produces four plays a year during its September–June season at the 400-seat Regency Theatre. The **Freeport Friends of the Arts** (tel. 809/373–1528) sponsors plays and musicals between November and May. A local amateur group, the **Grand Bahama Players,** produces a few Bahamian comedies each year. Tourist information centers (*see* Essential Information, above) have details on this group's performances.

Nightlife

Evening and late-night entertainment on Grand Bahama encompasses steel-drum bands, calypso music, discos, live music for dancing at hotel lounges, and lavish sequins-and-feathers revues straight out of Las Vegas. The major hotels usually organize their own late night entertainment. Nightclubs are open generally from 8 or 9 PM until 3 AM.

Bahamas Princess Country Club has the International Show musical revue on Wednesdays and the Goombay Festival, with a live calypso band and dinner, on Saturdays. *Tel. 809/352– 6721. Open evenings 6:30–9:30.*

Bahamas Princess Tower features a disco with multicolored lights that snake up and down mirrored columns on a stainless-steel dance floor, as well as whirling ceiling lights. *Tel. 809/ 352–9661. Open nightly 9 PM–3 AM.*

Casino Royale Show Room at the Bahamas Princess Resort & Casino puts on a twice-nightly French-style extravaganza, with glamorous costumes, dancing, and novelty acts. *Tel. 809/ 352–6721. Shows at 8:30 and 10:45. Reservations advised.*

Flamingo Showcase Theatre at the Lucayan Beach Resort & Casino rivals the Casino Royale at the Bahamas Princess with its twice-nightly, colorfully plumed revues, which include comedy acts. *Tel. 809/373–7777. Shows at 8:30 and 10:30. Reservations advised.*

Mates Lounge in the Captain's Charthouse Restaurant (tel. 809/373–3900) is where local residents meet to drink and dance to calypso music.

Panache at the Holiday Inn is a favorite nightclub, with dancing to a local reggae-calypso band. The hotel also has theme nights, with Bahamian festivals and Caribbean luaus. *Tel. 809/ 373–1333. Open 9 PM–3 AM.*

Port Lucaya Marketplace has become one of the liveliest places to be after dark, with live entertainment and calypso music at the Centre Bandstand from 8 PM till midnight and after.

Sir Winston Churchill Pub, next to the Strawmarket at the International Bazaar, specializes in theme nights: free champagne on Monday's Ladies Night; Gong Show, with prizes, on Wednesday; and Golden Oldie Night on Thursday. Every night, there's music to go along with the 5–7 happy hour. *Tel. 809/352–8866. Open nightly until 2 AM.*

Yellow Bird Showroom at the Castaways Resort has one of Grand Bahama's best shows of local performers, with calypso, limbo, and fire dancers. *Tel. 809/352–6682. Open nightly, except Tues., from 8.*

Yellow Elder Evening Bar at the Atlantik Beach Hotel has a calypso band and special theme nights, with a limbo competition on Mondays. *Tel. 809/373–1444. Open nightly 5 PM–2 AM.*

If you're after disco action, head for **Studio 69** (Midshipman Rd., tel. 809/373–2158), the **Connection Room** (E. Atlantic Dr., tel. 809/352–8666), **Lights** (Castaways Resort, E. Mall Dr. and W. Mall, tel. 809/352–6682), and **Orbit** (Pioneer's Way, tel. 809/ 352–8094).

Casinos   Whatever day and night activities are offered in Freeport and Lucaya, there's no doubt that the two casinos are among the area's top attractions. They offer a bewildering array of slot machines, aside from the temptations of the crap and blackjack tables, roulette, and baccarat. The last game is a special favorite with the high-rollers, because thousands of dollars often are staked on one hand. Dress in both casinos is casual, though you're not allowed to enter them in bare feet or in beach attire. You must also be at least 18 to gamble.

The 20,000-square-foot **Princess Casino,** with its flamboyant Moorish-style dome, has 450 slot machines (most are now computerized to the point where you can press a button and an attendant will come running with change), 40 blackjack tables, eight dice tables, eight roulette wheels, two money wheels, and assorted video games. The elevated circular bar is a great place from which to watch both the casino action and the live entertainment from the bandstand area. *Bahamas Princess Resort, W. Sunrise Hwy., tel. 809/352–7811, or 800/422–7466 in the United States. Open 9 AM–3:30 AM.*

The **Lucayan Beach Casino** covers exactly the same area as its rival, with 550 super slots, poker and video blackjack, and roughly the same number of tables for the other assorted games. Renovations begun recently were slated to include more slot machines and new games. Novices are invited to take free gaming lessons at the casino at 11 AM and 7 PM. The casino bar boasts "the longest happy hour in Grand Bahama," with 99-cent drinks from 11 AM until 7 PM. *Lucayan Beach Resort, Lucaya Beach, tel. 809/373–7777, or 800/334–6175 in the United States. Open 9 AM–3 AM.*

5 The Family Islands

Introduction

The quiet, simple way of life of the Family Islands—known traditionally as the Out Islands—is startlingly different from the fast-paced, more glittery worlds of Nassau and Freeport. On the dozen or so islands equipped to handle tourists outside of New Providence and Grand Bahama, the traveler no longer has access to sophisticated nightclubs, casinos, fancy restaurants, bazaars, or shopping malls. Sportsmen and outdoor enthusiasts, however, are luckier for virtually all of the Family Islands feature good-to-excellent facilities for fishing, boating, and diving, and you will often have endless stretches of beach all to yourself. You won't find hotels that provide the kind of costly creature comforts you take for granted in Nassau and Freeport. Accommodations in the Family Islands are generally modest lodges, rustic cottages, and small inns with balustraded balconies; many are without telephones and air-conditioning, relying instead on ceiling fans and breezes from the sea. A 40-room hotel is considered large, so don't be surprised if you only have a choice of a few, minimally furnished rooms at two or three inns.

Roughing it in Inagua—just for example—is a small price to pay for the glorious spectacle of 20,000 pink flamingoes taking off into the bright blue sky. A trip to these islands usually means a stress-free experience, a period of tranquillity in a mostly unspoiled environment. The meals in your hotel will be cooked by a local resident, with freshly caught fish being the staple diet. On some of the smaller islands, making a phone call to friends back home, or receiving one, may require an extra trip to the local telephone station.

Betting on the size of the next fish, the depth of dive to come, or the length of the next drive replaces the roll of the dice or the turn of the card. A day of sightseeing often simply entails a stroll down narrow, sand-strewn streets in fishing villages, past small pastel-colored homes where orange, pink, and bright-red bougainvillea spill over the walls. The taverns are tiny and usually noisy with chatter, but you will make friends with the locals over a beer and a game of darts or pool much more quickly than you would in a big-city cocktail lounge. Nightlife may involve listening to a piano player in a clubhouse bar, a small village combo playing calypso, or a guitarist on a moonlit terrace. If you're a television addict, you may wish to stay home—at most places, if you don't bring your own set, you'll have to do without.

The Family Islands were once the domain mostly of yachtsmen and private plane owners; the tourist who discovered a favorite hideaway on Andros or in the Exumas would cherish it and return year after year to find the same faces as before. But the islands are slowly becoming more and more popular, largely due to increased airline activity. Indeed, the frequency of airline service may play a part in your choice of destination. A few islands are served from Nassau or Florida daily; others may only have a couple of incoming and outgoing flights a week. If you want to sample a Family Island without feeling completely cut off, you may want to choose a slightly busier spot that is closer to the mainland United States, such as Bimini, Eleuthera, or Great Abaco Island. If you go farther away from the mainland, to a place like Cat Island or San Salvador, you will experience a deeper sense of getting away from it all.

Essential Information

Important Addresses and Numbers

Air Ambulances There are 13 health centers and 26 clinics scattered throughout the islands, but in the event of emergency illnesses or accidents requiring fast transportation to the United States, **Air Ambulance Associates** (in the Bahamas, call the Peace and Plenty Hotel, Exuma, tel. 809/336–2551/2; in the U.S., tel. 800/432–4086) provides aero-medical services out of Fort Lauderdale International Airport. Its Learjet 35 and Cessna 414 are equipped with sophisticated medical equipment and a highly trained staff of doctors and nurses.

Tour Groups

The following companies specialize in Family Islands tours:

In the U.S. **Adventure Tours** (9818 Liberty Rd., Randallstown, MD 21133, tel. 800/638–9040), **Aero International Tours** (638 S.W. 34th St., Fort Lauderdale, FL 33315, tel. 800/468–9876), **Bahamas Express** (545 8th Ave., New York, NY 10018, tel. 800/722–4262), **Cavalcade Tours** (450 Harmon Meadow Blvd., Box 1568, Secaucus, NJ 07096, tel. 800/521–2310), **Certified Tours** (Box 22350, Fort Lauderdale, FL 33335, tel. 800/221–6666), **Family Island Holidays** (1855 West S.R. 434, Suite 230, Longwood, FL 32750, tel. 800/288–0506), **Funway Holidays** (8907 N. Port Washington Rd., Milwaukee, WI 53217, tel. 800/558–3000), **GWV Travel** (300 1st Ave., Needham Heights, MA 02194, tel. 800/225–5498), **Lib/Go Travel** (69 Spring St., Ramsey, NJ 07446, tel. 201/934–3500), **Trade Mark Tours/Wylly's Tours** (149 Sevilla Ave., Coral Gables, FL 33134, tel. 305/442–2008), and **Travel Center Tours** (5413 N. Lincoln Ave., Chicago, IL 60625, tel. 800/621–8188).

In Canada **Americanada** (139 Sauve Ouest, Montreal, Quebec H3L LY4, Canada, tel. 514/384–6431) and **Holiday House** (110 Richmond St. E, Suite 304, Toronto, Ontario M5C 1P1, Canada, tel. 416/364–2433).

Dining

For the most part in the Family Islands, you will dine in your hotel. Few fine restaurants exist in the islands (or in the hotels, for that matter), and generally the food is not up to the standards of New Providence and Grand Bahama islands. Entrées will run anywhere from $10 to $20 per person, including 15% gratuity, without drinks. (Lobster, which is found all over the islands, costs the same as a New York strip steak, which has to be imported.)

Lodging

The small hotels of the Family Islands are mostly owner-operated, which ensures the personal touch, such as the owner's greeting guests in the bar for cocktails in the evening. "The cluster" is a term that may be applied to a number of hotels that form a community, such as those on tiny Harbour Island in Eleuthera. Some hotels specialize in the sports of fishing or diving, such as Brown's Hotel on Bimini and Small Hope Bay Lodge on Andros. There are also self-contained resorts which offer their own sports facilities, such as the Cotton Bay Club on Eleuthera. When you make a reservation, be sure to find out if the hotel offers any special packages.

Although accommodations may be small and out of the way, do not be deceived into thinking your vacation in the Family Islands will necessarily be inexpensive. Escapism does not always come cheap, and there are several resorts—such as the Cotton Bay Club, and the Treasure Cay Beach Hotel and Villas on Treasure Cay—that are every bit as expensive as you'll find on Cable Beach or Paradise Island on New Providence Island, though they are the exceptions. Lack of conveniences, such as television, room phones, and air-conditioning, can mean lower rates.

You'll find the **Bahamas Reservation Service** (tel. 800/327–0787) invaluable. The BRS represents nearly every hotel in the islands, and its agents have access to all hotel information, including availability, through a computerized service. Its hours are Monday–Friday 9–6.

The **Family Islands Promotion Board** (255 Alhambra Circle, Suite 420, Coral Gables, FL 33134, tel. 305/446–4111) has a helpful staff that provides information about certain hotels in the islands. The board has a plentiful supply of colorful brochures that show the features and facilities of these hotels.

Two firms in the United States specialize in renting private homes and villas in the islands. **Bahamas Home Rentals** (230 Lawrence Ave., Pittsburgh, PA 15238, tel. 412/828–1048; ask for Virginia Wellman) has access to properties that rent from $450 to $2,100 a week, including use of linens, laundry, utilities, and pickup at airports whenever possible. A part-time cook and complimentary fishing trips are sometimes part of the package. Monthly rentals may be a third less than the combined weekly rates. **Island Services, Inc.** (750 S.W. 34th St., Suite 105, Fort Lauderdale, FL 33315, tel. 800/825–5099), also has homes, villas, and condominiums available for rental, as well as all-inclusive packages at a number of island resorts.

The peak season is mid-December–mid-April; after that, room rates tend to drop by as much as a third. The categories that follow apply to all of the Family Islands hotels. An 8% tax is added to your hotel bill, representing resort and government levies. Some hotels may add a small gratuity for maid service or use of pool.

Highly recommended lodgings in each price category are indicated by a star ★.

Category	Cost*
Very Expensive	over $175
Expensive	$125–$175

Moderate	$75–$125
Inexpensive	under $75

All prices are for a double room, excluding tax and service charges.

The Abacos

In the northeastern Bahamas, the Abacos, a boomerang-shaped cluster of cays, stretch from the tiny Walker's Cay in the north to Hole in the Wall, which is more than 130 miles away to the southwest. Many of these cays are very small, providing exquisitely desolate settings for private picnics. The Abacos have their fair share of tranquil bays and inlets, lagoons, and pine forests where wild boars roam, but they also offer the commercial center of Marsh Harbour, the third-largest community in the Bahamas, with all the amenities of a small city, including a selection of shops, restaurants, and hotels. The two main islands, Great Abaco and Little Abaco, are fringed on their windward shore by an emerald necklace of cays that forms a barrier reef against the broad Atlantic.

The Abacos' calm, naturally protected waters, long admired for their beauty, have helped the area become the sailing capital of the Bahamas. The islands' excellent resorts are particularly popular with yachtsmen and fishermen because of the fine boating facilities available, among them the Treasure Cay Marina, the Boat Harbor Marina at Marsh Harbour, and Walker's Cay Club Marina. Man-of-War Cay remains the boatbuilding center for the Bahamas; its residents turn out traditionally crafted wood dinghies as well as high-tech crafts made of fiberglass. The Abacos play host annually to internationally famous regattas at Green Turtle Cay and Treasure Cay and to a half-dozen game-fish tournaments. Outside of the resorts, the oceanside villages of Hope Town and New Plymouth also appeal to tourists for their charming New England–style ambience.

The Abacos' first settlers, New England Loyalists, arrived in 1783. Other families soon followed from Virginia and the Carolinas, bringing with them their plantation lifestyle and their slaves. These early arrivals tried to make a living from farming, but the Abacos' land was resistant to the growing of crops. Next, many settlers turned to the sea for sustenance; some of them started fishing, while others practiced "wrecking."

By the end of the 18th century, charts of the Bahamian waters had not been drawn, and there were no lighthouses in the area until 1836. The wreckers of the Abacos worked at night, shining misleading lights to lure ships to destruction onto rocks and shoals—and then seizing the ships' cargo. Of course, not all these wrecks were caused by unscrupulous islanders; some ships were lost in storms and foundered on hidden reefs as they passed through the Bahamas. Nevertheless, by fair means or foul, wrecking remained a thriving industry in the Abacos until the mid-1800s.

The notorious deeds of the wreckers have long faded into history and legend. Today, about 7,300 residents live peacefully in the Abacos. Many of these enterprising, friendly people are seafarers, earning an honest living as boat builders, fishermen, and fishing guides. Because the Abacos are one of the most visited destinations in the Family Islands, an increasing number of residents work in the tourist industry.

Arriving and Departing

By Plane
Airports/Airlines

The Abacos have three airports: at Treasure Cay and Marsh Harbour on Great Abaco Island, and at Walker's Cay, which is a private airstrip served by its own airline, **Walker's Cay Air** (tel. 800/327–3714), out of Fort Lauderdale. Family Islands airports do not have direct telephone communication, so inquiries have to be made through the individual hotels where tourists are staying. **Bahamasair** (tel. 800/222–4262), the national carrier, flies from Nassau daily to Treasure Cay and Marsh Harbour. **Aero Coach International** (tel. 800/327–0010), and **USAir** (tel. 800/251–5720) have several flights daily to the two airports from Miami and Fort Lauderdale. Canadians should check with their travel agents about occasional flights from Montreal to Treasure Cay.

By Boat

Premier Cruise Lines (Box 573, Cape Canaveral, FL 32920, tel. 809/327–7113) offers three- and four-day trips on the *Majestic*, which departs Fridays and Mondays from Port Canaveral to the Abacos. Passengers can explore Treasure Cay, Green Turtle Cay, Great Guana Cay, and Man-of-War Cay. Premier Cruise Lines requests that all reservations be made through travel agents.

By Mailboat

From Potter's Cay, Nassau, the M/V *Deborah K II* sails Wednesdays to Cherokee Sound, Cooper's Town, Grand Cay, Green Turtle Cay, Guana Cay, Hope Town, Man-of-War Cay, and Marsh Harbour; it arrives back in Nassau on Monday. The one-way trip takes seven hours. The M/V *Champion II*, also out of Potter's Cay, calls on Thursday at Sandy Point, Moore's Island, Crossing Rock, and Bullock's Harbour, returning to Nassau on Saturday. Schedules are subject to change due to weather conditions or occasional drydocking. For details, call the **Dock Master's office** (tel. 809/393–1064) at Potter's Cay.

Getting Around

By Car

Although you can explore the main city of the Abacos, Marsh Harbour on Great Abaco Island, by foot, you will need a car to see the rest of Great Abaco and the other main island, Little Abaco. In Marsh Harbour, you may rent automobiles from **H & L Car Rentals** (Box 490, tel. 809/367–2854), **Shell Gas Station** (Box 438, tel. 809/367–2854), **Byrona's Car Rental** (Box 579, tel. 809/367–2165), **Agatha Archer Car Rental** (Box 463, tel. 809/ 367–2148), and **Cubel Davis** (Murphy Town, tel. 809/367–2671).

By Taxi

Taxi services meet arriving planes at the airports to take visitors to their hotels or to the dock, where they can take a water taxi to neighboring islands such as Green Turtle Cay or Elbow Cay. Hotels will arrange for taxis to take guests on short trips and back to the airport. Sample fares: A combination taxi and water-taxi ride from Treasure Cay Airport to Green Turtle Cay costs $12. The ride from Marsh Harbour Airport to Hope Town on Elbow Cay costs $10.

Important Addresses and Numbers

Emergencies Most areas in the Abacos do not have direct long-distance dialing, and emergencies usually have to be reported to the hotel management. BaTelCo (the Bahamas Telecommunications Corporation), however, recently completed a new system of microwave relay stations in the Abacos which provides some direct-dial connections to the outside world without going through an operator.

Marsh Harbour: **Police,** tel. 919; **Fire,** tel. 809/362–2000.

Medical Clinics The **Marsh Harbour** clinic (tel. 809/366–4010) has a resident doctor and a nurse. The **Treasure Cay clinic** (tel. 809/367–2570) has its own doctor.

Opening and Closing Times

Banks are located at Marsh Harbour and Treasure Cay on Great Abaco Island, New Plymouth on Green Turtle Cay, Hope Town on Elbow Cay, and on Man-of-War Cay. These banks are generally open Monday–Thursday 9:30–1, and Friday 9–5.

Guided Tours

In Marsh Harbour, **Albury's Ferry Service** (tel. 809/367–2306), at the dock near the Great Abaco Beach Hotel, offers expeditions to Hope Town, Man-of-War Cay, and Great Guana Cay and longer sightseeing trips to Treasure Cay and Green Turtle Cay. From Treasure Cay, the **Green Turtle Cay Ferry Service,** which has no telephone and must be contacted through the Treasure Cay Beach Hotel and Villas (tel. 809/367–2538), visits several areas on Green Turtle Cay.

Exploring the Abacos

Numbers in the margin correspond with points of interest on the Abacos map.

Great Abaco Island
Marsh Harbour
❶ Most visitors to the Abacos make their first stop on the east coast of Great Abaco Island at **Marsh Harbour,** the third-largest city in the Bahamas and the commercial center of the islands, with its own airport. Marsh Harbour, considered by boatmen to be one of the easiest harbors to enter, offers several fine full-service marinas, such as the 140-slip Boat Harbour Marina and the 65-slip Conch Inn Marina. This peaceful community is a good place to stock up on groceries and supplies on the way to other islands because its downtown area features several well-equipped supermarkets, department and hardware stores, banks, gas stations, and a few good, moderately priced restaurants.

The whole town can be explored on foot. The main street, where most of the gift shops are located, has the island's only traffic light. The **Loyalist Shoppe** (tel. 809/367–2701) specializes in pottery, china, and leather goods from England, Italy, and Poland. Situated near the harbor, **John Bull** (tel. 809/367–2473) is a branch of a leading Nassau shop where you can purchase watches and perfumes. Two restaurants worth sampling are the locally popular **Cynthia's Kitchen** (809/367–2268), which

The Abacos

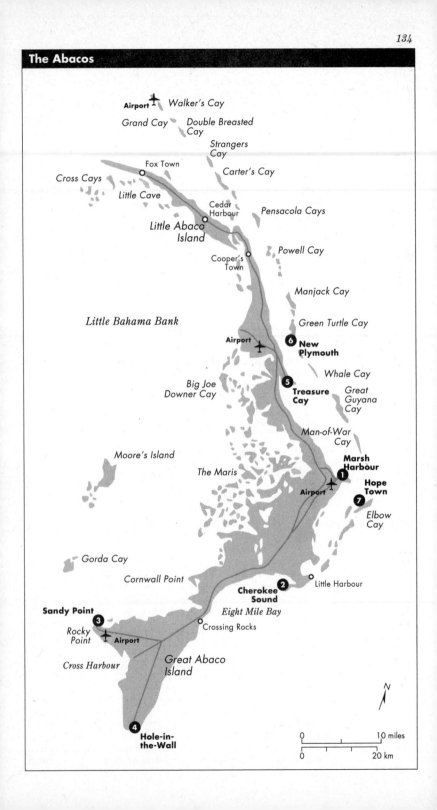

serves Bahamian fare, and the recently opened **Mangoes** (tel.
809/367–2366), a seafood dining spot located right on the active
harbor. Overlooking the town, on a hilltop, stands a miniature
castle built by Dr. Evans Cottman, a U.S. scientist who lived
on the island for many years and wrote about his experiences in
Out Island Doctor.

Time Out   For an inexpensive snack, pop into **Lovely's Pizza** (tel. 809/367–
2710) for a homemade pizza, hot patties (spicy beef sealed in a
light dough and deep-fried), fried chicken, or a crawfish burger, all made by owner Lovely Reckley. You can eat at one of two
picnic tables set up outside the eatery, which is open Monday–
Saturday.

Visitors to Marsh Harbour in November may wish to participate in the **Abaco Week Festival,** which commemorates the
arrival of the Loyalists after the Revolutionary War with fairs
and parades, as well as golf, tennis, and fishing tournaments.
For details, contact the **Abaco Chamber of Commerce** (Box 509,
Marsh Harbour, Abaco, tel. 809/367–2663).

If you take the rugged winding road south from Marsh Harbour, you'll pass through dense woodlands that are a **Bahamas
National Trust sanctuary** for the endangered Bahamian parrot;
more than a hundred other species have been sighted in this
area by avid bird-watchers. About 20 miles south of Marsh
❷ Harbour, you'll reach the little settlement of **Cherokee Sound**
(population 165), whose inhabitants make their living by
crawfishing and reside in wooden, shuttered houses with fruit
trees in the yards. More than 50 miles southwest of Marsh Har-
❸ bour lies **Sandy Point,** a rustic fishing village with a lovely
beach that attracts shell collectors. Although there are no communities to visit south of Sandy Point, a major navigational
❹ lighthouse stands at **Hole-in-the-Wall,** on the southern tip of
Great Abaco.

Treasure Cay   If you drive some 20 miles north on the main road out of Marsh
Harbour, through large pine forests that are still home to wild
❺ horses and boar, you'll reach **Treasure Cay,** which is not an island but a large peninsula connected to Great Abaco by a
narrow spit of land. Here you'll find a few small communities, a
3,000-acre farm that grows winter vegetables and fruit for export, and the Treasure Cay Mini Market (tel. 809/367–2570).
The main landmark of the area, however, is the sophisticated
Treasure Cay Beach Hotel and Villas (tel. 809/367–2570), situated on its own 3½-mile stretch of white sandy beach. This
residential and resort community, specializing in all-inclusive
packages, boasts an excellent 150-slip marina, an 18-hole golf
course, tennis courts, shops, and a full range of water-sports
activities. It has even expanded its activities to the small Great
Guana Cay, which has no roads and fewer than 100 inhabitants;
the island features a 450-acre water-sports and recreation complex named **Treasure Island,** also open to nonguests.

Green Turtle   Two miles off the shore of Treasure Cay is **Green Turtle Cay,** a
Cay/New Plymouth   tiny island steeped in Loyalist history, with several deep bays,
sounds, and a nearly continuous strip of fine ocean beach. Visi-
tors can take a 10-minute ferry ride from a dock on Treasure
Cay to the Green Turtle Club resort or New Plymouth on the
southern tip of Green Turtle Cay. An easy way to explore the
entire island is by small outboard dinghy or Boston whaler,

which can be rented by the hour or the day at most resorts and marinas.

6 **New Plymouth,** the main community on Green Turtle, was first settled in 1783; most of its approximately 450 residents eke out a living by diving for sponges or exporting lobster and fish through the Abaco Seafood Company. The village sits on a gentle hillside overlooking a harbor. Narrow streets flanked by wild-growing flora, such as amaryllis, hibiscus, and poinciana, wind between rows of white, New England–style clapboard cottages with pink-, brown-, and green-trimmed shutters. During the Civil War, New Plymouth provided a port of safety for Confederate blockade runners. One Union ship, the USS *Adirondack*, which was pursuing a gunrunner, was wrecked on a reef in 1862 at nearby Man-of-War Cay (*see* below). One of the ship's cannons now sits at the town harbor.

New Plymouth's most visited attraction is the **Albert Lowe Museum,** on the main thoroughfare, Parliament Street. The museum, dedicated to one of the island's original settlers by his son, artist Alton Roland Lowe, is housed in a nearly 200-year-old white-and-green clapboard building fronted by a picket fence. Visitors learn island history through displays of local 18th-century memorabilia, model schooners, and old photographs, including one of the aftermath of the 1932 hurricane that almost flattened New Plymouth. The museum also features a selection of Alton Lowe's paintings and a sculpture garden in the back. *Parliament St., tel. 809/365–4094. Admission: $3 adults, $1.50 children under 7. Open Mon.–Tues. and Thurs.–Sat. 9:30–4.*

Just a few blocks from the museum, on Victoria Street, is Green Turtle Cay's other main attraction, **Miss Emily's Blue Bee Bar** (tel. 809/363–5811), which stands next to a jail whose door is hanging on its hinges; it hasn't been used in 25 years. The bar's owner, Mrs. Emily Cooper, is well known for her stories and for making the best goombay smash in the islands. Visitors keep her busy serving the concoction of rum, pineapple juice, and apricot brandy (a devout church goer, the owner never touches the stuff herself). Mementos of customers—dollar bills, expired credit cards, business cards—cover the bar walls. Mrs. Lillian Carter, ex-President Jimmy Carter's mother, left her picture on the wall when she came here.

Man-of-War Cay Man-of-War Cay, the boatbuilding center of the Abacos south of Green Turtle and Great Guana cays, is an easily accessible 45-minute ride from Marsh Harbour by water taxi or by renting a small outboard dinghy. Many of the residents here are named Albury, descendants of early Loyalist settlers who started the tradition of handcrafting boats more than two centuries ago; they remain proud of their heritage and continue to build a few boats today. Joe Albury has a boat shop near the harbor; so does Sammy Albury. Boaters often stop at Norman Albury's **Sail Shop,** which stocks handmade skirts, blouses, and silk-screened island fabrics. Man-of-War Cay also has its own 60-slip marina. A mile north of the island divers can explore the unusual wreck of the USS *Adirondack*, which sank after hitting a reef in 1862. It lies among a host of cannon in 20 feet of water.

Visitors usually come to Man-of-War only for the day because there are no hotels. They are advised to dress conservatively—

scanty bikinis are definitely out of place here. The cay has one small road named Queen's Highway; the other thoroughfares are sandy paths. The island offers a few telephones and televisions, a one-room schoolhouse, and two churches, which most of the 170 residents faithfully attend. You won't be able to buy a drop of liquor on the island, but you can find a good conch salad at **Arlene's Hideaway** (tel. 809/365–6143) and tasty homemade coconut pie at the **Bite Site** (tel. 809/365–6051). The **Island Treasures Gallery** (tel. 809/365–6072) carries Bahamian-made jewelry, shell crafts, and straw work.

Elbow Cay/ Hope Town
❼

South of Man-of-War is another popular Abacos attraction, the village of **Hope Town** on Elbow Cay; the town is a 20-minute ferry or water-taxi ride from Marsh Harbour. Arrivals to Hope Town are greeted by the sight of a much-photographed Bahamas landmark, a 120-foot-tall, peppermint-striped **lighthouse** built in 1838. The lighthouse construction was delayed for several years by acts of vandalism because residents were afraid it would put an end to their profitable wrecking practice. Today, if you're feeling energetic, the lighthouse keeper will welcome you at the top (weekdays 10–4) for a superb view of the sea and the nearby cays. The Hope Town lighthouse is one of the last hand-powered kerosene-fueled beacons in the Bahamas.

Two narrow lanes circle the village and the harbor; follow either one for an interesting walking or bicycle tour of Hope Town, whose saltbox cottages, white picket fences, and flowering gardens will remind you of a New England seaside community—but with the grays and browns of northern climes replaced by the pretty pastels of the tropics. You may also want to stop at the **Wyannie Malone Historical Museum** on Queen's Highway, the main street. It contains memorabilia and photographs of Hope Town; many of the descendants of Mrs. Malone, who settled here with her children in 1875, still live on Elbow Cay. *Queen's Hwy., no telephone. Admission free, but donations are welcomed. Museum opening and closing hours vary because it is staffed by volunteers.*

Sports

Several sporting events are held annually in the Abacos. April brings the Walker's Cay Billfish Tournament, the International Billfish League "Warm Up" Tournament at the Treasure Cay Beach Hotel and Villas, and the Treasure Cay Powerboat Race Week. In May, fishermen can participate in the Treasure Cay International Billfish Tournament, the Green Turtle Club Fishing Tournament, the Annual Treasure Cay Bahamas Blue Marlin Tournament. The Green Turtle Cay Regatta takes place June 23–July 10, with fireworks and parties marking three weeks of races throughout the cays of the Abacos. For information, contact the **Bahamas Sports Line** (tel. 800/327–7678).

Golf

The only golf course in the Abacos is located on Treasure Cay. The club, a half-mile from the **Treasure Cay Beach Hotel and Villas,** has a par-72, 18-hole course designed by Dick Wilson. *Treasure Cay, tel. 809/367–2570. Cost: hotel guests free; visitors' greens fees $18 for 18 holes, $14 for 9. Electric carts: $20 and $15. Open winter 8–5, summer 8–6.*

Tennis

The Abacos offer only 13 courts. **Treasure Cay Beach Hotel and Villas** (tel. 809/367–2570) has six of the best, four lighted for night play. Guests play free, nonguests pay $10 an hour. **Walk-**

er's Cay Hotel (tel. 800/327–3714) has two courts, free to guests (not open to nonguests). **Great Abaco Beach Hotel** (tel. 809/ 367–2158) has two courts, allows guests complimentary play, and charges nonguests $5 an hour. **Bluff House** (tel. 809/365– 4247) at Green Turtle Cay has one court; guests play free, visitors pay $5. **Green Turtle Yacht Club** (tel. 809/367–2572), with one court, charges guests $5 an hour. **Abaco Towns by the Sea** (tel. 809/367–2221) at Marsh Harbour, with one court, is free to guests; visitors pay $5 an hour.

Water Sports *Boating and Fishing* Boats may be chartered by the week or longer, with or without crew, at Marsh Harbour and Hope Town. Weekly charter rates start at $900 a week (lower during the summer), with specials offering two weeks for the price of one. Arrangements can be made with **Abaco Bahamas Charters** (tel. 800/626–5690) in Hope Town and with **Bahamas Yachting Service** (tel. 305/484– 5246 or 800/327–2276) in Marsh Harbour. The Abacos offer several fine full-service marina facilities, including the Boat Harbor Marina, the Conch Inn Marina, and the Marsh Harbour Marina at Marsh Harbour; the Treasure Cay Beach Hotel Marina; the Green Turtle Club Marina; the Man-O-War Marina; and the Walker's Cay Marina.

These boating facilities are available at the main points on the islands. Great Guana Cay: **Pinder's** (tel. 809/367–2207); Green Turtle Cay: **Green Turtle Cay Club** (tel. 809/367–2572); Hope Town, Elbow Cay: **Elbow Cay Club** (tel. 809/367–2748); Man-of-War Cay: **Man-O-War Marina** (tel. 809/367–2306); Marsh Harbour, Great Abaco Island: **Boat Harbor Marina** (tel. 809/367– 2800), **Conch Inn Marina** (809/367–2800), **Marsh Harbour Marina** (809/367–2033); Treasure Cay: **Treasure Cay Beach Hotel and Villas** (tel. 809/367–2570); Walker's Cay: **Walker's Cay Hotel and Marina** (700 S.W. 34th St., Fort Lauderdale, FL 33315, tel. 305/522–1469).

Fishermen can find bonefish in the flats, yellowtail on the reefs, or marlin in the deep of the Abacos. Boat rental rates range from $35 a half-day to $300 a full day, depending on your preference for little Boston whalers or 25-foot Bertrams.

Scuba Diving The clear waters of the Abacos, which teem with marine life, waving corals and sea fans, and multihued fish, are ideal for diving. You can arrange expeditions through your hotel. Some main dive sites include the USS *Adirondack*, near Man-of-War Cay, a wrecked ship that lies among a host of cannon; Pelican Cays National Park at Marsh Harbour, with a full range of marine life; and ocean holes southwest of Hole-in-the-Wall.

These operators, which have equipment for rent, have daily dive trips to coral reefs, wrecks, and coral gardens: **Brendal's Dive Shop** (Green Turtle Cay, tel. 809/367–2572), **Island Marine Dive** (Hope Town, tel. 809/367–2822), **Chambered Nautilus** (Man-of-War Cay, tel. 809/367–2306), **Dive Abaco Ltd.** (Marsh Harbour, tel. 809/367–2014), **Treasure Cay Dive Center** (305/ 525–7711), and **Walker's Cay Dive Center** (tel. 800/327–3714).

Waterskiing **Treasure Cay Beach Hotel and Villas** (tel. 809/367–2570) charges $10 for 15 minutes on the water, $20 for 30 minutes, and $35 an hour.

Windsurfing **Abaco Inn** (Elbow Cay, tel. 809/367–2666) has rates of $30 a day, $15 a half-day; **Elbow Cay Beach Inn** (tel. 809/367–2748) charges $25 a day, $12 a half-day; **Green Turtle Yacht Club**

(Green Turtle Cay, tel. 809/367–2572) allows guests free windsurfing; **Pinder's Cottages** (Great Guana Cay, tel. 809/367–
2207) charges $20 a day; **Hope Town Harbour Lodge** (Elbow
Cay, tel. 809/367–2277) charges $20 a day; **Treasure Cay Beach
Hotel and Villas** (tel. 809/367–2142) has rates of $15 an hour,
$40 a half-day, $55 a day; and **Walker's Cay Hotel and Marina**
(tel. 800/327–3714) charges $15 an hour, $60 a day.

Dining and Lodging

Great Guana Cay **Guana Beach Resort.** This intimate resort, set against a background of thick tropical foliage, is the only hotel on one of the
Abacos' prettiest islands, Great Guana Cay; the island, which is
7 miles long, has only 80 residents. The property will suit you if
you just want to relax, because there aren't many activities to
distract you. The neat, simply furnished rooms are arranged
one next to the other, as in a motel; you can also rent a villa
(with a kitchen) that can accommodate four guests. Although
the resort has its own beach with thatched shelters, a five-
minute walk through a coconut grove will lead you to a more
spectacular stretch of sand that runs the length of the island.
*Box 474, Marsh Harbour, Abaco, tel. 809/367–2207. 15 rooms.
Facilities: Bahamian dining room bar, boutique, local entertainment, baby-sitting, laundry, marina. MC, V. Moderate.*

Green Turtle Cay **Bluff House.** Situated on 40 acres on top of the highest hill in
★ the Abaco chain, this romantic hideaway, surrounded by pine
trees, offers panoramic views of the sheltered harbor and ocean
reefs. Accommodations include simple poolside rooms with
sundecks, plush split-level town-house suites with ocean views,
and rustic one-, two-, and three-bedroom beachside villas (with
kitchens) that can accommodate eight people. The rooms feature wood paneling, tropical-style wicker furniture, wall-to-
wall carpeting, and private bathrooms. A wooden walkway
leads from the hotel marina to the nautical-themed clubhouse,
which offers a candlelighted dining room that serves complimentary wine and Bahamian and American fare, incorporating
local seafood. Guests have access to 2 miles of almost deserted
beach. The management will also arrange a water-taxi trip to
the town of New Plymouth, as well as boating, waterskiing,
and deep-sea fishing expeditions. The resort's gift shop carries
an extensive selection of swimwear. *Mail: c/o Green Turtle
Cay, Abaco, tel. 809/365–4247. 32 rooms. Facilities: pool, dining room, bar, lounge, marina. MC, V. Moderate–Expensive.*
Green Turtle Club. A well-groomed yet informal haven for boaters, this is a private-membership club with ties to the British
Royal Yachting Association and the Palm Beach Yacht Club; it
organizes the annual Green Turtle Yacht Regatta July 4–10.
Guests, however, are welcome and usually fit in quickly with
the always jovial crowd. The tasteful, well-maintained one- to
three-bedroom villas feature wood-paneled walls, full kitchens, dining and living areas, and terraces; the buildings are
nestled amid trees and shrubs on a hillside overlooking the harbor. The resort offers a small private beach and a 35-slip
marina, the largest and most complete yachting facility on the
island. Visitors can spend evenings at the congenial, flag-
festooned bar and at the fine, expensive restaurant that serves
just-caught grouper and lobster, as well as steaks, by candlelight. *Box 270, Green Turtle Cay, Abaco, tel. 809/367–2572. 31
rooms. Facilities: pool, dining room, bar, lounge, gift shop,*

laundry, marina, tennis, boating, diving, fishing. AE, MC, V. Moderate–Expensive.

New Plymouth Inn. Built in 1830, this charming, two-story historic hostelry with white balconies is in the center of New Plymouth. It was a French mercantile exchange, a warehouse (in which shipwreckers used to store their plunder), and a private residence before a Canadian Air Force colonel opened it as a hotel in 1946. Wally and Patti Davies, the present owners, have maintained the antique furniture, but they have also renovated the dining facilities, built a freshwater patio pool, and expanded the tropical gardens. The cozy, carefully restored high-ceilinged rooms offer solid chests and chairs, quilts on the beds, and private baths. The Galleon bar, with outdoor seating, is popular with local residents and tourists. You will need to make a reservation at the delightful Captain's Table restaurant, which serves Bahamian dishes, such as conch and turtle steaks, and vintage wines. Guests are provided with bicycles on which to ride around town. *Mail: c/o Green Turtle Cay, Abaco, tel. 809/365–4161 or 305/665–5309. 10 rooms. Facilities: pool, dining room, bar, lounge. No credit cards. Moderate.*

Hope Town/ Elbow Cay

Abaco Inn. About a mile south of Hope Town, this friendly beachfront resort, overlooking the ocean or bay, offers 10 shingled cottages scattered among palms and sea-grape trees. The simple and cheerful air-conditioned rooms with white-beamed ceilings are comfortably furnished; each cottage has its own hammock outside for dozing and reading. Visitors can daydream at a weathered gazebo facing the ocean, and a thatched solarium on the beach is available for nude sunbathing. Guests also have access to excellent nearby reefs for snorkeling and diving. The inn's restaurant, one of the best on the island, features creatively prepared seafood and vegetarian dishes in an indoor or outdoor setting. *Mail: c/o Hope Town, Abaco, tel. 809/367–2666. 10 rooms. Facilities: pool, dining room, lounge (with local entertainment), bar, baby-sitting, laundry, barber, marina, fishing and boating rentals. MC, V. Closed mid-Sept.–mid-Nov. Moderate.*

★ **Hope Town Harbour Lodge.** Perched on a hill that faces the Hope Town harbor, this amiable inn, the former dwelling of an Abaco family, draws a crowd at regatta time and remains a favorite with yachtsmen and locals, especially because of its bountiful Sunday champagne brunches (a buffet of beef, chicken, grouper, and lobster). Eight of the clean, unpretentious cottage rooms are clustered around the pool; the rest of the rooms in the main lodge overlook the harbor. Water sports can be arranged at the resort's marina; wonderful snorkeling opportunities on a reef are available only 15 yards out from the nearby beach. *Mail: c/o Hope Town, Abaco, tel. 809/367–2277 or 800/626–5690. 21 rooms. Facilities: pool, dining room, 2 bars, lounge, marina. AE, MC, V. Inexpensive.*

Marsh Harbour/ Great Abaco Island ★

Great Abaco Beach Hotel. At this hillside property, guests have a choice of a spacious room or one of the fancier two-bedroom, two-bath villas, complete with a kitchen, a living room, and a dining area; all the accommodations offer balconies with a grand view of the Sea of Abaco. The air-conditioned rooms, decorated in a tropical fashion, feature attractive white-wicker furniture and baths with dressing areas. Palm trees surround the pool, only a few steps from the beach. Local bands and singers perform regularly at the Below Decks lounge and nightclub. The hotel provides cable TV in the lounge, which is unusual in the Family Islands. Guests will enjoy the excellent fresh-caught seafood served in the 200-seat restaurant. Golfers have access to a bus to take them to the 18-hole Treasure Cay course. The resort arranges fishing charters, diving trips, boat rentals, and sightseeing tours. *Box 419, Marsh Harbour, Abaco, tel. 809/367–2158. 25 rooms and 5 villas. Facilities: pool, bar, lounge, restaurant, laundry, 2 tennis courts, boating, diving, fishing. AE, MC, V. Expensive.*

Abaco Towns by the Sea. This complex contains elegant two-bedroom, two-bath villas, each featuring a kitchenette, a dining area, a master bedroom, a guest bedroom, and a private patio. All the apartments can accommodate up to six people, which can be a thrifty arrangement; they're surrounded by well-landscaped gardens, including bougainvillea and hibiscus plants. The sparkling pool and two tennis courts overlook a lovely beach and the Sea of Abaco. A snack bar is available on the premises, but you will have to go out to have larger meals or to buy your own groceries. Guests may purchase time shares or opt for a vacation rental. *Box 486, Marsh Harbour, Abaco, tel. 809/367–2221. 48 apartments. Facilities: pool, 2 tennis courts, fishing, snorkeling. AE, MC, V. Moderate–Expensive.*

Conch Inn. This casual hotel, situated between the ferry dock and the town center, provides one of the most popular gathering spots on Great Abaco Island for yachtsmen, private fliers, local residents, and guests from other resorts. Its full-service 65-slip marina is one of the best and busiest in Marsh Harbour. The comfortable, air-conditioned rooms offer nautical-themed decor, full bathrooms, and small patios overlooking the harbor, and you can also rent a cozy two-bedroom cottage with a kitchen. The congenial Conch Out Bar often provides musical entertainment. Guests can try the Conch Crawl for good burgers and snacks and the Conch Inn Restaurant for fine, Bahamian-style candlelight dining. The inn, which is located 3 miles from the airport, also has a large swimming pool, a well-stocked boutique, and a pleasant beach nearby. *Box 434, Marsh Harbour, Abaco, tel. 809/367–2800. 10 rooms. Facilities: pool, dining room, bar, laundry, marina. AE, MC, V. Inexpensive–Moderate.*

Treasure Cay
★

Treasure Cay Beach Hotel and Villas. This plush, all-inclusive complex, only 10 minutes from the airport, combines the sophistication of a major international resort with the charm and style of an island village. An intimate hotel is centered on the 1,400 lush, tropical acres that overlook a 3½-mile curving white beach; additional accommodations with water views are available in town houses, rustic cottages, and villas scattered among gardens of palm trees and flowering shrubs. The most recent addition is Harbour House, a group of lovely villas with private terraces near the marina. The various rooms, generally decorated in pastel colors such as light green and beige, feature handsome bamboo and rattan furniture. The marina behind the complex can handle 150 boats and provides a full range of high-tech yachting services. The owners have developed the north end of Great Guana Cay and named it Treasure Island. Guests can travel there by the *Treasure Queen* ferry boat to dive, play volleyball, or just relax in hammocks. Additional boat trips can be arranged to Elbow Cay, Man-of-War Cay, and Green Turtle Cay. You can bicycle through shady lanes and find secluded beaches nearby, or participate in a variety of water sports; an underwater garden is available for divers and snorkelers. The complex has an excellent 18-hole championship golf course and 10 tennis courts. Guests can choose between two good seafood restaurants, the Abaco Room and the Spinnaker Restaurant (with a piano bar). The resort offers its own shopping center, and guests have access to a doctor's office, a bank, and a post office. *2301 S. Federal Hwy., Fort Lauderdale, FL 33316, tel. 305/444–8381; or Box TC-4183, Treasure Cay, Abaco, tel. 809/ 367–2570/2535/2845 or 800/327–1584. 205 rooms. Facilities: 4 pools, 2 dining rooms, 3 bars, lounge with entertainment, baby-sitting, laundry, barber/beauty shop, gift shops, marina, snorkeling, diving, fishing, boating, waterskiing, golf, 6 tennis courts (4 lighted at night). AE, CB, DC, MC, V. Very Expensive.*

Walker's Cay **Walker's Cay Hotel and Marina.** A self-contained resort on the northernmost island of the Bahamas, this property is served by its own airline out of Fort Lauderdale. The complex is a favorite with the yachtsmen and fishermen who flock to the Annual International Billfish League Tournament in May; the waters around here are renowned for their spectacular fishing opportunities. Not surprisingly, the resort specializes in fishing and diving packages; if you are not involved in these sports, this place may not be for you. The full-service 75-slip marina offers some of the best yachting facilities in the Bahamas, but you'll certainly find better beaches elsewhere in the Abacos. Accommodations include elegant hotel suites and modern, octagonal-roofed villas, nicely secluded in a wooded area; the rooms are cheerfully decorated with tropical-style furniture. The bar and lounge, whose walls are covered with huge stuffed fish, serve as gathering spots for sportsmen to swap fish tales. A pleasant dining room with an ocean view features Bahamian and American specialties, complemented by a superb wine list. *700 S.W. 34th St., Fort Lauderdale, FL 33315, tel. 305/522–1469 or 800/ 327–3714. 62 rooms and 4 villas with living rooms. Facilities: 2 pools (1 freshwater), dining room, bar, disco, lounge, baby-sitting, laundry, marina, gift shop, dive shop, boating, fishing, 2 tennis courts, water sports. AE, DC, MC, V. Expensive.*

Andros

Andros, the largest of the Bahamian islands (100 miles long and 40 miles wide), is the least explored of them all, a land serrated by channels and tiny inlets with names such as North Bight, Middle Bight, and South Bight. Although not a heavily visited island, Andros is popular with sportsmen for its excellent deep-sea fishing and its diving opportunities. The Spaniards who came here in the 16th century called it *La Isla del Espiritu Santo*—the Island of the Holy Spirit—and it has retained its eerie mystique to this day.

In fact, the descendants of a group of Seminole Indians, runaway slaves who left the Florida Everglades in the mid-19th century, settled in Andros and remained hidden from the outside world until a few decades ago. They continue to live as a tribal society with a leader they acknowledge as their chief. Their village, near the northern tip of the island, is called Red Bay, and they make a living by weaving straw goods. The Seminoles are credited with originating the myth of the island's legendary (and elusive) chickcharnies—red-eyed, bearded, green-feathered creatures with three fingers and three toes which hang upside down by their tails from pine trees. These mischievous characters supposedly wait deep in the forests to wish good luck to the friendly trespasser and vent their mischief on the hostile.

Andros's western shore, which lies 170 miles southeast of Miami and 30 miles west of Nassau, is utterly barren and not recommended to yachtsmen. The island's lush green interior is covered with dense forests of pine and mahogany, fringed on its western edge by miles of mangrove swamp. The forests provide nesting grounds for parrots, partridges, quail, white-crowned pigeons, and whistling ducks. Hunters come to Andros from September to March in search of game. Only a dozen settlements and a handful of hotels are located on the eastern shore; along the length of the shore the Andros Barrier Reef runs for 140 miles. The third-largest reef in the world, its enchanting variety of marine life, within a mile of the shore, is easily accessible to divers. Sheltered waters within the reef average 6 to 15 feet, but on the other side of the reef ("over the wall") lies the fathomless depths of the Tongue of the Ocean, which is used for testing submarines and underwater weapons by the U.S. and British navies, which operate under the acronym AUTEC (Atlantic Underwater Test and Evaluation Center). AUTEC's base is located near Andros Town.

Arriving and Departing

By Plane Andros has three airports: at San Andros in the north, at An-
Airports and dros Town in Central Andros, and at Congo Town in South
Airlines Andros. **Bahamasair** (tel. 800/222–4262) has twice-daily flights from Nassau to Andros Town and San Andros, and four times a week to Congo Town. Guests should check with their travel agent to find the airport closest to their hotel. The two best-known resorts are Small Hope Bay Lodge at Fresh Creek near Andros Town, and Andros Beach Hotel and Villas in the north at Nicholl's Town, both of which also fly in guests on charter flights from Fort Lauderdale.

By Mailboat From Potter's Cay Dock in Nassau, the M/V *Lisa J II* sails to Morgan's Bluff, Mastic Point, and Nicholl's Town in the north of the island every Wednesday, returning to Nassau the following Tuesday. M/V *Central Andross Express II* leaves for Fresh Creek, Behring Point, and Blanket Sound in Central Andros every Wednesday, returning to Nassau the following Sunday. M/V *Big Yard Express* leaves Nassau for Victoria Point and Little Harbour in South Andros every Wednesday at 7 AM, returning to Nassau the following Sunday. Schedules are subject to change due to weather conditions or occasional dry docking. For information on fares and sailing, contact the **Dock Master's office** (tel. 809/393–1064) at Potter's Cay.

Getting Around

By Car Rental cars are available on Andros, but potential drivers should be aware that this is an exercise in adventure, for the roads can be difficult; many are unpaved, and there are few gas stations along the way. Visitors are advised to arrange for a local driver through their hotels. The following companies rent cars: **Bereth Rent-A-Car** (Fresh Creek, tel. 809/368–2102), **Benjamin Rolle** (Lowe Sound, tel. 809/329–2562), **Alan Russell** (Lowe Sound, tel. 809/329–2153), **Basil Martin** (Mastic Point, tel. 809/329–3169), and **Cecil Gaitor** (Mastic Point, tel. 809/329–3043/2273).

By Taxi Taxis meet incoming planes at all airports, and they can also be arranged through the hotels. Rates are around $1.50 a mile. The average fare from Andros Town Airport to the Small Hope Bay Lodge is around $14.

By Bicycle/Scooter **Andros Beach Hotel** (Nicholl's Town, tel. 800/327–8150) has scooters and bicycles for hire. Bicycles are also available at **Chickcharnie's Hotel** (Andros Town, tel. 809/368–2025), **Longley's Guest House** (Mangrove Cay, tel. 809/329–4311), and **Small Hope Bay Lodge** (Fresh Creek, tel. 809/368–2014).

Important Addresses and Numbers

Emergencies Telephone service is available only through the front desk at Andros hotels, so emergencies should be reported to the management.

Police: North Andros, tel. 919; Central Andros, tel. 809/368–2626; South Andros, tel. 809/329–4733.

Medical Clinics North Andros, tel. 809/329–2121/2291; Central Andros, tel. 809/368–2038; South Andros, tel. 809/329–4620.

A doctor lives in San Andros. Medical clinics are located at Mastic Point, Nicholl's Town, and Lowe Sound, each with a resident nurse. A health center at Fresh Creek has both a doctor and a nurse. A clinic at Mangrove Cay has a nurse.

Opening and Closing Times

The **Canadian Imperial Bank of Commerce** is located in San Andros. It is open Wednesday 10:30–2:30. The bank visits Andros Town once a week.

Exploring Andros

Numbers in the margin correspond with points of interest on the Andros map.

Andros has no tour operators, and cabdrivers will charge around $50 for a half-day tour of the island. Most visitors opt to get around by bicycle or scooter over the few paved roads.
❶ **Nicholl's Town,** at the northeastern corner of Andros, is the largest village on the island, with a population of about 600. This friendly community has stores in which to buy supplies and groceries, a few hotels, a public medical clinic, a telephone station, and small restaurants that serve Bahamian fare. A few miles north of Nicholl's Town is a crescent beach and a headland
❷ known as **Morgan's Bluff,** named after the 17th-century pirate Henry Morgan, who allegedly dropped off some of his stolen loot in the area.

About 30 miles south from Nicholl's Town on the east coast is
❸ the small hamlet of **Andros Town;** visitors often stay at the ar-
❹ ea's main dive resort, the Small Hope Bay Lodge at **Fresh Creek.** Five miles inland from Andros Town is **Captain Bill's Blue Hole,** one of several on the island, a delightful freshwater spring with ropes for swinging across. Also near Andros Town, visitors may commune with nature by strolling along forest paths and taking in the wild orchids. Bob Dean, an expert on

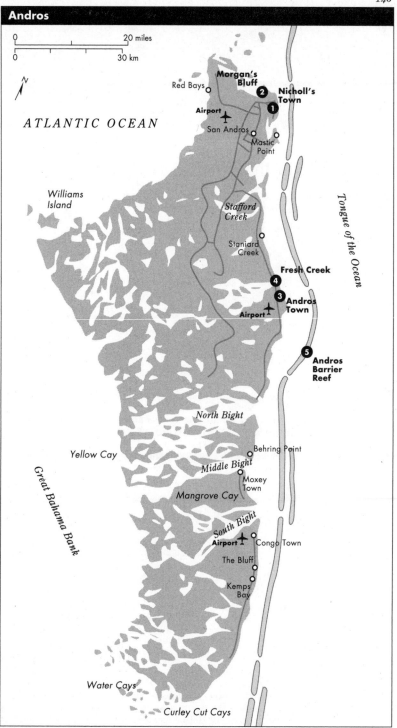

Andros

0 — 20 miles
0 — 30 km

ATLANTIC OCEAN

Williams Island

Red Bays

Morgan's Bluff

2

Nicholl's Town

1

Airport

San Andros

Mastic Point

Stafford Creek

Staniard Creek

Tongue of the Ocean

Fresh Creek

4

3 **Andros Town**

Airport

5 **Andros Barrier Reef**

North Bight

Yellow Cay

Behring Point

Middle Bight

Moxey Town

Mangrove Cay

Great Bahama Bank

South Bight

Airport

Congo Town

The Bluff

Kemps Bay

Water Cays

Curley Cut Cays

Andros flora and fauna, leads groups along the trails around the middle of the island and happily expounds on herbal medicines derived from the various plants. He charges $2.50 per person, and can be contacted through the Small Hope Bay Lodge (tel. 809/329–2582).

Andros is also the island where Androsia batik fabric is made. This brilliantly colored fabric is designed and dyed by more than 75 people at the **Androsia Batik Works Factory** (tel. 809/368–2020) in Fresh Creek, a 3-mile drive out of Andros Town; the batik fabric is turned into wall hangings and clothing for men and women these are sold throughout the Bahamas and the Caribbean. Tourists can visit the factory to observe how the material is made.

⑤ But the fabulous bonefishing on the flats of Andros and the diving on the **Andros Barrier Reef** lure most of the island's visitors. Here is a world offering a variety of underwater experiences; divers can explore reefs such as the Three Sisters, where visibility is clear 15 feet to the sandy floor, and jungles of elkhorn snake up to the surface; others can delve into the 60-foot-deep coral caves of the Petrified Forest, beyond which the wall slopes down to depths of 9,000 feet. Undersea adventurers also may investigate wrecks that have become home to multitudes of fish. The *Potomac*, a steel-hulled freighter that sank in 1952, lies in 40 feet of water close to the Andros Beach Hotel in Nicholl's Town. And off the waters of Fresh Creek, at 70 feet, lies the 56-foot-long World War II LCM (landing craft mechanized) known only as the Barge Wreck, which was sunk in 1963 to create an artificial reef.

Divers also have the chance to explore an uncounted number of blue holes throughout the east coast and around the island. These huge submarine networks can extend more than 200 feet down into the coral. Blue holes are named for their inky-blue aura when viewed from above and for the light-blue filtered sunlight that is visible from many feet below. Some of the holes that have been explored include vast cathedrallike interior chambers with stalactites and stalagmites, offshoot tunnels, and seemingly endless corridors.

Sports

Boating and Fishing
The **Chickcharnie Hotel** (tel. 809/328–2025) at Fresh Creek has a dock, with three small boats available for fishing. Rates are $40–$150, depending on total time of use. In Nicholl's Town, the **Andros Beach Hotel and Villas** (tel. 809/329–2021) has charter boats available; call ahead for rates. **Charlie's Haven** (tel. 809/329–5261) at Behring Point offers bonefishing for $80 a day, with guides.

Scuba Diving
Andros probably has the largest number of dive sites in the country. Almost all the diving is connected with the Andros Barrier Reef; the island offers about 100 miles of drop-off diving into the Tongue of the Ocean. Two major dive sites are the Barge Wreck, and Over-the-Wall near Fresh Creek. Divers can also explore the numerous blue holes along the barrier reef and around the island.

Andros Undersea Adventures BDA (tel. 809/329–2582 or 800/223–6961) at the Andros Beach Hotel and Villas, in Nicholl's Town, and **Small Hope Bay Lodge BDA** (tel. 809/368–2014 or

800/327–8150), in Fresh Creek, both have facilities for diving on the Andros Barrier Reef. A half-day reef trip with boat, guide, and equipment runs about $50.

Dining and Lodging

Andros Town/
Fresh Creek
★

Small Hope Bay Lodge. Canadian Dick Birch, looking for the simple life, built this easygoing, well-known dive resort on Fresh Creek's Small Hope Bay more than a quarter of a century ago. The property has long been popular with families and a favorite with divers because of the excellent undersea opportunities at the nearby Barrier Reef. The resort features 20 rustic cottages made of coral rock and Andros pine, set on a beautiful beach amid tall coconut palms. All cottages offer showers and ceiling fans and are decorated with original batik prints, but none of them have phones or televisions. The central lodge, where guests check in, houses a large fireplace for cool evenings (with throw pillows for sprawling), a game room, a dining room, and the *Panacea*, a fishing boat that serves as a bar. Meals served here tend to be hearty, with a choice of seafood or meat at dinner. Nearly everyone samples the snorkeling; novices are trained in a few hours and don mask and gear to explore the shallow reefs, while dive trips to the barrier reef are arranged frequently for more experienced divers. When you make a reservation, be sure to ask for the all-inclusive packages. The hotel is located 4 miles from the Andros Town airport. *Box N 1131, Nassau, tel. 809/368–2014; or Box 21667, Fort Lauderdale, FL 33335, tel. 305/463–9130 or 800/ 223–6961. 20 rooms. Facilities: dining room, bar, lounge, gift shop, laundry service, private sunbathing, hot tub, bicycles, diving, fishing, boating. AE, MC, V. Expensive.*

Chickcharnie's Hotel. This whitewashed, two-story resort at Fresh Creek has small, air-conditioned rooms. Only some rooms have a private bath. The inn is popular with anglers because of its economy rates and the availability of fishing boats and guides. Guests can stock up at the grocery store on the premises. The hotel is located 3 miles from the Andros Town airport. *Mail: c/o Fresh Creek, Andros Town, Andros, tel. 809/368– 2025. 8 rooms. Facilities: dining room, bar. No credit cards. Inexpensive.*

Mangrove Cay

White Sands Beach Hotel. The 12 rooms here stretch in a motellike line along a beach fringed with palm trees. Six of them offer private baths; the other six share two baths. Aside from swimming, guests must make their own sports arrangements. *Mail: c/o Pinder's, Mangrove Cay, Andros, tel. 809/ 329–4159. 12 rooms. Facilities: dining room. Inexpensive.*

Nicholl's Town
★

Andros Beach Hotel and Villas. This informal, low-rise hotel, which includes two cottages and a villa with kitchen facilities, sits on a 3-mile beach against a background of palm trees and grassy lawns. The air-conditioned rooms are clean, if not luxurious, which is fine with the guests: Activities center mostly on hotel manager Neal Watson's Underseas Adventures dive shop. The success of the hotel and dive operation owe much to Watson's personality and colorful past; he holds a master's rank in karate, flies his own plane, has doubled for James Bond in 007's filmed underwater scenes, has dived on the *Andrea Doria*, and has salvaged Spanish gold. Dive trips to the Barrier Reef, as well as fishing and boating expeditions, can all be arranged at the hotel, which is 8 miles from the San Andros air-

port. *Box 21766, Fort Lauderdale, FL 33335, tel. 305/763–2188
or 800/327–8150. 15 rooms. Facilities: pool, dining room, bar,
disco, lounge, laundry, dock, boating, fishing, water sports.
AE, MC, V. Inexpensive.*
Donna Lee Guest House. The rooms here are housed in two low-
rise buildings a five-minute walk from the beach. The hotel features neat landscaping and palm trees and has nearby flats for
bonefish aficionados. The restaurant serves seafood, and a
package store is also available. *Box SS 5213, Nicholl's Town,
Andros, tel. 809/329–2194. 12 rooms. Facilities: dining room,
bar. No credit cards. Inexpensive.*

South Andros **Emerald Palms by the Sea.** At press time, this Hotel Corporation of the Bahamas property was scheduled to open in the
early summer of 1990 at Driggs Hill, served by the airport at
Congo Town. The air-conditioned rooms, including two lanai
suites, feature four-poster double beds. Planter's chairs on the
private lanais and hammocks among the palms on the beach add
to the tropical ambience. The hotel offers indoor and outdoor
restaurants decorated with Spanish tiles. *Box 800, Driggs
Hill, Andros, tel. 809/329–4661 or Bahamas Reservation Service, tel. 800/327–0787. 20 rooms. Facilities: pool, tennis, volleyball, library, snorkeling gear, TV, VCR and videotapes,
stocked refrigerator, hair dryers, tubs. AE, MC, V. Moderate.*

The Berry Islands

The Berry Islands consist of more than two dozen little cays
stretching in a curve like a new moon north of Andros and New
Providence Island. Although a few of the islands are privately
owned, most of them are uninhabited, except by rare birds es-
tablishing the territory as their nesting grounds or by visiting
yachtsmen dropping anchor in secluded havens. The Berry Islands start in the north at Great Stirrup Cay, where a lighthouse guides passing ships, and they end in the south at Chub
Cay, whose club and marina attract anglers in search of bonefish in the nearby flats. Chub Cay lies only 35 miles north of
Nassau.

Most of the islands' 500 residents live on Great Harbour Cay,
which is 10 miles long and 1½ miles wide. Its main settlement,
Bullock's Harbour, offers a couple of small restaurants and a
grocery store. The Great Harbour Cay resort, a few miles away
from Bullock's Harbour, was developed in the early '70s; it includes a golf course, a marina, and privately owned villas and
town houses, which are now rented out. Like its counterpart at
Chub Cay, the resort is geared toward fishermen. Both Chub
and Great Harbour cays are located close to the Tongue of the
Ocean, where the big game fish roam.

Arriving and Departing

By Plane The **Chub Cay Club** (tel. 305/445–7830 or 800/662–8555) has
Airports and charters from Miami and Fort Lauderdale to the Chub Cay air-
Airlines port. **Stanair** (tel. 407/586–5748/3650) has a daily charter service from Palm Beach to Great Harbour Cay's airstrip, a
quarter-mile from the main resort. **Trans Island Airways** (tel.
809/327–8329) has two daily flights from Nassau to Great Harbour Cay's airstrip.

Between the Airports and Hotels	The Chub Cay Club picks guests up at the airport in buses. Arrangements for getting to Great Harbour Cay resort from the airstrip have to be made through the resort.
By Mailboat	M/V *Champion II* leaves Potter's Cay, Nassau, every Thursday for the Berry Islands. For schedules and specific destinations, call the **Dock Master's office** (tel. 809/393–1064) at Potter's Cay.

Getting Around

The resort on **Great Harbour Cay** (tel. 809/322–4782) rents bicycles, though there is nothing much to explore on the island.

Important Addresses and Numbers

Emergencies **Police,** Bullock's Harbour, Great Harbour Cay, tel. 2344. **Great Harbour Cay medical clinic,** tel. 2400.

Sports

The **Chub Cay Club** (tel. 809/325–1490 or 800/662–8555) offers charter boats with guides, diving facilities through Undersea Adventures, and two tennis courts. The resort at **Great Harbour Cay** (tel. 809/322–4782) can arrange guides for its guests for bonefishing, sportfishing, and diving.

Dining and Lodging

Chub Cay **Chub Cay Club.** The huge marina at this semiprivate club can handle more than 90 oceangoing craft, so fishing and diving are the main pursuits here. The 15 fair-sized rooms overlook a freshwater pool open to the public; the 40 villas scattered around the marina and facing the ocean are reserved for club members. All the rooms feature twin beds, small refrigerators, and dressing rooms. The casual and formal dining areas specialize in well-prepared seafood dishes. Visitors who are not interested in fishing and diving may get bored. The only other diversions available are tennis, ping-pong, or bicycling around the tiny island. *Box 661067, Miami Springs, FL 33266, tel. 305/445–7830, 809/325–1490, or 800/662–8555. 15 rooms. Facilities: dining room, pool, cable TV, boating, fishing, diving. AE, MC, V. Moderate–Expensive.*

Great Harbour Cay **Great Harbour Cay.** You can rent the villas and colonial-style town houses on the beach or marina by the day or week. The villas each feature an upstairs bedroom, a downstairs living room, and a kitchen; some kitchens are larger than others. The spacious town houses overlook the circular 80-slip marina; they each offer attractive wicker and rattan furnishings, two bedrooms and two baths upstairs, living and dining areas, a full kitchen, a washer and dryer, and sun decks downstairs. A grocery store is located on the premises. Guests can hire the services of fishing guide Percy Darville, who has four boats for bonefishing, bottom fishing, and deep-sea fishing. You can find snacks at the Beach Club, full meals at Basil's Restaurant on the marina, and a more expensive fish-and-seafood buffet at the resort's Tamboo Club, which is popular with local residents. *Box N 918, Nassau, tel. 809/322–4782 or 800/343–7256. 8 villas, 8 town houses. Facilities: dining room, air-conditioning,* *bar, golf, 4 tennis courts, rental bikes, beauty shop, diving, fishing. AE, MC, V. Moderate–Expensive.*

The Biminis

The Biminis have long been known as the big-game-fishing capital of the Bahamas. The nearest Bahamian islands to the U.S. mainland, they consist of a handful of islands and cays just 50 miles east of Miami, across the Gulf Stream that sweeps the area's western shores. Most visitors spend their time on North Bimini. Throughout the year, more than a dozen billfish tournaments draw anglers to the Gulf Stream and the Great Bahama Bank from the United States, Canada, Britain, and the rest of Europe. Marinas such as Brown's, Weech's Bimini Dock, the Bimini Big Game Fishing Club, and Bimini's Blue Water, all on the eastern side of skinny North Bimini, provide almost 130 slips for oceangoing craft, many of them belonging to weekend visitors who make the short trip from Florida ports. The western side of North Bimini, along Queen's Highway, is one long stretch of beautiful beach.

All of the hotels, restaurants, churches, and stores in the Biminis are located along North Bimini's King's and Queen's highways, which run parallel to each other. Everything on North Bimini, where most of the islands' 1,400 inhabitants reside, is so close together you do not need a car to get around. Sparsely populated South Bimini, separated from its big brother by a narrow ocean passage, is where Juan Ponce de León allegedly looked for the Fountain of Youth in 1513. Tourists are sometimes still approached by locals offering to show them the exact site of the Fountain of Youth, which is supposedly close to South Bimini's little airstrip.

Ernest Hemingway did many a battle with big fish around North Bimini, which he visited for the first time in 1935 from his home in Key West. He made frequent visits here, where he wrote much of *To Have and Have Not* and *Islands in the Stream*. He is remembered in the area as a picaresque hero, not only for his graphic descriptions of his fishing exploits, but for his drinking and brawling, including a fistfight he had with his late brother Leicester on the Bimini dock. Other notables lured to the island include Howard Hughes, Richard Nixon, and the latter's faithful friend Bebe Rebozo.

The Biminis also have a notorious history as a jumping-off place for illicit dealings; first during the Civil War, when it was a refuge for profiteers bringing in war supplies from Europe, and then during Prohibition, when it was a haven for rumrunners. Until a few years ago, it is believed that the airstrip on South Bimini was used nocturnally by smugglers bringing marijuana into the nearby Florida Keys. The dope peddlers, who also made drop-offs in the surrounding waters, have since been forced out by U.S. Customs officers in cooperation with Bahamian officials. Today, the Biminis attract only friendly tourists, especially Floridians; during spring recess, students rent sailboats and cruise over from Fort Lauderdale for wild nights at Papa Hemingway's former favorite watering hole, the Compleat Angler.

Arriving and Departing

By Plane

Airports and Airlines

Chalk's International Airline (tel. 800/432–8807) has several 25-minute flights daily into Alice Town, North Bimini, from Miami's terminal at Watson Island on the MacArthur Causeway, and from Fort Lauderdale (40 minutes). If you've just arrived at Miami International Airport, the taxi drive (cost: about $10) to the Watson Island terminal across from the Port of Miami will take about the same time it takes to get to North Bimini. North Bimini is also served from Chalk's base in Nassau (tel. 809/326–2845/6); at press time, Chalk's was owned by Resorts International, which also runs the Paradise Island Resort & Casino. Chalk's uses 17-passenger Grumman Mallard amphibians, with takeoffs and landings on water. Baggage allowance is 30 pounds per passenger.

Aero Coach International (tel. 800/432–5034) has daily flights from Fort Lauderdale and Miami to the small landing strip on South Bimini.

Between the Airports and Hotels

If you don't have heavy luggage, you can walk to your hotel from the place where the Chalk International plane lands in Alice Town, the main settlement on North Bimini. The Bimini Bus Company takes incoming passengers to Alice Town in 12-passenger vans. The cost is $3. A $5 taxi-and-ferry ride takes visitors from the South Bimini airport to Alice Town.

By Ship

SeaEscape (1080 Port Blvd., Miami, FL 33132, tel. 305/379–0000 or 800/432–0900) has one-day cruises to Alice Town, North Bimini, from the Port of Miami on Wednesday, Thursday, and Friday, leaving in the morning and returning in the evening. Fares, which include buffet, floor shows, casino, and exploring time in North Bimini, are $79–$89.

By Mailboat

M/V *Bimini Mack* sails from Potter's Cay, Nassau, to Cat Cay and Bimini every Thursday, returning to Nassau on Monday. For information, call the **Dock Master's office** (tel. 809/393–1064) at Potter's Cay.

Getting Around

By Car

Visitors do not need a car on North Bimini and usually walk wherever they go; there are no car-rental agencies.

By Bus

The Bimini Bus Company has minibuses available for a tour of the island. Arrangements can be made through your hotel.

By Bicycle/Scooter

At **Sawyer's Rentals** (tel. 809/347–2555), however, across the street from the Bimini Big Game Fishing Club and up the hill toward Queen's Highway, you can rent a moped for $40 a day or $8 an hour, with a deposit. You can also rent bicycles at the **Bimini Big Game Fishing Club** (tel. 809/347–2391).

Important Addresses and Numbers

Emergencies

Police and **fire**, tel. 919. The **North Bimini medical clinic** (tel. 809/327–2210) has a resident doctor and a nurse.

Exploring North Bimini

Alice Town, the main community of the Biminis, is situated at the southern end of North Bimini; here, Chalk International's

The Biminis

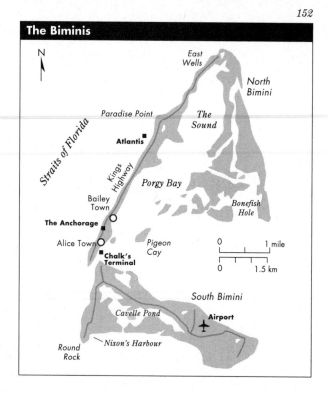

N

East
Wells

North
Bimini

Straits of Florida

Paradise Point

*The
Sound*

■
Atlantis

Kings Highway

Porgy Bay

Bailey
Town

○

*Bonefish
Hole*

The Anchorage ■

Alice Town ○

*Pigeon
Cay*

■ **Chalk's
Terminal**

0 _____ 1 mile

0 _____ 1.5 km

South Bimini

Cavelle Pond

✈ **Airport**

Round
Rock

＼*Nixon's Harbour*

seaplanes splash down in the harbor, lumber up a ramp, and
park on the other side of King's Highway. Near the Chalk landing area is a customs and immigration office. Close by this
office, along the narrow King's Highway, one of two main thoroughfares, stand the ruins of Bimini's first hotel, the **Bimini
Bay Rod and Gun Club,** a resort and casino built in the early
1920s and destroyed by a hurricane in 1926.

A hundred yards away from the club ruins, as you walk north
on King's Highway (cars that meet head-on have to slow down
so they can scrape by each other), you'll find on your right the
End of the World Bar (tel. 809/347–2370), a small, noisy tavern
that has a sandy floor; its back door is always open to the harbor. This place offers a good spot to meet some local folk over a
beer. The bar became a hangout in the late '60s for the late New
York Congressman Adam Clayton Powell when he came to
North Bimini while Congress investigated his alleged misde-
meanors; Powell entertained American reporters, who knew
they could find him here, ready to dispense flowery quotes. A
marble plaque in his honor is displayed in the bar, which still
draws curious tourists. An annual Bimini fishing tournament is
named in Powell's memory.

If you continue from the bar along King's Highway on the eastern side of Bimini, which is dominated by marinas, you'll come
to a huge arch on the roadway inscribed THE GATEWAY TO THE
BAHAMAS. Across the street from the arch, you'll find the
Compleat Angler Hotel (tel. 809/347–2122), Ernest Hemingway's hideaway in the '30s. Ossie Brown, who runs the place,

perpetuates the Hemingway legend with a room full of memorabilia related to the author, including pictures of the writer with gigantic fish and framed excerpts from his writings, most of them concerning battles with sharks. A photo of Cuban fisherman Angelmo Hernández, the supposed model for the hero of *The Old Man and the Sea*, also hangs in the bar. Brown claims a Cuban man named Bruce Garmendia walked into the hotel a few years ago, said he was Hernández's grandson, and gave the photograph to Brown.

A few hundred yards farther north of the Compleat Angler stands another Hemingway hideaway, the **Bimini Blue Water Hotel and Marina** (tel. 809/347–2291). Although the entrance to the hotel is on King's Highway, the hotel also sits on top of a 20-foot hill, facing Queen's Highway on the western side. The hotel restaurant, the **Anchorage,** was formerly the home of Michael Lerner, who opened a laboratory on the island devoted to dolphin and shark research in 1947 (it was closed in 1974); the former home is believed to have been the main setting for Hemingway's novel *Islands in the Stream.* You can still rent **Marlin's Cottage,** where the author wrote much of the novel. The cottage remains the best place on the island for watching the sunset and, on a clear evening, the reflection of Miami's lights on the water.

Bailey Town, the island's second-largest settlement, lies on Queen's Highway north of the Bimini Blue Water Hotel. Many of the island's residents live here in small, pastel-colored, concrete houses, a higgledy-piggledy combination of different shapes and sizes. Here you'll also find the attractive **Wesley Methodist Church,** built in 1858, with a bell tower on the roof.

Time Out   If you return east to King's Highway, drop in at **Priscilla's Epicurean Delights** (no phone), which is just across from the Big Game Fishing Club. The tasty conch fritters sell for $3 a dozen. Only one table is available at Priscilla Bain's restaurant, which is open from 11:30 AM until early evening; most tourists order the deep-fried morsels through a window in the wall and munch on them as they amble up the highway. You will have to sit inside, however, if you wish to try her inexpensive dishes of chicken, fried fish, or peas 'n' rice.

Continue walking north on King's Highway; you will pass a few liquor stores, grocery shops, clothing stores, a small strawmarket, and a bakery that turns out the mouth-watering Bimini bread (it is sold warm, soft, and sweet). At the northwestern part of the island, you will find the ruins of a planned luxury development that was begun only a few years ago, a $350 million resort community that was to include a marina, private homes, and a hotel. The developers ran out of money and abandoned the project, leaving the frames of a half-dozen homes looking out on an untrampled, shell-strewn beach.

Just offshore from this ghost settlement lies a controversial dive site called **Atlantis,** some 40 feet under water. This oddshaped 300-foot-long rectangular rock formation is purported to be a lost city, and archaeologists do estimate it to be between 5,000 and 10,000 years old. Carvings in the rock appear to some scientists to resemble a network of highways. Sceptics have pooh-poohed the theory, conjecturing that they are merely turtle pens built considerably more recently.

Time Out If your walk takes you back down King's Highway after 5 PM, you can stop in for a beer at the one above-average, nonhotel restaurant on the island, the russet-colored **Red Lion Pub** (tel. 809/347–2259), near the Bimini Big Game Club. The small bar with weatherbeaten tables can fill up quickly. Owner Dolores Saunders serves moderately priced dinners at a cost of $12–$16, including native turtle tidbits sautéed with wine, a combination seafood platter, grouper baked in wine, and ribs barbecued over charcoal and wood in a pit at the rear.

Cat Cay

This gorgeous little island 8 miles off South Bimini offers a 75-slip marina and other luxurious facilities maintained by the 250 members of a private club. Members of the public are not permitted to stay overnight. Recently the club decided to branch out and extend its membership; it invited applications, added 30 slips to its marina, and started work on a 2,450-foot airstrip.

Until the airstrip is completed, members who don't have their own yachts have to be ferried to the crucifix-shaped island from North Bimini, a $50 ride. Facilities for members include a fancy dining room (The Captain's Table), more than 100 rooms for rent in houses and villas ($150 a day and up), a golf course, a pool, tennis courts, and a cabana club. Membership fees start with a $7,500 initiation fee, plus $1,750 a year and up, depending on one's age. For additional details, contact Jim Rydell at the **Cat Cay Yacht Club** (2000 S. Dixie Hwy., Suite 205A, Miami, FL 33133, tel. 305/858–6856 or 305/361–7666).

Sports

The Biminis play host to the following sporting events throughout the year. February: Bimini Benefit Billfish Tournament; March: Annual Bacardi Rum Billfish Tournament and Hemingway Billfish Tournament; May: Championship Tournament; June: Championship Tournament (on Labor Day), Bimini Blue Water Tuna Tournament, and Blue Marlin Tournament; July: Independence Day All Billfish Tournament and Jimmy Albury Memorial Blue Marlin Tournament; August: Native Tournament and Big Game Rodeo; September: Small Bimini Open Angling Tournament; December: Annual Bonefish Willie Bonefishing Tournament and Adam Clayton Powell Memorial Wahoo Tournament.

For information on dates and tournament regulations, tel. 800/327–7678.

Boating and The **Bimini Big Game Fishing Club** (Box 699, tel. 809/347–
Fishing 2391), which has a first-class, full-service 100-slip marina serving as headquarters for many spring and summer fishing tournaments, charges $400 a day, $200 a half-day for deep-sea fishing. **Bimini Blue Water Marina** (Box 627, tel. 809/347–2166) charges $450 a day, $350 a half-day, with captain, mate, and all gear; this marina features 32 modern slips and usually hosts the annual Hemingway Billfish Tournament, among several other fishing events. **Brown's Marina** (Box 601, tel. 809/347–2227), a full-service 22-slip marina, will take you reef, shark, or deep-sea fishing for $350 a day, $225 a half-day. **Weech's Bimini Dock** (mail c/o North Bimini, tel. 809/347–2391), with 15 slips, has

four Boston whalers, which it rents for $80 a day, $40 a half-day.

Scuba Diving The Biminis offer several excellent diving opportunities. **Atlantis,** a 300-foot rectangular long rock formation in shallow water off North Bimini, is thought by some scientists to be a lost city. *Sapona,* off the coast of South Bimini, is a landmark wreck of a concrete-and-steel ship. *Piquet Rock* at Gun Cay features wreck debris from a Spanish ship, including ballast rocks, cannonballs, and ribs.

Bimini Undersea Adventures (Box 21766, Fort Lauderdale, FL 33335, tel. 800/327–8150) charges $35 for a one-tank dive, $60 for three dives. It also has package rates from $299 (two days/one night) to $675 (eight days/seven nights), which includes round-trip airfare from Fort Lauderdale, transfers, breakfast and dinner, and diving. Guests taking advantage of the package stay at the Bimini Big Game Fishing Club, Brown's Hotel, or the Compleat Angler.

Tennis The **Bimini Big Game Fishing Club** (tel. 809/347–2391; *see* Dining and Lodging, below) has one court, complimentary to guests and lighted for night play.

Dining and Lodging

Expensive **Bimini Big Game Fishing Club and Hotel.** This hotel is the larg-
★ est resting spot on the island, a favorite not only of fishing and yachting types who take advantage of the full-service 100-slip marina, but also of casual visitors who receive a warm welcome from veteran manager Mike Kaboth. Owned by the Bacardi Corporation, the rum company, it offers 35 large and comfortable air-conditioned guest rooms that overlook King's Highway, as well as four elegant penthouse apartments (often rented by VIPs) and 12 pleasant cottages on the marina that have kitchenettes with refrigerators. Sportsmen often prefer the roomy cottages, where they can easily prepare a lucky catch on an outdoor grill. The club has the only tennis court on North Bimini. Televisions were recently installed in the rooms, a purely protective measure to keep guests from hanging around the tiny lobby and give them an added diversion during rainy days. A broad beach is only a few minutes' walk away. If you plan to stay here during one of the major fishing tournaments, you will need to make a reservation well in advance. The club's Fisherman's Wharf restaurant on the harbor is the best on the island, specializing in fresh boiled grouper, a Bimini bouillabaisse, and cracked conch; steaks and lamb chops imported from Miami, which are more expensive, are also served. *Box 699, Alice Town, Bimini, tel. 809/347–2391 or 800/327–4149. 51 rooms. Facilities: 2 dining rooms, 2 bars, pool, marina, baby-sitting, laundry, tennis, boating, fishing, scuba diving. AE, MC, V.*

Moderate **Bimini's Blue Water Resort.** The main building of this resort is a white-painted, blue-shuttered house on top of a hill. The hotel has generous-sized, air-conditioned rooms offering white furniture, wood-paneled walls, and private balconies. It also features a full-service marina with 32 modern slips. The grounds extend to Queen's Highway and face a beautiful stretch of beach. On the property stands Marlin Cottage, where Hemingway stayed in the '30s; he used it as the main setting for *Islands* *in the Stream*. Ask the manager to lead you up the stairs of the cottage to the little room where the author worked. Guests may walk down a grassy hill to King's Highway and its little shops. The lovely Anchorage dining room specializes in conch and lobster dishes and provides a gorgeous view of the Gulf Stream. The resort belongs to a pioneer family in the islands, the Browns, who also own Brown's Hotel and the Compleat Angler (*see* below). *Box 627, Alice Town, Bimini, tel. 809/347–2291. 12 rooms. Facilities: dining room, bar, pool, marina. AE, MC, V.*

Inexpensive **Brown's Hotel.** Bimini pioneer Captain Harcourt Brown founded the hotel, which has long been a cherished hangout for visiting fishermen. The property is conveniently located only a few steps from Chalk's seaplane ramp. Its simple rooms and two apartments offer private baths and look out over the 22-slip marina; they may be unadorned, but they are also bargain buys. *Box 601, Alice Town, Bimini, tel. 809/347–2227. 30 rooms. Facilities: dining room, bar, boating, fishing, diving. No credit cards.*

★ **Compleat Angler Hotel.** This well-worn, informal, and friendly wooden-sided hotel dates back to the early '30s and will forever be associated with Hemingway, who often drank here after a day of stalking marlin. The cozy, unpretentious rooms have televisions and wooden-balustraded balconies. The walls of the bar are plastered with fishing photographs and personalized auto license plates. Hemingway memorabilia are kept in a separate room off the bar, hung on varnished, paneled walls. Visitors can have a drink either inside or at the outdoor bar, which encircles a huge almond tree. The bar remains the liveliest night spot on the island; this can be of doubtful merit if you're trying to sleep upstairs. *Box 601, Alice Town, Bimini, tel. 809/347–2122. 12 rooms. Facilities: bar, lounge, boating, fishing. AE.*

Diandrea's Inn. This attractive gabled former house from the '30s stands back from King's Highway and retains the warmth of a private residence. The owner recently added televisions to the comfortable, low-ceilinged rooms, which offer plain furnishings, carpeting, private baths, and air-conditioning. One of the larger rooms features two double beds. *Mail: c/o Alice Town, Bimini, tel. 809/347–2334. 13 rooms. Facilities: bar. AE, MC, V.*

Sea Crest Hotel. For an economical stay, try this adequate, unassuming three-story hotel with a splendid view of the harbor. The large air-conditioned rooms are modestly furnished. A two-minute walk will take you up to Queen's Highway and the beach. *Box 654, Alice Town, Bimini, tel. 809/347–2071. 17 rooms. No credit cards.*

Cat Island

At the summit of Cat Island's 206-foot Mt. Alvernia, the highest point in the Bahamas, you will find a tomb that is almost considered a shrine by the 2,140 inhabitants of this boot-shaped land. Above the tomb's entrance, carved in stone, is the epitaph BLESSED ARE THE DEAD WHO DIE IN THE LORD, and inside, past the wooden gate that hangs on its hinges, lies interred the body of an extraordinary man named Father Jerome; in 1956, at age 80, he was buried, supposedly with his arms outstretched, the pose resembling a crucifixion. The mystique surrounding Father Jerome seems to envelop Cat Island, one of the Bahamas' farthest-flung destinations. It's 130 miles southeast of Nassau and is a close neighbor of San Salvador, the landing place of Columbus. Little is known of Cat Island's history, perhaps because of its infrequent visitors. Nevertheless, the island's unofficial biographer, Mrs. Frances Armbrister, a member of a pioneer family, known simply throughout the island as Mrs. A, has many tales to tell about the place; some of her stories involve the practice of Obeah, the Bahamian version of voodoo.

The island may have been named after a frequent notorious visitor, Arthur Catt, a piratical contemporary of Edward "Blackbeard" Teach. Then again, the name may derive from the fact that if you look at the island from on high, you can see the shape of a cat sitting on its haunches. Slender Cat Island is 50 miles long, featuring high cliffs and dense forest. Its shores are ringed with mile upon mile of exquisite, untrampled beaches, edged with casuarina trees. Perhaps the tranquillity of the place is one of the reasons why some of the original inhabitants' descendants, who migrated long ago to New York, Detroit, and Miami, are slowly returning to the island; large, new homes have started to appear throughout the island.

Its inhabitants fish, farm, and live a peaceful existence. The biggest event of the year here remains the Annual Cat Island Regatta, which during the summer brings the most fervent yachtsmen to this faraway island. Otherwise, its resorts' guests are professional people who definitely want to get away from it all.

Arriving and Departing

By Plane   From Nassau, **Bahamasair** (tel. 800/222–4262) flies into Arthur's Town Airport on northern Cat Island every Tuesday and Saturday.

Between the   Taxis are not available on Cat Island. Resort owners make ar-
Airport and   rangements beforehand with guests to pick them up at the
Hotels   airport.

By Mailboat The *North Cat Island Special* leaves Potter's Cay, Nassau, every Tuesday for Bennett's Town and Arthur's Town, returning on Thursday. M/V *Maxine* leaves Potter's Cay on Tuesday for Old and New Bight, returning on Saturday. For information, call the **Dock Master's office** (tel. 809/393–1064) at Potter's Cay.

Getting Around

By Car   **Russell Brothers** (Bridge Inn, New Bight, tel. 809/354–5013), toward the southern part of the island, rents cars to explore the island.

Important Addresses and Numbers

Emergencies Cat Island has three medical clinics—at Smith Bay, Old Bight, and Arthur's Town. There are few telephones on the island, but the front desk of your hotel will be able to contact the nearest clinic in case of an emergency.

Exploring Cat Island

Numbers in the margin correspond with points of interest on the Cat Island map.

❶ **Arthur's Town,** where Bahamasair planes drop off the Cat Island visitors who aren't brought in by private plane, is located almost at the island's northernmost tip. Its main claim to fame is that it was the boyhood home of actor Sidney Poitier, who has written about growing up there in his autobiography; his parents and other relatives were farmers. The village has little of interest, except for the telephone station and a few stores. If you drive south from Arthur's Town, the winding road passes through small villages and bays where fishermen's boats are tied up. At times, the road offers views of the sea and beaches lined with coconut palms. One of the island's oldest settlements
❷ of small, weatherbeaten houses is situated at **Bennett's Bay,** some 15 miles south of Arthur's Town; at the Bluff, you can see bread baked daily in whitewashed ovens beside many of the homes.

❸ Just outside the settlement of **New Bight,** on the western coast
❹ about 30 miles from Arthur's Town, you'll reach the **Hermitage,** Father Jerome's resting place at the top of **Mt. Alvernia.** Early in this century, Father Jerome, whose original name was John Hawes, had traveled the world and eventually settled in the Bahamas. An Anglican who converted to Roman Catholicism, he built two fine churches, St. Paul's and St. Peter's, on hills on Long Island (in the Bahamas), as well as the St. Augustine Monastery in Nassau, before he retired to Cat Island to live out the last dozen years of his life as an ascetic hermit. His final, supreme act of religious dedication was carried out here, where he carved steps up to the top of Mt. Alvernia. Along the way, he also carved the 14 Stations of the Cross representing incidents from the passion of Christ, and, at the summit, he built a child-sized abbey with a small chapel, a conical bell tower, and three closet-sized rooms that he used as living quarters.

The pilgrimage to the Hermitage begins next to the commissioner's office at New Bight, at a dirt path that leads to the foot of Mt. Alvernia. No one visiting the island should miss the experience of making the slightly laborious climb to the top. The Hermitage provides a perfect, inspired place to pause for quiet contemplation; it also has glorious views of the ocean on both sides of the island. The previously mentioned Frances Armbrister takes guests from the Fernandez Bay Village resort (*see* Dining and Lodging, below) on pilgrimages to the Hermitage. She regularly makes the trip by herself, clears the weeds around the tomb, and lights a candle to Father Jerome's memory.

At the bottom of Mt. Alvernia, some 3 miles north of New
❺ Bight, you'll find the resort of **Fernandez Bay Village** (tel. 305/764–6945), which sits on a long, curved bay. The resort is usually the final destination for many of Cat Island's visitors. About 10 miles south of here is **Old Bight,** where the road leads to a large pond called Great Lake. As the road curves around to-
❻ ward **Port Howe** at the bottom of the island, you'll see the ruins of the **Deveaux Mansion,** a stark, two-story, whitewashed building overrun with wild vegetation. Once, however, it was a grand house on a cotton plantation, home of Col. Andrew Deveaux, who had been granted thousands of acres of Cat Island

Cat Island

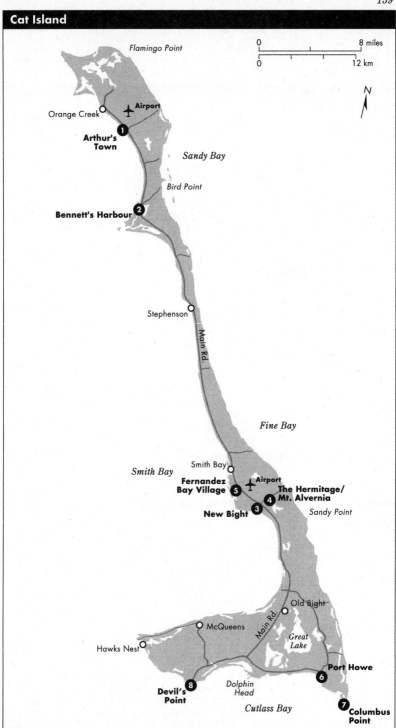

property as reward for his daring raid in 1783 that recaptured Nassau from the Spaniards.

The road now swings westward around the bottom of Great Lake, skipping the easternmost point of the island, **Columbus Point,** a name that conjures up more speculation about the great explorer's actual landing spot. About 10 miles west of Columbus Point, on the way toward the little village of **Devil's Point,** with its pastel-colored, thatch-roofed homes, you'll pass more ruins, those of the **Richman Hill–Newfield plantation.** Although there is little to see here now, the estate once stretched from the lake to the ocean.

At the southwestern tip of the island is the Hawk's Nest Club on a channel dredged out from the sea. In the past, the club's hotel, restaurant, bar, and marina have been popular with visiting yachtsmen. The club was closed when this guide went to press, as was the Cutlass Bay Club a few miles east on the south coast. For the latest information on the status of these two resorts, check with the Bahamas Reservation Service (tel. 800/327–0787).

Sports

At press time, the Hawk's Nest Marina and the Cutlass Bay Club, the two resorts that specialized in diving and water sports, were not in business. The other hotels listed below, however, can make arrangements for boating and fishing.

Dining and Lodging

Moderate ★ **Fernandez Bay Village.** Enterprising Tony Armbrister and wife Pam run this resort, which Armbrister built on land owned by his parents. Situated on a stunning white sand beach, the large villas, made from brick and stone, can accommodate four to six persons. The villas feature kitchens (there's a handy grocery store at the resort), terraces facing the sea, and individual gardens, where guests can shower; an outside wall ensures privacy. Only one telephone is available on the property, at the front desk. The dinner menu relies on freshly caught fish and locally grown vegetables; meals are often served under a chikee hut on the beach, though a comfortable, mahogany-beamed dining room is also used. Nightlife here usually involves conversation and sing-alongs. Guests who do not fly via Bahamasair are picked up at Nassau International Airport by Armbrister in his small plane every Friday and Sunday; he flies them to the New Bight airport close to the resort, and returns them to Nassau after their stay. *Mail: c/o Tony Armbrister, Box 2126, or Fort Lauderdale, FL 33303, tel. 305/764–6945 or 305/792–1905. 10 cottages. Facilities: dining room, bar, laundry service, waterskiing. No credit cards.*

Inexpensive **Bridge Inn.** This motellike property, run by Cat Islanders Mr. and Mrs. Russell, has glass doors at the back that lead to the beach 300 yards away. Its wood-paneled, high-ceilinged rooms (each can fit up to four people) have just been redecorated with blue drapes and carpeting; they offer private baths, ceiling fans, and cable TV. The inn features a small dining room, and guests who are on special diets will find the managers very accommodating. Mr. Russell arranges pickups of his guests in Nassau seven days a week, landing them at the nearby New

Bight airport. *Mail: c/o New Bight, Cat Island, tel. 809/354–5013. 12 rooms. Facilities: dining room, bar, game room, baby-sitting, car rentals, boating arranged. No credit cards.*

Greenwood Inn. This modest establishment, the most isolated hotel on Cat Island, is located at Port Howe on the southern coast, 6 miles from the little airstrip at Cutlass Bay, where guests are flown in by the owners. The rooms feature private baths and terraces; they are situated close to the beach and next to a dining room and a bar. Guests have access to a pool amid the landscaped gardens. Boating, diving, and fishing trips can be arranged. *Mail: c/o Greenwood Inn, Port Howe, Cat Island, tel. ask for overseas operator, New Bight. 16 rooms. Facilities: dining room, bar, disco, pool, rental cars, bicycles. No credit cards.*

Crooked Island

Historians of the Bahamas tell us that as Columbus sailed down the lee of Crooked Island and its southern neighbor Acklins Island (the islands are separated by a short water passage), he was aroused by the aroma of native herbs wafting out to his ship. Soon after, Crooked Island, which lies 225 miles southeast of Nassau, became known as one of the "fragrant islands." The first known settlers, however, didn't arrive in Crooked Island until the late 18th century, when Loyalists brought their slaves from the United States and established cotton plantations. It was a doomed venture because of the island's poor soil, and those who stayed made a living of sorts by farming and fishing. Today the 1,100 inhabitants who live on Crooked and Acklins islands continue to farm and fish. A salt and sponge industry flourished for a while on Fortune Island, south of Crooked Island, but the place is now a ghost town.

Arriving and Departing

By Plane **Bahamasair** (tel. 800/222–4262) offers two flights weekly, on
Airports and Tuesday and Saturday, from Nassau to Crooked and Acklins is-
Airlines lands. Airports are located in Colonel Hill, Crooked Island, and at Spring Point on Acklins Island.

Between the Taxis wait at the airport for the twice-weekly flights from Nas-
Airports and sau. Resorts can also arrange transportation by prior arrange-
Hotels ment.

By Mailboat M/V *Windward Express* sails from Potter's Cay in Nassau to Acklins Island, Crooked Island, Long Cay, and Mayaguana. For schedules, check with the **Dock Master's office** (tel. 809/393–1064) at Potter's Cay. A government ferry service operates daily between Crooked Island and Acklins Island 9–4.

Important Addresses and Numbers

Emergencies **Police** on Crooked Island, tel. 809/336–2197.

Medical Clinics Government medical clinics are located on both islands. On Acklins Island they are situated at Spring Point and Chesters Bay. Crooked Island's clinic is found at Landrail Point. The resident doctor and nurse for the area live in Spring Point. Nurses are also available at Colonel Hill, Chesters Bay, and Masons Bay. You can contact any of these medical professionals through your hotel.

Exploring Crooked Island

Although the plantations have long crumbled, two relics of those days are preserved by the Bahamas National Trust on the northern part of the Crooked Island, which overlooks the Crooked Island Passage separating the cay from Long Island. One ruin, **Marine Farm,** may have been used as a fortification, for old Spanish guns have been discovered there; the other old structure, **Hope Great House,** has orchards and gardens that are still tended by the Trust.

Crooked Island is surrounded by 45 miles of barrier reefs that are great for diving; they slope from 4 to 50 feet, then plunge to 3,600 feet in the Crooked Island Passage, once one of the most important sea roads for ships following the southerly route from the West Indies to the Old World. From **Colonel Hill,** where the airport is located, you get an uninterrupted view of the region all the way to the narrow passage between Crooked Island and Acklins Island. There are two lighthouses on these islands. The sparkling white **Bird Rock** lighthouse (built in 1872) in the north used to guard the Crooked Island Passage. The rotating flash from its 115-foot tower still welcomes pilots and sailors to the **Pittstown Point Landings** resort. The **Castle Island** lighthouse (built in 1867), at the southern tip of Acklins Island, formerly served as a haven for pirates who used to retreat there after attacking ships.

Dining and Lodging

Moderate **Pittstown Point Landings.** Guests stay here to take advantage of Crooked Island's fabulous fishing and diving. This beach-front hideaway on the north end of the island has its own 2,300-foot landing strip for small private planes; the main Colonel Hill Airport is located 12 miles away. The large, airy rooms with private bathtubs and showers are adequate. The very plain but well-kept dining room and lounge are situated in a mid-18th-century building that once housed the British West Indies Naval Squadron and, later, a post office. The completely isolated property features miles of open beach that will delight the au naturel sun worshiper. *Bahamas Caribbean International, Box 9831, Mobile, AL 36691, tel. 205/666–4482. 12 rooms. Facilities: bar, lounge, dining room, boating, snorkeling, diving. AE.*

Inexpensive **Crooked Island Beach Inn.** This attractive, rustic resort, only a 10-minute walk from the Colonel Hill Airport, is conveniently located on the waterfront. The clean, self-sufficient units allow the choice of preparing your own food or eating the inn's tasty Bahamian dishes; owner Rev. Ezekiel Thompson, minister of the local Evangelical Chapel, is happy to cater to his guests' requests. Children under 12 stay free. *Mail: c/o Crooked Island Beach Inn, Crooked Island, tel. 809/336–2096. 12 rooms. Facilities: boating, diving, boat rental. No credit cards.*

T & S Guest House. This little inland resort belongs to the owner of the Crooked Island Beach Inn (*see* above), which is a mile away. Scooters and bicycles are available for the pleasant ride to the beach. The small rooms are modestly furnished; guests share bathrooms. You can tell the owner what you would like for meals, and he will try to accommodate you. *Mail: c/o T & S Guest House, Cabbage Hill, Crooked Island, tel. 809/336–2096. 5 rooms. Facilities: boating, fishing. No credit cards.*

Eleuthera

Eleuthera is considered by many people who know the Family Islands well to be one of the most desirable destinations in the Bahamas. Its appealing features include miles and miles of unspoiled beach, green forests, rolling hills, and rich, red soil that produces pineapples and a variety of vegetables. The locals are extremely friendly people who live in bold-colored houses adorned with bougainvillea; they wave at you when you pass in your rental car, and if you come upon a few of them thumbing a ride, do not hesitate to oblige. In return for the favor, they will tell you interesting stories about their island, though you'll have to listen intently, for their lilting, fast-spoken words often skitter into one another.

On your own, you may explore the sumptuous, exclusive joys of resorts such as the Windermere Island Club or the Cotton Bay Club, but the locals will let you know where to find bargains at a little tucked-away strawmarket or tell you the name of the best restaurant on the island for conch chowder. Have a drink with an old-timer, and he'll tell you about some of the bush medicines that have contributed to his longevity: the kill-or-cure bush, crushed and sprinkled on wounds; the crab bush for stomach pains; the aralia bush for tuberculosis; and the blue flower leaves that cure constipation. If the casual narration takes longer than you have anticipated, despite its staccato delivery, remember one maxim valid throughout the Bahamas that sums up the way of life there: Where time stands still, so, sometimes, do the natives.

Shaped like a praying mantis, Eleuthera, which is 100 miles long, and, for the most part, less than 2 miles wide, has 10,600 inhabitants, the largest population of all of the Family Islands. It lies 200 miles southeast of Florida and 60 miles east of Nassau. The island was named by a group from Britain who came here seeking religious freedom in 1648. Led by William Sayle, a former governor of Bermuda, the group took the name of the island from the Greek word for freedom. The Eleutheran Adventurers, as these Europeans called themselves, gave the Bahamas its first written constitution, which called for the establishment of a republic.

The Eleutheran Adventurers landed first on the middle of the island, close to what is now called Governor's Harbour. After quarreling among themselves, however, the group split up, and Sayle led some of them around the northern tip of the island by boat. This faction was shipwrecked and took refuge at Preacher's Cave, where they held religious services. The cave, and the crude altar at which they worshiped, is still in existence, close to North Eleuthera.

Later in 1648, Sayle journeyed to the United States to seek help in settling his colony; but the people he left behind began to drift away from the island. By 1650, most of them had fled to New England, leaving only a few of the original Adventurers on Eleuthera to trade with passing ships in salt and brasiletto wood. Around 1666, Sayle returned to the Bahamas, this time to the island now called New Providence, which was ideally situated for shipping routes. New Providence eventually became the commercial center of the islands. Eleuthera was "revisited" at the end of the Revolutionary War by Loyalists who fled America with their slaves. The new settlers constructed colonial-style homes that still stand, and they started a shipbuilding industry. Today the population of Eleuthera (and of Harbour Island and Spanish Wells, which lie offshore in the north) consists of descendants of the original Adventurers, Loyalists, and the Loyalists' slaves.

Arriving and Departing

By Plane
Airports and Airlines
Eleuthera has three airports; at North Eleuthera; at Governor's Harbour, near the center of the island; and at Rock Sound, in the southern part of the island. **Bahamasair** (tel. 800/222–4262) offers daily service from Nassau to North Eleuthera, Governor's Harbour, and Rock Sound. **Aero Coach International** (tel. 800/432–5034) has several flights a day to all three airports from Miami, Fort Lauderdale, and West Palm Beach. Other airlines flying to Eleuthera include **Airway International** (tel. 305/526–3852), **USAir** (tel. 800/842–5374), and **Continental** (tel. 800/525–0280) from Miami.

Because Eleuthera's resorts are scattered throughout the island, you'll need to find out in advance which airport is nearest your hotel. If you're staying in Harbour Island and Spanish Wells, for example, your destination will be North Eleuthera Airport, and you'll take a taxi and ferry trip from there. If you are going to Cotton Bay or Windermere Isle, you will land at Rock Sound. For Club Med Eleuthera, you will fly to Governor's Harbour.

Between the Airports and Hotels
Taxis wait for incoming flights at all three airports and can also be found at most resorts. If you land at North Eleuthera and need to get to Harbour Island, off the north coast of Eleuthera, take a taxi ($2) to the ferry dock on Eleuthera ($3), a water ferry ($3) to Harbour Island, and, on the other side, another taxi ($2 to Coral Sands, for example); some hotels are within walking distance from the Harbour Island dock. You follow a similar procedure to get to Spanish Wells, which is also off the north shore of Eleuthera. Other sample rates: Rock Sound Airport to the Cotton Bay Club (12 miles), $25; Rock Sound to the Windermere Island Club (22 miles), $40; Governor's Harbour Airport to the Rainbow Inn, Hatchet Bay (15 miles), $30. Make sure you head for the airport closest to your hotel. If, for instance, you were to fly mistakenly to Governor's Harbour Airport instead of to Rock Sound, your taxi fare to Cotton Bay would be around $80 instead of $25.

By Mailboat
All of the following mailboats leave from Nassau at Potter's Cay; for schedules, contact the Dock Master's office (tel. 809/393–1064).

M/V *Current Pride* sails to Current Island, Lower Bogue, and Upper Bogue on Thursday, returning Tuesday. M/V *Bahamas Daybreak II* leaves for North Eleuthera, Spanish Wells, Harbour Island, and The Bluff on Thursday, returning Monday. M/V *Harley and Charley* leaves on Friday for Central Eleuthera, Hatchet Bay, Governor's Harbour, South Palmetto Point, and Tarpum Bay, returning Sunday. The same mailboat also leaves on Monday for South Eleuthera, Davis Harbour, Rock Sound, Green Castle, Wemyss Bight, Deep Creek, and Bannerman Town, returning on Thursday.

Getting Around

By Taxi To explore the island, you would be well advised to rent a car, which is a more economical way than hiring a taxi, unless you don't mind paying the driver to be your tour guide. Taxis, however, are available through your resort should you need one.

By Car Renting a car is a good idea for the visitor to Eleuthera. The roads are well paved, and this picturesque island is worth exploring at leisure. You may rent at **Cecil Cooper** (Palmetto Point, tel. 809/322–2575), **Dingle Motor Service** (Rock Sound, tel. 809/334–2031), **El-Nik's Rent-A-Car** (Palmetto Point, tel. 809/332–2523), **Griffin Rent-A-Car** (Governor's Harbour, tel. 809/332–2077), **Johnson's Rental** (Harbour Island, tel. 809/333–2376), **Ross Garage and U-Drive-It Cars** (tel. 809/333–2122), **Wellington Johnson** (Palmetto Point, tel. 809/322–2530), and **Yvette Rent-A-Car** (North Palmetto Point, tel. 809/332–2256).

Important Addresses and Numbers

Emergencies **Police:** Governor's Harbour, tel. 809/332–2111; Rock Sound, tel. 809/334–2244; Harbour Island, tel. 809/333–2111; and Spanish Wells, tel. 809/333–4030.

Medical clinics Harbour Island, tel. 809/333–2227, and Governor's Harbour, tel. 809/332–2001.

Exploring Eleuthera

Numbers in the margin correspond with points of interest on the Eleuthera map.

❶ Begin your driving tour of Eleuthera at its largest settlement, **Rock Sound,** whose airport serves the southern part of the island; the village has a small shopping center, where locals in the area come to stock up on groceries and supplies.

Front Street, Rock Sound's main thoroughfare, runs along the seashore, where fishing boats are tied up. If you walk down the street, you'll eventually come to the pretty, whitewashed **St. Luke's Lutheran Church,** a contrast to the deep blue and green houses nearby, with their colorful gardens of poinsettia, hibiscus, and marigolds. If you pass the church on a Sunday, you'll be sure to hear fervent hymn-singing, for the windows are always open to catch the breeze. A small, brand-new supermarket shopping center is located on the west side of the street. Also, stop by Janice and Michael Knowles' **Goombay Gifts** (tel. 809/334–2191), where you'll find shell necklaces, straw work, and souvenirs.

Time Out In Rock Sound, pop in for a taste of Bahamian food at **Sammy's Place** (tel. 809/334–2121) on Albury's Lane. Owned by Sammy Culmer, maître d' at the Cotton Bay Club, but managed mainly by his personable daughter Margarita, the eatery serves conch fritters, fried chicken and fish, and peas 'n' rice. Customers sit at leather booths in this spotlessly clean place, which is inexpensive and accepts no credit cards.

If you drive just a few miles south from the Rock Sound Airport, look for the little graveyards on your left; the tombs here are all built aboveground because of the difficulty of digging into and burying beneath the coral surface in the area. The

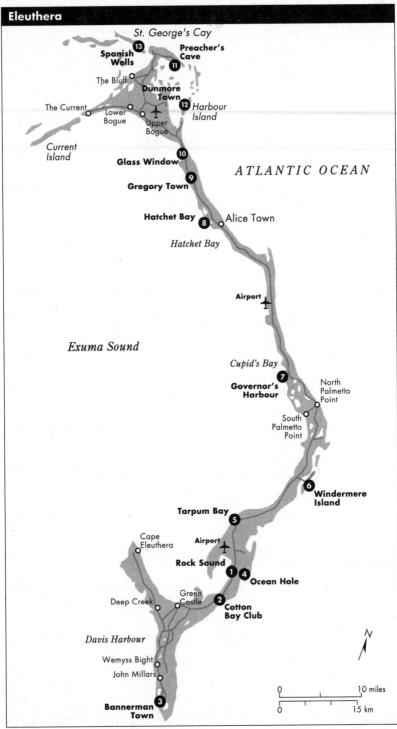

Eleuthera

St. George's Cay

Spanish Wells ⑬

Preacher's Cave

⑪

The Bluff

Dunmore Town

The Current

Lower Bogue

⑫ *Harbour Island*

Current Island

Upper Bogue

⑩ **Glass Window**

ATLANTIC OCEAN

⑨ **Gregory Town**

Hatchet Bay ⑧ Alice Town

Hatchet Bay

Airport ✈

Exuma Sound

Cupid's Bay

⑦ **Governor's Harbour**

North Palmetto Point

South Palmetto Point

⑥ **Windermere Island**

Tarpum Bay ⑤

Cape Eleuthera

Airport ✈

Rock Sound

① ④ **Ocean Hole**

Deep Creek

Green Castle

② **Cotton Bay Club**

Davis Harbour

Wemyss Bight

John Millars

③ **Bannerman Town**

0 ⸻ 10 miles

0 ⸻ 15 km

2 chic, 450-acre **Cotton Bay Club** (tel. 809/334–2101) is only 12 miles from the Rock Sound Airport. A famed Robert Trent Jones golf course, studded with tree groves and nestled against the sea, dominates the property. Cotton Bay was once a private club, the domain of Pan Am founder Juan Trippe, who would fly his friends into the island on a 727 Yankee Clipper for a weekend of golf. The resort is now open to the public—the well-heeled section of the public, that is. Visitors are welcome to use the golf course, but guests are given preference and the greens fees are high. The management recently acquired the 50-acre summer retreat of U.S. industrialist Edgar Kaiser, which overlooks the club. It includes his six-bedroom villa, which rents for a minimum of $2,000 a day and holds up to 12 persons.

3 If you wish, you can also take a pleasant drive south to the **Bannerman Town** lighthouse, about 30 miles from the Cotton Bay Club; you'll pass through the quiet, little fishing villages of **Wemyss Bight** and **John Millar's,** barely touched over the years.

4 From Rock Sound, you can also drive a mile east on the main road out of town to **Ocean Hole,** a large inland saltwater lake connected by tunnels to the sea. Steps have been cut into the coral on the shore so that visitors can climb down to the lake's edge and feed the rainbow fish that find their way in from the sea and return to it at will. The hole is estimated to be more than 100 fathoms deep, but, in fact, its depths have never been actually measured.

5 Next, head from Rock Sound to **Tarpum Bay,** a waterfront town less than 10 miles north. Just before you reach the village, you'll find the new **Tarpum Bay Shopping Center** (tel. 809/334–4022), where you can purchase groceries, T-shirts, snacks, and Bahamian souvenirs. Tarpum Bay, one of the island's loveliest settlements, offers hilly roads flanked by weatherbeaten homes with colored shutters; goats roam the streets. The town is also the site of a small artists' colony.

One of the island's more unusual characters lives in this community—a self-proclaimed mystic and prodigious painter named G. MacMillan Hughes. A bearded, ponytailed Scotch-Irish expatriate, he resides in a stone castle he built himself and from which pennants fly from the top. Behind a monumental, sculptured front gate, triangular steps lead to his gallery (tel. 809/334–4091); other forms—pyramidic, circular, arched—can be found around the gallery, and the artist is constantly adding mosaic touches to the decor. His striking paintings, which are modestly priced, depict themes of the sea; several canvases include mermaids. If he takes a liking to you (and he will know instantly, because he's psychic), he will lead you up to his battlement for a glass of wine and a panoramic view of his island world.

Time Out Ma Cilla (her real name is Priscilla Clark) owns a five-table restaurant (tel. 809/334–4210) worth trying, tucked away on a side road; it serves inexpensive meals of fresh grouper and crawfish. You'll recognize the place by the sculpted mermaid on the outside wall.

6 About 10 miles farther north from Tarpum Bay, a road cuts east, and a bridge takes you into the rarefied world of **Winder-**

mere Island (tel. 809/332–2538), Eleuthera's other plush resort besides Cotton Bay. Here you're likely to find yourself standing at the bar next to a world-renowned socialite or watching a member of British royalty as he or she takes a stroll through the pines. Lord Mountbatten's daughter has a home here; in 1982, the club played host to Prince Charles and a very pregnant Princess Diana; the pine trees on the grounds were festooned with Fleet Street's paparazzi.

7 **Governor's Harbour,** 15 miles north of Windermere Island (and home to one of the ubiquitous Club Med resorts), nestles in **Cupid's Bay,** the spot where the intrepid Eleuthera Adventurers landed. This attractive little town features faded Victorian houses confined to a half-dozen blocks near the local harbor. If you're here when the mailboat M/V *Harley and Charley* chugs in, you'll be treated to the sight of residents from around the island as they unload mattresses, lumber, mail, stacks of vegetables, and other household necessities. You'll probably also see the same Eleutherans loading their own vegetables and pineapples for export to Nassau. While they are here, the locals also will check their mail boxes at the small post office in the town's pink government building.

Time Out **The Buccaneer Club** (tel. 809/332–2500) serves good Bahamian dishes incorporating vegetables plucked fresh from the restaurant's own garden.

---

8 Next you can drive to **Hatchet Bay,** 25 miles north of Governor's Harbour. Side roads here are named even before houses are built on them, with such colorful designations as Lazy Road, Happy Hill Road, and Smile Lane. A sign will lead you to **The Cave,** a subterranean, bat-haunted tunnel, complete with stalagmites and stalactites, that supposedly once was used by pirates to hide their loot. An underground path leads for over a mile to the sea, ending in a lofty, cathedrallike cavern; within its depths fish swim in total darkness. The adventurous may wish to explore this area with a flashlight, but it would be wise to inquire first at one of the local stores for a guide.

9 Continue north for 5 miles to the village of **Gregory Town,** which sits on top of a cliff, though many of its charming pastel homes are located in a gully; you can drive down one side of the gully and up the other. One of the town's most colorful and popular characters is a Roman Catholic priest, Philadelphia-born Father Joe Guzinski, an authority on orchids. His home and greenhouse are bulging with species of orchids that he is crosspollinating. Father Guzinski sells the exotic plants to support his little **St. Gregory's Church** (tel. 809/332–2269, ext. 204); he claims the reason he has a church at all is due largely to the generous financial help of a frequent Eleuthera visitor, actor Raymond Burr (television's Perry Mason). You can always tell if Father Guzinski is on the island: The church doors will be open.

This area of North Eleuthera is pineapple country; its rich, red soil yields an abundance of the sweet-tasting fruit, which is exported and also made locally into a flavored rum. On the eastern shore of this region is an incredible formation of limestone cliffs called **The Grotto,** stratified and shaped over millions of years. In the yawning cave that is the centerpiece, one could house a good-sized restaurant, though the surrounding jagged rock might make access something of a problem.

⑩ At a very narrow point of the island a few miles north of Gregory Town, you'll find the **Glass Window,** where a slender wooden
bridge links two sea-battered bluffs that separate the Governor's Harbour and North Eleuthera districts. Sailors going
south in the waters between New Providence and Eleuthera
supposedly named this area the Glass Window because they
could see through the narrow cavity to the Atlantic on the other
side.

⑪ The main road now turns west through the villages of **Upper
Bogue** and **Lower Bogue** and goes by some small farms, and
then it swings north toward **Preacher's Cave** at the tip of the
island, where the Eleutheran Adventurers took refuge and
held services when their ship hit a reef more than three centuries ago. You can see inside the cave, with its original stone
altar. If you return south from here to **Lower Bogue** and head
northeast to the North Eleuthera dock, you can take the 20-
minute ferry-boat ride (cost: $3) to Harbour Island.

Harbour Island **Harbour Island** has often been considered the prettiest of all
the Family Islands because of its 3 miles of powdery pink beach
(perhaps the most beautiful beach in the Bahamas), and its
white gingerbread clapboard houses edged by picket fences
and tropical flowers. The residents have long called it Briland,
their faster way of pronouncing "Harbour Island." Old trees
⑫ line the narrow streets of **Dunmore Town,** named after the
18th-century royal governor of the Bahamas, Lord Dunmore; it
was once second only to Nassau in terms of its prosperity. Dunmore built a summer home here and laid out the town's plans.
You can take in all of Dunmore Town's attractions during a 10-
minute stroll. Stop off at **Curline Higgs** (tel. 809/333–2065) for
coral bead necklaces, and at **Frank's Art Gallery** (tel. 809/333–
2151) for local artists' paintings and prints. You will also enjoy a
visit to the oldest Anglican church in the Bahamas, **St. John's**
(built in 1768), and the distinguished **Wesley Methodist Church**
(built in 1848); services are still held there. **Loyalist College**
(built about 1792), one of the original settlers' homes, has also
survived. Offshore lies a long coral reef, which protects the
beach and offers excellent snorkeling; you can see multicolored
fish and a few old wrecks.

Although cars are available, you can explore the island without
too much exertion, for it is little more than 3 miles long. Within
its 2 square miles, however, are tucked away nine resorts
where you can fall asleep with the windows open and listen to
the waves lapping the pink beach.

Spanish Wells On the other side of northern Eleuthera from Harbour Island
⑬ lies **Spanish Wells,** on **St. George's Cay.** You reach Spanish Wells
by taking a 20-minute ferry-boat ride (cost: $3) from the North
Eleuthera dock. In the 17th century, the Spaniards, taking
their riches from the New World to the Old, found this a safe
harbor, and supposedly they dug wells from which they drew
water on their frequent visits. Today, however, water comes
from the mainland.

The people live on the eastern end of the island in clapboard
houses that look as if they've been transported from a New England fishing village. Tourists have little to do but hang out on
the beach or dive. You'll find sanded shell frames and lamps at
Roy Roberts' Ponderosa shop. **Walton's Langusta Restaurant**

and Bar, near the ferry dock, serves good turtle steaks and crawfish salad.

You can bet the seafood you will find on Spanish Wells is fresh. Descendants of the early Eleutherans, many of whom still have the same blond hair and blue eyes as their ancestors, continue to sail these waters, and bring back to shore fish and lobster (most of the Bahamas' langoustes are caught in these waters), which are prepared and boxed for export in a factory at the dock. The 700 inhabitants, many of them interbred, may be the most prosperous out-islanders in the Bahamas, so lucrative is the trade in crawfish. Those who don't fish here grow tomatoes, onions, and the inevitable pineapples.

Sports

Golf The Robert Trent Jones course, an 18-hole, 7,068-yard, par-72 course at the **Cotton Bay Club** (Box 28, Rock Sound, tel. 809/334–2101 or 800/THE–BAYS), charges $20 for all-day play, guests and nonguests alike. A caddie costs $8 for 18 holes, and an electric cart costs $20 to rent. The club has a free golf clinic, a bar, a lounge, and a pro shop. Affable Sean O'Connor, member of a famous Irish golfing family, has been the pro at the club for a quarter of a century.

Tennis Twenty courts are scattered around the island. Guests of the resorts play free; nonguests should call for information about rates. **Club Med** (Governor's Harbor, tel. 809/332–2270) has the largest complex, with eight courts. The **Cotton Bay Club** (Rock Sound, tel. 809/334–2101) has four of the possibly best-kept courts on the island and a resident pro. **Pink Sands Lodge** (Harbour Island, tel. 809/333–2030) has three courts in a elite setting. Each of the following has one court: **Coral Sands Hotel** (Harbour Island, tel. 809/333–2350), **Dunmore Beach Club** (Harbour Island, tel. 809/333–2200), **Romora Bay Club** (Harbour Island, tel. 809/333–2325), **Valentine's Yacht Club** (Harbour Island, tel. 809/333–2142), and **Spanish Wells Beach Resort** (tel. 809/333–4371).

Water Sports At many spots around the island, anglers can go bonefishing (at
Boating and a cost of around $75 a half-day), bottom fishing ($75 a half-day),
Fishing reef fishing ($20 an hour), and deep-sea fishing ($250–$500 a full day). On Harbour Island, **Coral Sands Hotel** (tel. 809/333–2350) offers bonefish, bottom, and deep-sea fishing. **Romora Bay Club** (tel. 809/333–2325) has Boston whaler and Sunfish boats for rent, and **Valentine's Yacht Club** (tel. 809/333–2142) can arrange various types of fishing and has small boats for rent. **Spanish Wells Beach Resort** (tel. 809/333–4371) has reef or bonefishing for $25 per person a half-day. At Rock Sound, the **Cotton Bay Club** (tel. 809/334–2156) charges $20 an hour for reef fishing and has sailboats for rent at $6 an hour.

Scuba Diving Eleuthera offers several fine diving options, including **Train Wreck,** an old railway train in 15 feet of water near Harbour Island; **Current Cut,** which is loaded with marine life and provides a roller-coaster ride on the tides; and **Devil's Backbone** in North Eleuthera, offering a tricky reef area with a nearly infinite number of dive sites and a large number of wrecks.

Cotton Bay Club (Rock Sound, tel. 809/334–2101) arranges dive trips. **Romora Bay Club BDA** (Harbour Island, tel. 809/333–

2325) rents equipment and offers diving instruction, certification, dive packages, and daily dive trips. The **Valentine's Dive Center** (Harbour Island, tel. 809/333–2142) rents and sells equipment and provides free scuba lessons to beginners, advanced instruction, certification, dive packages, and daily group and custom dives. **Spanish Wells Dive Center DBA** (tel. 809/333–4371) rents and sells equipment and features a dive program for beginners, instruction, certification, and daily group and custom dives.

Waterskiing/   **Valentine's Yacht Club** (Harbour Island, tel. 809/333–2142) of-
Windsurfing   fers waterskiing and windsurfing. Waterskiing is offered at **Cotton Bay Club** (Rock Sound, tel. 809/334–2101). **Club Med** (Governor's Harbour, tel. 809/332–2270) and **Romora Bay Club** (Harbour Island, tel. 333–2325) have windsurfing.

Dining and Lodging

Governor's   **Club Med Eleuthera.** This all-inclusive mammoth resort fea-
Harbour   tures a distinctive carefree Bahamian ambience. The 300 rooms have been freshly decorated in white and pastels, with twin beds, wood furniture, and marble fixtures in the private baths; they front either a long stretch of pink sand beach or tropical gardens. Social life revolves around the main complex, which houses a relatively new dining room, an open-air cocktail lounge, a dance floor, a theater, a disco, and a boutique. Certainly, there's no place else on Eleuthera that offers a circus workshop in which you can swing on a trapeze or bounce on a trampoline. The club also offers a scuba course for beginners. Parents can leave toddlers ages 2–3 at the new Petit Club, and the Mini Club caters to older kids, who can learn to dive and sail. The resort is located 8 miles from Governor's Harbour Airport. *Box 80, Governor's Harbour, Eleuthera, tel. 809/332–2270; book through a travel agent or call 800/CLUB–MED. 300 rooms. Facilities: pool, dining room, bar, diving, sailing, fishing, 8 tennis courts, aerobics, volleyball, circus workshop. AE, MC, V. Moderate.*

Gregory Town   **Oleander Gardens.** The white stucco villas of this property house informal one- and two-bedroom rental apartments with kitchens and living and dining areas; the buildings, which are spaced apart on a hillside running down to the sea, offer privacy and their own tranquil beach on the northern part of the island. This is an ideal place to rent if you want to cook your own meals. Boating, fishing, and snorkeling trips can be arranged. The hotel is located about 20 miles from the North Eleuthera Airport and 2 miles from Glass Window. *Box 5165, Gregory Town, Eleuthera, tel. 809/333–2058. 20 rooms. Facilities: dining room, bar, tennis, fishing, diving. AE, MC, V. Moderate.*

Pineapple Cove. The attractive setting here offers 28 acres of pineapple fields, tropical trees, and flowers, and you can also explore the nearby coral coves and cliffs. The villa-style rooms are tastefully decorated in rattan furniture and pastel colors; all of them have private porches with enchanting views of the sea. *Box 1548, Gregory Town, Eleuthera, tel. 809/332–0142 or 800/552–5960. 32 rooms. Facilities: dining room, bar, pool, tennis, indoor games, laundry, fishing. AE, MC, V. Moderate.*

Cambridge Villas. This two-story, motellike resort of well-maintained private rooms and apartments (some of the larger apartments have kitchens) is run by a helpful Eleutheran family. The complex surrounds a shady terrace and a saltwater pool. In the evening, the hotel serves good Bahamian food, including conch chowder and broiled grouper, in a restaurant on the premises. The cheerful bar and disco is popular with locals and visitors. A bus shuttles guests to a beautiful beach just a mile and a half away. The resort is located 20 miles from the North Eleuthera Airport. *Box 5148, Gregory Town, Eleuthera, tel. 809/332–2269, ext. 212. 25 rooms. Facilities: pool, dining room, bar, disco, entertainment, baby-sitting, rental cars, scooters. AE, MC, V. Inexpensive.*

Harbour Island   **Pink Sands Lodge.** Considered by some travelers to be the
★ grande dame of the island, this 40-acre resort of forest glen, paved pathways, and tropical greenery has been designated a bird sanctuary by the Audubon Society. The lodge, which has an ambience of dignified informality, is a private club that also accepts guests. The comfortable stone cottages feature large well-furnished living rooms, bedrooms, dressing rooms, private baths, kitchens, and spacious patios. In the evening, men and women dress up for American- and Bahamian-style dinners, which are merely adequate. *Box 87, Harbour Island, Eleuthera, tel. 809/333–2030. 49 rooms. Facilities: dining room, bar, lounge, library, tennis, boating, fishing, rental cars, scooters, bicycles. No credit cards. Expensive.*

Romora Bay Club. This red-roofed, Mediterranean-style resort, once a private club and now popular with young couples, fronts the harbor; the island's famed pink beach is a short stroll away down a tropical path. The brightly furnished villas have balconies or patios that overlook the beach and beautiful gardens with coconut palms and pine trees. In the evening, you watch the sun set from the clubhouse perched on the water; the building houses a pleasant dining room, a rustic bar, and a relaxing lounge. After exploring Dunmore Town, guests can take advantage of the resort's complete diving program. *Box 146, Harbour Island, Eleuthera, tel. 809/333–2325 or 800/327–8286. 34 rooms. Facilities: dining room, bar, lounge, entertainment, laundry, diving, fishing, scooters, bicycles. AE, MC, V. Expensive.*

Runaway Hill Club. Perched on a bluff, this elegant yet intimate hotel on 7 nicely landscaped acres offers a steep flight of stairs that leads right to the beach. Once a private residence, the place maintains a homey ambience with spacious, colorfully decorated rooms upstairs or in an adjacent wing; most of them face the sea to catch the cool breezes. Locals know the main house as the best place to dine on the island; chef Rica Thompson's shrimp scampi and conch and fish dishes have become renowned in the area. (There's a fixed-price menu.) *Box 31, Harbour Island, Eleuthera, tel. 809/333–2150. 8 rooms. Facilities: pool, dining room, bar, lounge, entertainment. AE, MC, V. Expensive.*

★ **Valentine's Yacht Club.** Owners John and Gloria Valentine brought their antiques and Oriental art with them when they moved from their mid-18th-century Virginia home to Harbour Island, thus following somewhat in the footsteps of fellow Virginian Lord Dunmore, who also once resided here. This friendly, small marina resort with its pagodalike roof blends tropical and colonial furnishings in the lounge and lobby, giving the place a country-house look. Island-hopping yachtsmen like to tie up at the marina and sip a cool drink at the nautical bar replete with old ships' lanterns and wheels turned into chandeliers. The hotel food is well above average; specialties include lobster almondine, curried conch, and grouper Creole. The club offers a complete dive program with free lessons for beginners and fascinating reefs waiting to be explored nearby. *Box 1, Harbour Island, Eleuthera, tel. 809/333-2142. 21 rooms. Facilities: pool, dining room, bar, barber/beauty shop, laundry, diving, fishing, tennis. AE, MC. V. Expensive.*

★ **Coral Sands Hotel.** Former movie actor Brett King and wife Sharon have run this easygoing, two-story yellow resort for 20 years. Its 14 hilly acres stretch along the pink beach to the center of Dunmore Town. A congenial host, King counts well-heeled Europeans among his guests; he is always ready to play pool with visitors in the game room. The number of repeat guests says something about his likable personality. King recently opened his Nightclub-in-the-Park for dancing under the stars; a plaque on a tree carries its name: "Harbour Island's Carnegie Hall." The pleasing green decor of the rooms complement the palm trees right outside the windows. Upstairs rooms are reached by attractive, curving steps. Bahamian and American food are served at dinner; picnics to other islands can be arranged. *Mail: c/o Coral Sands Hotel, Harbour Island, Eleuthera tel. 809/333-2350. 33 rooms. Facilities: dining room, 3 bars, TV, game room, laundry, tennis, fishing, diving. AE, DC, MC, V. Moderate.*

Hatchet Bay **Rainbow Inn.** The villas and apartments that dot the beachfront grounds offer unadorned rooms with exposed wood, complete kitchens, large private porches, and air-conditioning. The bar is a favorite with locals, for you'll usually find a Bahamian folk singer strumming away during the evening. The inn's Eleutheran cook presents good Bahamian fare in the simply furnished dining room, located in the octagonal wooden main complex by the swimming pool. *Box 53, Governor's Harbour, Eleuthera, tel. 809/332-0294 or 800/327-0787. 15 villas and apartments. Facilities: dining room, bar, pool, tennis. AE. Moderate.*

Rock Sound **Cotton Bay Club.** Some 200 palm trees line the 2-mile drive
★ from the main road to this prestigious resort, once privately owned by Pan Am founder Juan Trippe. The sandy pink villas face the curving beach, with the superb 18-hole Robert Trent Jones golf course nearby. Interior designer Melvin Doty decorated the rooms with mahogany trim and rattan-style headboards, tables, chairs, and armoires. The pastel bedspreads and draperies were imported from France. Gardener Godfrey Cartwright, who planted the palms dotted around the golf course, keeps the grounds beautifully landscaped. Guests take lunch on the patio overlooking the 16-foot freshwater pool in a courtyard; nearby, local resident Mrs. Mackey weaves straw hats and bags for sale. In the evening, fine cuisine is served indoors (jackets for men are a must). Austrian chef Johan Kaufmann serves what is arguably the best food on the island. Among his specialties are hearts of palm soup, Long Island duckling with raspberry sauce, and poached grouper with julienne zucchini and lobster sauce. Manager Ron Lindemann positively pampers his guests, often joining them to watch late-night television on the huge screen in the game room. The resort is located at Powell Point, 12 miles from the airport. *Box 28, Rock Sound, Eleuthera, tel. 809/334-2101 or 800/334-3523. 77 rooms. Facilities: pool, dining room, bar, game room with*

TV, golf, tennis (4 excellent courts and a pro), boating, diving, fishing. AE, MC, V. Very Expensive.

Winding Bay Beach Resort. This resort, whose wide, white-balustrated entrance is guarded by a magnificent ficus tree, is reached by a 1-mile drive east from the main road, which at one point goes through a gorge gouged out of coral. Guests experience a happy sense of isolation when they stay here. Eleven peaceful cottages are nestled in a horseshoe-shaped bay; the pleasant rooms offer refrigerators, wicker furniture, and private patios. The grounds feature palm trees and other tropical vegetation, especially around the curved pool and the tennis courts, as well as shaded walkways. The all-inclusive rates include cocktails and wine at dinner, which is prepared by a European chef. *Box 93, Rock Sound, Eleuthera, tel. 809/334–4055 or 800/327–0787. 36 rooms. Facilities: pool, dining room, bar, tennis, water sports, activities program, tennis, bicycling, evening entertainment. AE, MC, V. Very Expensive.*

Spanish Wells **Spanish Wells Beach Resort and Spanish Wells Harbour Club.** The Beach Resort, with one of the best locations on the island, features six white cottages with kitchens and dining areas and 21 well-maintained rooms that overlook a pristine beach. Its sister hotel, the Harbour Club, has 14 plain, tidy rooms that face a marina, from which boats leave frequently for fishing and diving expeditions. Both hotels offer good dive and honeymoon packages, sunset cruises, island picnics, and beach shell-gathering. You can dine on Bahamian and American cuisine at both hotel restaurants. *Box 31, Spanish Wells, Eleuthera, tel. 809/333–4371. 41 rooms. Facilities: dining rooms, bars, entertainment, tennis, diving, fishing, private beach. AE, MC, V. Moderate.*

Tarpum Bay **Hilton's Haven.** This hotel is not part of the well-known U.S. hotel chain; instead, it's an unassuming 12-room motel across the road from a beach and just around the corner from that unique attraction, the MacMillan Hughes Gallery and Castle. The establishment is run by a local nurse named Mary Hilton, and you'll get more personal attention here than at some of the larger resorts. The cozy rooms have private baths and patios. Ms. Hilton serves good home cooking in her small restaurant. This is the kind of neat, unpretentious place you'll be happy to stay at overnight during a leisurely tour of the island. You can also ramble Tarpum Bay's narrow streets in the daytime to meet some of the residents and local artists. The hotel is about 6 miles from the Rock Sound Airport. *Mail: c/o Tarpum Bay, Eleuthera, tel. 809/334–4231/4125. 12 rooms. Facilities: dining room, bar, air-conditioning. No credit cards. Inexpensive.*

Windermere Island **Windermere Island Club.** If you drive over a bridge east of the ★ main road north of Tarpum Bay, you'll enter a world of the elite—a hideaway for European royalty, VIPs, and others of assorted claims to fame. Guests have several options. They can stay in huge villas (some can sleep eight) with lavish interiors reflecting the tasteful personalities of the owners; these are hidden among casuarina trees. For less money, they can rent attractive tropical-style apartments with sitting rooms overlooking the beach or more modest carpeted club rooms, with rattan furniture. Palm trees surround the large octagonal swimming pool. This is the sort of place where you eat a breakfast of papaya and pineapple on your balcony, relax over afternoon tea at the club after tennis (there's a resident pro), loll on the private island beach, and dress up for dinner on the terrace or dining room. The American/Continental dishes are good, but guests have been known to drive the 30-odd miles to the Cotton Bay Club for Chef Kaufmann's more satisfying fare. The resort is 18 miles from the Rock Sound Airport. *Box 25, Rock Sound, Eleuthera, tel. 809/332–2538 or 800/243–5420. 22 rooms. Facilities: 2 pools, dining room, bar, lounge, laundry, baby-sitting, 6 tennis courts, boating, snorkeling. AE, V. Closed Sept.–Oct. Very Expensive.*

The Exumas

On the Exumas, you'll still find wild cotton, which was first grown on plantations established by Loyalists after the Revolutionary War, and breadfruit trees, which a local preacher bought from pirate Capt. William Bligh in the late 18th century. The islands are also known as the onion capital of the Bahamas. Many of the 3,670 residents earn a living by fishing and farming. Your first impression of the friendly people on the Exumas may be that almost all of them have the surname Rolle. Lord John Rolle, who imported the first cotton seeds to these islands, had more than 300 slaves, to whom he bequeathed not only his name but also the 2,300 acres of land that were bestowed on him by the British government in the late 18th century. This land, in turn, has been passed on to each new generation and can never be sold to outsiders. Not surprisingly, recognition of his generosity was perpetuated by the two settlements that bear his name, Rolleville and Rolle Town.

The Exumas begin less than 40 miles southeast of Nassau and stretch south for about 130 miles, flanked by the Great Bahama Bank and Exuma Sound. They are made up largely of some 365 fragmented little cays. The two main islands, Great Exuma and Little Exuma, lie in the south, connected by a bridge. The islands' capital, George Town, on Great Exuma, is the site of one of the Bahamas' most prestigious and popular sailing events, the April Family Island Regatta, when locally built wooden work boats compete with one another. During the winter, Elizabeth Harbour is a haven of yachts; the surrounding waters are legendary for their desolate islands, coves, bays, and harbors.

The Exumas certainly offer their share of impressive characters. One of them, Gloria Patience, who is in her seventies and lives near George Town, is known as the Shark Lady because she goes out regularly in her 13-foot Boston whaler and catches sharks with a 150-foot-long handline. Ms. Patience brings the sharks home and dissects them. She then drills holes in their teeth and vertebrae to make pendants, necklaces, and earrings, which she sells to visitors at George Town's unofficial social center, the Hotel Peace and Plenty (tel. 809/336–2551) on Elizabeth Harbour. At the hotel, you're also likely to run into Christine Rolle, known as the Bush Medicine Woman, who says the island has "the spoonbush for anemia and stomach pains, blue flowers for a cough, the horse bush for backaches, and black buttonwood for arthritis."

Arriving and Departing

By Plane George Town has the only major airstrip in the Exumas and is the only official port of entry. Little Staniel Cay, however, near the top of the chain, has a 3,000-foot airstrip that accepts private planes flying in U.S. citizens with homes there. **Bahamasair** (tel. 800/222–4262) has daily flights from Nassau to George Town, and **Aero Coach** (tel. 800/432–5034) schedules several flights a day from Fort Lauderdale to George Town.

Taxis wait at the George Town airport for incoming flights. The cost of a ride from the airport to the hotel is about $10.

By Mailboat M/V *Lady Roslyn* travels from Nassau to George Town weekly. M/V *Capt. Moxey* leaves Nassau on Thursdays for Staniel Cay, Farmers Cay, Black Point, and Baraterre, returning to Nassau on Saturdays. M/V *Grand Master* leaves Nassau on Tuesdays for George Town, Rolleville, Forest, Farmers Hill, and Black Point, returning to Nassau on Saturdays. For information on specific schedules and fares, contact the **Dock Master's office** (tel. 809/393–1064) at Potter's Cay.

Getting Around

By Car In George Town, you can rent an automobile through **Exuma Transport** (tel. 809/336–2101), **Hotel Peace and Plenty** (tel. 809/336–2551), and **R & M Tours** (tel. 809/336–2112). Hotels also can arrange rentals of cars, scooters, and bicycles.

By Taxi Your hotel will arrange for a taxi if you wish to go exploring or need to return to the airport.

Important Addresses and Numbers

George Town: **Police,** tel. 809/336–2666. **Medical Clinic,** tel. 809/336–2088.

Opening and Closing Times

The **Bank of Nova Scotia** in George Town is open Monday–Thursday 9–3, and Friday 9–1 and 3–5.

Exploring the Exumas

Numbers in the margin correspond with points of interest on the Exumas map.

❶ Begin your tour at the southern tip of **Little Exuma Island,** where you'll find **Williams Town,** an old village whose main landmark is the **Hermitage,** a former plantation house that is now a private home; the ruins of slave cottages are situated nearby. Next, drive the 10 miles north to **Great Exuma Island,** linked by a bridge at the settlement called The Ferry; on the way, you'll pass the lovely **Pretty Molly Bay;** Molly is a mermaid, according to local legend, whom some residents have seen at night, possibly after a few of bartender "Doc" Rolle's special rum concoctions at the Hotel Peace and Plenty (*see* below).

Queen's Highway runs in an almost straight line across the length of Great Exuma, and some 5 miles before you get to George Town you'll run into the first of the Rolle settlements,

The Exumas

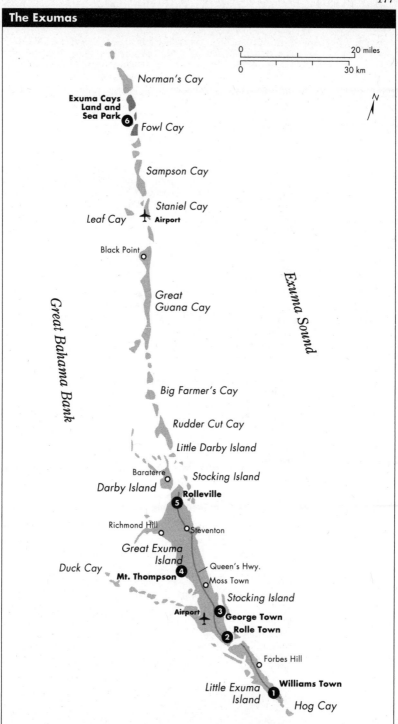

Norman's Cay

Exuma Cays Land and Sea Park ⑥ Fowl Cay

Sampson Cay

Staniel Cay
✈ **Airport**

Leaf Cay

Black Point

Great Bahama Bank

Great Guana Cay

Exuma Sound

0   20 miles
0   30 km

N

Big Farmer's Cay

Rudder Cut Cay

Little Darby Island

Baraterre   Stocking Island

Darby Island   **Rolleville** ⑤

Richmond Hill   Steventon

Great Exuma Island

Duck Cay

Queen's Hwy.

Mt. Thompson ④

Moss Town

Stocking Island

Airport ✈ ③ **George Town**

② **Rolle Town**

Forbes Hill

Little Exuma Island   **Williams Town** ①

Hog Cay

②
③ **Rolle Town,** whose inhabitants grow onions, mangoes, bananas, and other crops. Although **George Town** is the island's main settlement, it is hardly a hive of activity; the town does not even have a traffic light. The most imposing structure here is located in the town's center, the white-pillared, sandy pink colonial-style **Government Administration Building,** modeled on Nassau's Government House and containing the commissioner's office, police headquarters, courts, and a jail. Atop a hill across from the government building is the whitewashed **St. Andrew's Anglican Church** (built around 1802), whose blue painted doors welcome many of the locals every Sunday. Behind the church is the small Lake Victoria.

A leisurely stroll around town will take you past a strawmarket and a few shops, such as **Olga's Variety Store, Patrice's Department Store,** the **Two Turtles Gift Shop, Maynard's Boutique,** and **Liz and Jim's** ice-cream shop. You can buy fruit and vegetables and bargain with fishermen for some of the day's catch at the **Government Wharf,** where the mailboat comes in. The wharf is close to **Regatta Point** (tel. 809/336–2206), an attractive guest house named after the annual April sailing event, the Family Island Regatta, which curls around Kidd Cove, where the 18th-century pirate Captain Kidd supposedly tied up.

Overlooking Elizabeth Harbour stands one of the island's best-known landmarks, the **Hotel Peace and Plenty** (tel. 809/336–2551), a historic inn that got its name from a slave ship that sailed near the Exumas in the late 18th century. Part of the hotel once served as slave quarters; the lively bar was the slaves' kitchen. Because the hotel has no beach, owner Stanley Benjamin, a Cleveland industrialist, bought part of **Stocking Island** (with only six inhabitants) just over a mile away; hotel manager Charlie Pflueger ferries his guests there daily. The 7-mile-long island has a pier and a long stretch of white beach rich in seashells. Stocking Island also features the 400-foot-deep **Mystery Cave,** where divers can find a variety of marine life.

④ About 30 miles north of George Town, you'll reach **Mt. Thompson,** which is actually just a hill rising from the beach. It affords a pleasing view of the **Three Sisters Rocks** jutting above the water just offshore. During your peregrinations, you may glimpse a flock of roaming peacocks on Great Exuma. Originally, a peacock and a peahen were brought to the island as pets by a man named Shorty Johnson, but when he left to work in Nassau, he abandoned the birds, who gradually proliferated into a colony. Some locals hunt these birds because they eat crops, but they are difficult to catch because they run so fast.

If you continue north, you'll pass the small villages of **Moss Town** and **Steventon,** and then reach the last stop on this driving
⑤ tour, **Rolleville,** on a hill above a harbor; here old slave quarters still stand, but they have been transformed into livable cottages. The town's most prominent citizen, Kermit Rolle, runs the **Hilltop Tavern** (tel. 809/336–6038), a pink seafood restaurant and bar guarded by an ancient cannon. The place is a popular meeting spot for the locals. Rolleville's **Church of God of Prophecy** was built by one of the Rolle families.

North of Great Exuma lies a world of cays, with names such as Rudder Cut, Big Farmer's, Great Guana, and Leaf. **Staniel Cay** is a favorite destination of yachtsmen. The island has one paved road, from the airstrip to a yacht club. At the two grocery stores, boat owners replenish their supplies. The village also offers a small, red-roofed church, a post office, and a straw-market. The island has one nightclub, the **Royal Entertainer Lounge** at the **Happy People Marina** (tel. 809/355–2008), where Bahamians and visitors mix to enjoy lively out-island music performed by local talent twice a week.

Near the northern end of the **Exumas** is the 200-square-mile **Exuma Cays Land and Sea Park,** where the rare Bahamian iguana is a protected species. Snorkelers, beachcombers, and bird-watchers need to charter a small boat to reach the park, which has more than 20 miles of protected little cays. Part of the Bahamas National Trust (which enforces strict laws about taking coral or plants away as souvenirs), the park appeals to divers who find here a vast underworld of limestone, coral reefs, drop-offs, blue holes of freshwater springs, caves, and a multitude of exotic marine life.

Also at the northern end of the Exumas lies a beautiful, and now-abandoned, little island with 10 miles of rarely trodden white beaches that attract an occasional yachtsman. **Norman's Cay** was once the private domain of convicted Colombian drug smuggler Carlos Lehder, whose planes left from there for drop-offs in Florida.

Sports

In January, the Annual New Year's Day Cruising Regatta is held at the Staniel Cay Yacht Club, with international yachts taking part in a series of races. April sees the most important yachting event of the year in the Bahamas, the Family Island Regatta, starting from Elizabeth Harbour in George Town, where island-made wooden sailing boats compete against one another for trophies; onshore, the town is a three-day riot of Junkanoo parades, goombay music, arts and crafts fairs, and continuous partying in the hotels. In November, the Bonefish Bonanza II Tournament, sponsored by the Hotel Peace and Plenty, takes place in the shallows off George Town.

Boating and Fishing The Exumas offer some of the finest cruising areas in the Bahamas. The Upper Exumas offer a nature wonderland, and yachtsmen can observe a variety of wildlife, including birds and iguanas. The Exuma Cays Land and Sea Park from Wax Cay to Conch Cay is a protected area also worth visiting. George Town on Great Exuma Island is generally the final destination of yachtmen visiting the area; it offers good anchorages and stores to stock up on supplies.

Deep-sea fishermen will find plenty of gamefish sport in Exuma Sound, off the Great Exuma's east coast, and good boneing off the west coast. In George Town, make arrangements for boating and fishing at **Exuma Docking Services** (tel. 809/336–2578), **Minn's Watersports** (tel. 809/336–2604), and the **Out Island Inn** (tel. 809/336–2171). **Sampson Cay Colony Ltd.** (tel. 809/325–8864) has guides for hire. On Staniel Cay, contact the **Happy People Marina** (tel. 809/355–2008), and the **Staniel Cay Yacht Club** (tel. 809/355–2024). You can also book fishing trips through your hotel.

Scuba Diving Some major dive sites in the Exumas include the **Exuma Cays Land and Sea Park,** a 200-square-mile fish-and-bird sanctuary that runs from Wax Cay Cut to Conch Cut in the Upper Exumas;

Thunderball Grotto, north of Staniel Cay; and **Stocking Island Mystery Cave,** near George Town, which is full of schools of colorful fish.

Exuma Dive Company (Box 152, George Town, tel. 809/336–2170) offers a 38-foot houseboat that takes divers to coral reefs, sea gardens, and the Mystery Cave at Stocking Island off George Town. **Staniel Cay Yacht Club** (4250 S.W. 11th Terrace, Fort Lauderdale, FL 33315, tel. 305/467–6850 or 809/355–2024) has Boston whalers that can each take four divers to the Exuma Cays Land and Sea Park.

Tennis The **Out Island Inn** (tel. 809/336–2171), in George Town, has two Flexipave hard courts. Guests play free, nonguests are charged $3 an hour.

Dining and Lodging

George Town **Flamingo Bay Club and Villas.** Located a half-mile from George Town Airport, this complex boasts 1,300 acres of rolling hills and dense tropical vegetation that extend down to a long, secluded, golden beach on Flamingo Bay. On the beach is a marker that notes the Tropic of Cancer runs through here. The two- and three-bedroom villas, which are clustered by a freshwater pool, feature tasteful contemporary furnishings, kitchens, and full baths. The resort offers access to sports instructors, a private dock, and beach picnic areas. *Box 90, George Town, Exuma, tel. 809/336–2661. 9 villas. Facilities: kitchens, satellite TV, maid service, baby-sitting, laundry, tennis court. No credit cards. Expensive.*

★ **Out Island Inn.** The largest of the Exuma resorts, this casual establishment features low-rise stone buildings that house large and comfortable air-conditioned rooms with private baths. The resort sits on a peaceful stretch of white sand with thatch-roof shelters. Guests and locals meet at the Reef Bar that overlooks the beach and the 30-slip marina, where guests can take a ferry to nearby Stocking Island. The attractive oceanside dining room offers hearty Bahamian and American specialties. The all-inclusive rate includes meals, drinks, afternoon tea, sports activities, and gratuities. The resort is located 5 miles from the airport. *Box 49, George Town, Exuma, tel. 809/336–2171. 80 rooms. Facilities: pool, dining room, live entertainment, lounge, baby-sitting, laundry, powerboat rentals, bicycles, fishing, tennis, windsurfing, bus tour of the island, diving. AE, MC, V. Expensive.*

★ **Hotel Peace and Plenty.** Much of this two-story pink hotel's ongoing success may be attributed to the amiable personality of Charlie Pflueger, who has managed the place for more than 20 years. You'll find him joining guests nightly at the bar and introducing them to Lermon "Doc" Rolle, who has been a hotel bartender for a quarter of a century, serving his special drinks to such celebrities as Britain's Prince Philip and Greece's King Constantine. The bar attracts locals and a yachting crowd, especially during the Family Islands Regatta; its walls are suitably decorated with ships' name boards, anchors, rudders, and assorted lights. The cheerful, air-conditioned rooms, all with balconies, face the water. Guests can take a ferry to the hotel's private beach on Stocking Island. In early 1990, work began on Peace and Plenty West, a 16-room facility with a bar and restaurant that is situated a mile west of George Town. *Box 55, George Town, Exuma, tel. 809/336–2551. 32 rooms. Facilities:*

pool, dining room, bar, entertainment, private baths, free Sunfish sailing, boating, fishing, diving. AE, MC, V. Moderate.

Pieces of Eight. Coconut palms dot the pool area of this two-story stone resort situated on a slope of Queen's Highway. Its bright, air-conditioned rooms with balconies offer a good view of Elizabeth Harbour and Stocking Island. The place shares beach and dining privileges with the Out Island Inn, its sister resort. Exuma Aquatics, which is located on the property, features PADI instructors and a dive shop with an underwater photo lab, camera rentals, and photography lessons from a resident pro. *Box 49, George Town, Exuma, tel. 809/336–2600. 32 rooms. Facilities: dining room, bar, pool, lounges, babysitting. AE, MC, V. Moderate.*

Regatta Point. This pleasant apartment complex with kitchens, which looks on to Kidd Cove, sits on a small cay connected to George Town by a short causeway. The hotel has a delightful view of the yachts in Elizabeth Harbour. The large, high-ceilinged rooms are well designed to catch the cool, incoming trade winds. Rental cars, scooters, and bicycles are available, and the resort also has its own beach and dock. Children may share a room for a small charge. The resort has no restaurant; you'll have to eat in town or stock up on groceries. *Box 6, George Town, Exuma, tel. 809/336–2206. 5 apartments. Facilities: kitchens, laundry. No credit cards. Moderate.*

★ **Two Turtles Inn.** This two-story hotel with a small cannon guarding its entrance is made of local stone; overlooking Elizabeth Harbour, it is also situated near the village green, where you'll find a straw market. Its plain, wood-paneled rooms feature balconies, private baths, and cable TV. All the rooms are cooled with ceiling fans, and some have air-conditioning. A few efficiency units provide stove/sink/refrigerator combinations. Guests can dine on good Bahamian fare at tables and benches on the patio. Hostess Valerie Noyes, an Englishwoman, is a veritable font of local lore. *Box 51, George Town, Exuma, tel. 809/ 336–2545 or 800/327–0787. 14 rooms. Facilities: dining room, bar, rental cars, scooters. AE, MC, V. Inexpensive.*

Staniel Cay   **Staniel Cay Yacht Club.** A half-mile from the small Staniel Cay Airport in the Upper Exumas, this relaxed club with a nautical-theme decor is a favorite of yachtsmen. The four trim cottages on the edge of the water contain only six well-kept rooms with private baths; each cottage can house two people. The two-bedroom guest house with full kitchen facilities, set among casuarina trees, can accommodate four to six guests. An additional houseboat is available for rental, with space for four guests. The resort rents small boats for sailing or fishing, as well as scuba gear for diving. *Mail: c/o Transmar International, 4250 S.W. 11th Terr., Fort Lauderdale, FL 33315, tel. 809/ 355–2024. 4 cottages, 1 guest house, 1 houseboat. Facilities: bar, dining room, baby-sitting, marina, boating, fishing, windsurfing. AE. Expensive.*

Happy People Marina. You may find this casual hotel a bit isolated if you're not interested in yachting. The property is close to Staniel Cay, but it's a long way from the George Town social scene. A local band, however, plays at the Royal Entertainer Lounge, and a small but adequate restaurant is available for dining. The simple but comfortable motel-style rooms are situated along the beach. Children under 12 can stay at half-price. *Mail: c/o Staniel Cay, Exuma, tel. 809/355–2008. 11 rooms, pri-*

*vate or connecting with bath. Facilities: dining room, bar, ma-
rina. No credit cards. Inexpensive.*

Inagua

Little Inagua, only 20 miles wide and 40 miles long, is strictly
for the birds—that is, for the ones who reside in the island's
vast national park. Bird lovers constitute the majority of the
tourists who brave the long trip to this southernmost of the
Family Islands. Inagua's unusual climate of little rainfall and
continual trade winds created rich salt ponds, which have
brought prosperity to the island over the years. The Morton
Salt Company has a successful operation at its Matthew Town
factory: It produces upwards of a million tons of sea salt annually. Most Inaguans earn their living by working for the
company.

Arriving and Departing

By Plane **Bahamasair** (tel. 800/222–4262) has two flights weekly, on
Airport and Tuesday and Saturday, from Nassau to Matthew Town Air-
Airlines port.

Between the Taxis meet incoming flights. The two hotels are situated at
Airport and Matthew Town on the southwest coast, slightly more than a
Hotels mile from the airport.

By Mailboat M/V *Windward Express* makes weekly trips from Nassau to
Matthew Town. For information on specific schedules and
fares, contact the **Dock Master's office** (tel. 809/393–1064) at
Potter's Cay.

Getting Around

Check with your hotel about arranging tours of Inagua's park
through the Bahamas National Trust.

Important Addresses and Numbers

In Matthew Town, you can call the **police** at 4263 and the **hospital** at 4249.

Exploring Inagua

Fewer than a thousand people live on Inagua, whose capital,
Matthew Town, is on the west coast. On a clear day, you can see
the coast of Cuba, just over 50 miles west, from atop the lighthouse (built in 1870) at **Southwest Point,** a mile or so south of the
capital.

The desire to marvel over the salt process entices few visitors
to Inagua, but the **Bahamas National Park,** which spreads
over nearly 290 square miles and occupies most of the western
half of the island, draws nature lovers, ornithologists, and photo-
graphers—for a very colorful reason. As many as 20,000 flamingos (the pink creature is the national bird of the Bahamas)
fly in every spring to mate at **Lake Windsor,** a 12-mile-long
brackish body of water in the center of the island. The sight of
many flocks of the spindle-legged, long-necked birds flying
across a backdrop of the setting sun may be worth the trip here,
even if you're not an ornithologist. Bird-watchers can also ogle

rare Bahamas parrots, cormorants, herons, and egrets. Trust wardens run guided tours through this winged paradise, but, frankly, the flamingos may have the most fun here.

Dining and Lodging

Inexpensive **Ford's Inagua Inn.** A plain, two-story building with basic rooms, the inn features a dining room (where you'll be served good fresh fish), a bar, and beach privileges. The nearby marina offers deep-sea fishing opportunities. The hotel is located 1 mile from the airport. *Mail: c/o Matthew Town, Inagua, tel. 809/555–1222; ask operator for Inagua, 4277. 5 rooms. No credit cards.*

Main House. The Morton Salt Company operates this small, simple resort. The comfortable rooms are air-conditioned, and the place also offers a dining room with fresh fish on the menu. The hotel is 1½ miles from the airport. *Mail: c/o Matthew Town, Inagua, tel. 809/555–1222; ask operator for Inagua, 4267. 8 rooms. No credit cards.*

Long Island

Long Island, one of Columbus's stopping-off places, lives up to its name, for its Queen's Highway runs for close to 60 miles, never more than 4 miles wide, through some 35 villages and farming towns where you'll always find a little strawmarket beckoning to the tourist. (One of the island's 3,300 residents nicknamed the highway Rhythm Road, a reference perhaps to the many potholes that make driving along it an undulating experience.) The scenery changes from shelving beaches and shallow bays on the west coast to rugged headlands that drop suddenly to the sea on the east coast.

Arriving and Departing

By Plane **Bahamasair** (tel. 800/222–4262) flies four times a week to Long
Airports and Island's two airports, Stella Maris and Deadman's Cay. The
Airlines **Stella Maris Resort Club** (tel. 305/359–8236, 809/336–2106, or 800/426–0466) also has charter flights from Fort Lauderdale and Nassau to Stella Maris.

By Mailboat M/V *Nay Dean* makes a weekly trip from Nassau to Salt Pond, Simms, and Stella Maris. M/V *Windward Express*, also out of Nassau, calls weekly at Clarence Town, South End, and Roses. For information on specific schedules and fares, contact the **Dock Master's office** (tel. 809/393–1064) at Potter's Cay.

Getting Around

By Car The **Stella Maris Resort Club** (tel. 809/336–2106) and **Joseph B. Carroll** (tel. Operator, Deadman's Cay) both have automobiles for rent.

Important Addresses and Numbers

Police: Clarence Town, tel. 231; Simms, tel. 233.

Exploring Long Island

The island's northern tip is named **Cape Santa Maria,** the name given to it by Columbus in honor of one of his ships. This area features stunning beaches, and it's a popular short trip from **Stella Maris,** home of the island's largest resort. Divers can explore the wreck of a ship, the M/V *Combebaca,* which lies just off the headland.

Stella Maris (Star of the Sea) lies about 12 miles south of Cape Santa Maria, off Queen's Highway and past the ruins of the 19th-century **Adderley's Plantation.** This was another Bahamian island where fleeing Loyalists attempted, with little success, to grow cotton. You can still see parts of the plantation's three buildings up to roof level; the remains of two other plantations, **Dunmore's** and **Gray's,** are also on the island.

The all-encompassing **Stella Maris Resort Club** (tel. 809/336–2106) has a 4,300-foot airstrip to handle guests. In a world of its own, the resort features a shopping complex, a bank, a post office, a pub, and a marina. Nearby, at the famous **Stella Maris shark reef,** divers can watch the less voracious of the species being fed fish by a divemaster with whom the sharks must be happily familiar by now.

One of the oldest settlements on Long Island is at **Simms,** 8 miles south of Stella Maris, past little pastel houses; some of these abodes sport emblems to ward off evil spirits, an indication of the presence of Obeah, the superstitious culture found in many of the Bahamian islands voodoo-like. When the mailboat comes to Simms once a week, local islanders bring their fruit and vegetables to be sold in Nassau. Ten miles south of Simms lies **Salt Pond,** where the annual Long Island Regatta is held every May among competing Bahamian-made boats, attracting contestants from all over the islands.

Deadman's Cay, an additional 15 miles south of Salt Pond, is the location of the commercial airport. This town serves as the home for most of the island's population; here you'll find a few shops (such as **J. B. Carroll's Food Store**), churches, and schools. Deadman's Cay features a cave that has stalactites and stalagmites and eventually leads to the sea. The cave has apparently never been completely explored, though Indian drawings were found on one wall. (There are several other caves, supposedly pirate-haunted, around Millerton and Simms; knock on any door and the resident will point you in the right direction.)

An additional 10 miles south of Deadman's Cay is **Clarence Town,** the setting for Long Island's most celebrated landmarks, **St. Paul's Church** (Anglican) **and St. Peter's Church** (Catholic). They were both built by a legendary priest, Father Jerome, who lies in a tomb in the Hermitage atop Mt. Alvernia on Cat Island. He constructed St. Paul's as he practiced the Anglican faith while named John Hawes, and St. Peter's after his conversion to Catholicism. The two churches' architectural style is similar to that of the missions established by the Spaniards in California in the early 18th century.

Sports

The **Stella Maris Resort Club** (tel. 809/336–2106) offers fishing and boating ($440 for a full day of deep-sea fishing), scuba diving, tennis (two courts), waterskiing, and windsurfing.

Dining and Lodging

Moderate **Stella Maris Resort Club.** Built on the grounds of the original
★ Adderley plantation, this hotel, which sits atop a hill overlooking the ocean, continues to attract an international clientele. The rooms and apartments here surround the clubhouse. The bungalows are scattered throughout the grounds, which are close to the eight beaches spreading east and west. Although the rooms are not luxurious, they offer small refrigerators and a view of the ocean; the apartments have kitchenettes. Both the rooms and apartments feature rattan furnishings and tiled floors. The two-bedroom, two-bath bungalows have vaulted ceilings, living rooms, and kitchens. Visitors can swim in three pools, two of them freshwater. Diving and fishing are popular pursuits here, but you can also explore some of the island by bicycle. The resort also has its own cabana preserve on Cape Santa Maria. Guests can enjoy a weekly "Out Islands Cave" night of music and dancing on Mondays. *Box 105, Stella Maris, Long Island, tel. 809/336–2106, 305/467–0466, or 800/426–0466. 50 rooms. Facilities: dining room, bar, entertainment, marina, pools, game room, barber, lounge, boating, fishing, diving, waterskiing, snorkeling, tennis. AE, MC, V.*

Inexpensive The following properties offer more modest alternatives to the Stella Maris Resort Club. They all have simple, clean rooms. All can be contacted by mail direct, or by telephoning the overseas operator (809/555–1212) and asking for the individual properties on Long Island.
Carroll's Guest House. This well-maintained wood and stone guest house, located near the Deadman's Cay Airport and several good beaches, offers four bedrooms downstairs (two share baths) and two one-bedroom apartments upstairs, each with a living room, a dining room, a kitchen, and a bath. The management offers free transportation to the property from the airport. *Deadman's Cay, Long Island. 6 rooms. Facilities: dining room, boating and fishing can be arranged. AE, V.*
Thompson Bay Inn. Guests stay in a neat, comfortable two-story building featuring a dining room and a popular bar and lounge. The inn, located near Stella Maris, will help guests arrange boating, fishing, and sightseeing excursions. *Thompson Bay, Long Island. 8 rooms. Facilities: TV in rooms, bar, dining room, baby-sitting, laundry, nearby beach privileges. No credit cards.*
Windtryst Guest House. This place is essentially just a clean, no-frills place to sleep. Its location, Salt Pond, hosts the annual Long Island Regatta in May. *Salt Pond, Long Island. 4 rooms. No credit cards.*

San Salvador

On October 12, 1492, Christopher Columbus disturbed the lives of the peaceful Lucayan Indians by landing on San Salvador; he knelt on the beach and claimed the land for Spain. (Never mind that doubting Thomases, spurred by the findings of a computerized study published in a 1986 *National Geographic* article, point to Samana Cay, 60 miles southeast, as the exact point of the weary explorer's landing.) Three monuments on the 7-by-12-mile island commemorate Columbus's arrival, and the 500th-anniversary celebration of the event will be officially focused here in 1992.

A 17th-century pirate named George Watling, who frequently sought shelter on the island, changed San Salvador's name to Watling's Island. The Bahamas Government switched the name back to San Salvador in 1926.

Arriving and Departing

By Plane Bahamasair (tel. 800/222–4262) has two direct flights weekly on Tuesday and Saturday from Nassau to Cockburn Town Airport.

Taxis meet arriving planes at Cockburn Town Airport.

By Mailboat M/V *Maxine*, out of Nassau, calls on Tuesdays at San Salvador, Cat Island, and Rum Cay. For information on specific schedules and fares, contact the **Dock Master's office** (tel. 809/393–1064) at Potter's Cay.

Getting Around

The **Riding Rock Inn** (tel. 800/272–1492) rents cars for $65 a day, motor bikes for $30 a day, and bicycles for $5 a day.

Important Addresses and Numbers

Emergencies Police, tel. 218. **Medical Clinic,** tel. 207.

Exploring San Salvador

Numbers in the margin correspond with points of interest on the San Salvador map.

In 1492, the inspiring sight that greeted Christopher Columbus by moonlight at 2 AM was a terrain of gleaming beaches and far-reaching forest. The peripatetic traveler and his crews— "men from Heaven," the locals called them—led the *Santa Maria,* the *Nina,* and the *Pinta* warily among the coral reefs and anchored, so it is recorded, in **Fernandez Bay,** close to what is now the main community of **Cockburn Town,** midway on the western shore of the island.

A cross erected in 1956 by Columbus scholar Ruth C. Durlacher Wolper Marvin stands at his approximate landing spot. (Ms. Marvin's New World Museum near North Victoria Hill on the east coast contains artifacts from the era of the Lucayana, who called the island Guanahani.) An underwater monument marks the place where the *Santa Maria* anchored; nearby, an-

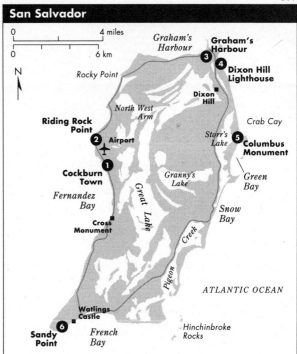

other monument commemorates the passage of the Olympic flame on its journey from Greece to Mexico City in 1968.

Queen's Highway encircles the island from Cockburn Town, where the twice-weekly plane flights land and where the weekly mailboat docks. This small village's narrow streets feature two churches, a commissioner's office, a police station, a courthouse, a library, and a telephone station.

About a mile north of the town is **Riding Rock Point,** which Columbus spotted and recorded. The area now serves as the home for the **Riding Rock Inn** (tel. 809/322–2631), a popular resort for divers.

In a northeasterly direction from Cockburn Town to the tip of the island, you'll find **Graham's Harbour,** which Columbus describes in his diaries as large enough "to hold all the ships of Christendom." Here a complex of buildings near the harbor houses the **College Center of the Finger Lakes' Bahamian Field Station,** a biological and geological research institution that attracts scientists and students from all over the world. A couple of miles south of Graham's Harbour stands the **Dixon Hill Lighthouse** (built around 1856), which is still hand-operated; its light from a small kerosene lamp beams out to sea every 15 seconds. The lighthouse keeper must continually wind the apparatus that projects the light. A climb to the top of the 160-foot landmark, the last lighthouse of its kind in the Bahamas, offers a fabulous view of the island, which includes a series of inland lakes. The keeper is present 24 hours a day. Knock on his door and he'll give you free admittance.

If you drive south down the east coast an additional 3 or 4 miles,
⑤ you'll pass the **Columbus Monument** on Crab Cay. No road
leads to the monument; you have to make your way along a
bushy path. This initial tribute to the explorer was erected by
the *Chicago Herald* newspaper in 1892, far from the presumed
site of Columbus's landing. Continue south for a dozen miles
through a series of little villages, such as **Holiday Track** and
Polly Hill, that once contained plantations. On the southern
⑥ end of the island you'll reach **Sandy Point,** on French Bay. On a
hill overlooking the bay lie **the ruins of Watling's Castle,** named
after the 17th-century pirate. The ruins are more likely the remains of a Loyalist plantation house than a castle from the
buccaneering days. You can walk from Queen's Highway up a
hill to see what is left of the ruins, which are now engulfed in
vegetation.

Sports

Guanahani Ltd., which is affiliated with the **Riding Rock Inn**
(tel. 809/322–2631), has year-round dive packages. It also offers one-, two-, and three-dive trips for $30, $45, and $65.
Diving and snorkeling gear can be rented. The Riding Rock Inn
can also arrange for fishing and boating, and it has a tennis
court that is free to guests.

Dining and Lodging

Cockburn Town **Riding Rock Inn.** This white, motel-style resort attracts divers
because of its excellent reefs offshore and its variety of packages appealing to these sportspeople. You'll also have access to
the spot where Columbus landed. If you're thinking of staying
here for the big Columbus celebration in 1992, you would be
wise to book now. The inn's two buildings—one facing the
ocean, the other near the freshwater pool—offer small rooms
painted off-white, with modern wooden furniture and redwood
patios. The restaurant, which can seat 60 people, serves Bahamian dishes, such as fried grouper, conch, and peas 'n' rice.
*Mail: 750 S.W. 34th St., Suite 206, Fort Lauderdale, FL 33315,
tel. 305/761–1492, 809/322–2631, or 800/272–1492. 24 rooms.
Facilities: pool, restaurant, lounge, marina. AE, MC, V. Moderate.*
Ocean View Villas. At North Victoria Hill, these pleasant two-
bedroom cottages feature small kitchenettes and sitting rooms.
*Mail: c/o San Salvador, tel. 809/555–1212; ask for Cockburn
Town operator. 4 rooms. Facilities: water sports can be ar-
ranged. No credit cards. Inexpensive.*

Index

Personal Itinerary

Departure *Date*

Time

Transportation

Arrival *Date*   *Time*

Departure *Date*   *Time*

Transportation

Accommodations

Arrival *Date*   *Time*

Departure *Date*   *Time*

Transportation

Accommodations

Arrival *Date*   *Time*

Departure *Date*   *Time*

Transportation

Accommodations

Addresses

Name

Address

Telephone

Name

Address

Telephone

Name

Address

Telephone

Name

Address

Telephone

Name

Address

Telephone

Name

Address

Telephone

Name

Address

Telephone

Name

Address

Telephone

Name

Address

Telephone

Name

Address

Telephone

Name

Address

Telephone

Name

Address

Telephone

Name

Address

Telephone

Name

Address

Telephone

Name

Address

Telephone

Name

Address

Telephone

Fodor's Travel Guides

U.S. Guides

Alaska
Arizona
Boston
California
Cape Cod
The Carolinas & the
  Georgia Coast
The Chesapeake
  Region
Chicago
Colorado
Disney World & the
  Orlando Area

Florida
Hawaii
The Jersey Shore
Las Vegas
Los Angeles
Maui
Miami & the Keys
New England
New Mexico
New Orleans
New York City
New York City
  (Pocket Guide)

New York State
Pacific North Coast
Philadelphia
The Rockies
San Diego
San Francisco
San Francisco
  (Pocket Guide)
The South
Texas
USA
The Upper Great
  Lakes Region

Virgin Islands
Virginia & Maryland
Waikiki
Washington, D.C.

Foreign Guides

Acapulco
Amsterdam
Australia
Austria
The Bahamas
The Bahamas
  (Pocket Guide)
Baja & the Pacific
  Coast Resorts
Barbados
Belgium &
  Luxembourg
Bermuda
Brazil
Budget Europe
Canada
Canada's Atlantic
  Provinces
Cancun, Cozumel,
  Yucatan Peninsula
Caribbean
Central America
China

Eastern Europe
Egypt
Europe
Europe's Great
  Cities
France
Germany
Great Britain
Greece
The Himalayan
  Countries
Holland
Hong Kong
India
Ireland
Israel
Italy
Italy's Great Cities
Jamaica
Japan
Kenya, Tanzania,
  Seychelles
Korea

Lisbon
London
London Companion
London
  (Pocket Guide)
Madrid & Barcelona
Mexico
Mexico City
Montreal &
  Quebec City
Morocco
Munich
New Zealand
Paris
Paris (Pocket Guide)
Portugal
Puerto Rico
  (Pocket Guide)
Rio de Janeiro
Rome
Saint Martin/
  Sint Maarten
Scandinavia

Scandinavian Cities
Scotland
Singapore
South America
South Pacific
Southeast Asia
Soviet Union
Spain
Sweden
Switzerland
Sydney
Thailand
Tokyo
Toronto
Turkey
Vienna
Yugoslavia

Special-Interest Guides

Bed & Breakfast
  Guide to the Mid-
  Atlantic States

Bed & Breakfast
  Guide to New
  England
Cruises & Ports
  of Call

A Shopper's Guide
  to London
Health & Fitness
  Vacations
Shopping in Europe

Skiing in North
  America
Sunday in New York
Touring Europe